THE BEST SEAT IN THE HOUSE

THE
BEST SEAT
IN THE HOUSE

The Golden Years of
Radio and Television

PAT WEAVER

WITH THOMAS M. COFFEY

Alfred A. Knopf   New York   1994

THIS IS A BORZOI BOOK
PUBLISHED BY ALFRED A. KNOPF, INC.

Library of Congress Cataloging-in-Publication Data
Weaver, Pat.
The best seat in the house : the golden years of radio and
television / by Pat Weaver. — 1st ed.
p.   cm.
ISBN 0–679–40835–5
1. Weaver, Pat. 2. National Broadcasting Company, Inc.
3. Television broadcasting—United States—Biography.
4. Executives—United States—Biography.   I. Title.
PN1992.4.W43A3   1994
384.55′092—dc20
[B]   93–1685
CIP

Manufactured in the United States of America

FIRST EDITION

TO LIZ
Dimidium Animae Meae

ACKNOWLEDGMENTS

First, Tom Coffey, not only for his writing, but for the time he had to spend reading through tons of my memos, projects, et al, from my NBC days, and for hours of taping with me about my earlier life. Then to Garry Ross, who extracted from my usual pronouncement of the promise of the communications revolution "the best seat in the house," the phrase that is the book's title. And my longtime associates and friends who prodded a faulty memory: Everard Meade who came to Young & Rubicam with Fred Allen and me, and was my right hand there, and at American Tobacco, and again at Y&R, where he took over for me when I left for NBC; my agent Frank Cooper, who made me do the book; Dick Pinkham, almost lifetime pal and associate; Tommy Loeb, who helped and will be disappointed that I did not confine the book to all the funny stuff; Murray Bolen, my ex-roommate in our beautiful apartment above the bay in San Francisco, where I persuaded Murray to leave show business as a performer and become a producer, which he did later at Y&R and Wells Rich Greene; and Prince Azamat Guirey, who helped me reminisce . . . not easy.

Most of all, I want to acknowledge all the unnamed friends who helped me so much in all my undertakings described here. Most of them will not know, for they have gone on, but I will not forget how much they meant to me how often and how long ago.

THE BEST SEAT IN THE HOUSE

THE QUESTION MOST OFTEN ASKED OF ME DURING MY later career has been, "Why did you leave NBC?"

That was a long time ago—1956. To explain why I left, I'll have to explain why I went there in the first place, in 1949, exchanging a marvelous situation at the powerful Young & Rubicam advertising agency for a very hazardous one at the network.

At the agency I was vice president in charge of television, radio, and movies. I was also a member of the executive committee and the plans board, and a stock-holding partner in a company that was owned by its employees. I was well satisfied, but I could see many things that, in my opinion, needed doing for the broadcasting industry, and especially for television, which was then an infant, though already a potential giant in the eyes of anyone who looked at it closely.

The National Broadcasting Company, as it happened, had offered me a situation that I thought would give me an extraordinary opportunity. But unfortunately, the offer also required that I work for David Sarnoff, the president of Radio Corporation of America, which owned NBC. That was something my financial friends on Wall Street had been almost unanimous in telling me not to do. They said things like: "Sarnoff! You can't work for that bastard. He's a monster. You know the Sarnoff joke on Wall Street? With all those great RCA electronic patents he owns, he should be pushing the world of tomorrow instead of the world of yesteryear. They say that if RCA stock opened at ten, and he dropped dead, it would hit a hundred by closing. And on top of that, he doesn't really give a damn about radio or television, except the hardware."

I hadn't listened to these friends, and in many ways I was glad. My years at NBC put me in the forefront of a suddenly burgeoning television industry and left me with many happy memories and many accomplishments—the creation of programs like *Today* (originally with Dave Garroway) and *Tonight* (originally with Steve Allen), which are still anchoring the NBC-TV schedule after forty years; the launching of programs like *Your Show of Shows* with Sid Caesar and Imogene Coca, the *Comedy Hour, Producers' Showcase, Matinee Theater*, and *Wide Wide World*; the introduction of NBC "spectaculars," which took the viewer out of his living room and made him a witness to wondrous events in the theater and in real life—events he would not otherwise have ever had a chance to experience. But most important, I was proud of the broadcasting revolution I had started—an upheaval that put the networks back in control of radio and television.

When I went to NBC in 1949, the networks were no more than facilities that the big advertising agencies used to broadcast shows they created, owned, and controlled. They hired the producers, the writers, and the stars, and, in effect, decided what was to go on the air. I knew all about that, because it was exactly what I had been doing at Young & Rubicam. Among the stars I had handled at Y&R were Fred Allen, Jack Benny, George Burns and Gracie Allen, Phil Baker, Kate Smith, Phil Silvers, and Jackie Gleason.

Advertising agencies were remarkable institutions. I had no quarrel with them, but I saw their limitations. An advertiser went to an agency because he wanted to market his product, and that was the end of his responsibility. He didn't advertise either to do good or to make enemies. He expected to sell without offending people. The net result was the bland leading the bland, as the well-known advertising man Paul Cunningham put it. Agency people were often blamed for this, but, in fact, there were no heavies—unless they were the network executives, who had allowed the agency-ownership system to develop.

After taking part in this system for some time, I gradually came to realize, while I was still at Y&R, that it could be radically improved. I found myself becoming less and less interested in the commercial aspects of broadcasting and more and more interested in what was happening in the world. Television seemed to offer tremendous potential for upgrading humanity—for making the common man uncommon—but not unless its course could be altered to make room for cultural and educational as well as commercial entertainment programs. And I felt that the networks would be more likely to accomplish this if they were in control. The advertisers and their agencies had to think primarily of sales and ratings.

I joined NBC as head of television with an unspoken determination to change the existing system—unspoken, because I didn't dare make too public an issue of it. What I had in mind was a real revolution in broadcasting. And during my years at NBC, I actually managed to carry it off. At first, a lot of people disapproved of what I was doing, especially my former colleagues at the ad agencies. But very soon, as the cost of television sponsorship rose, most of them realized that there were advantages in the new system, especially for the smaller advertisers, who couldn't afford to sponsor an entire program.

By the time I left NBC, it owned most of the shows it put on the air, and the other networks had begun to follow. I was proud of that, but it didn't make me happy on that day in September 1956 when I resigned.

It was a pleasant morning in New York. The leaves on the trees in Rockefeller Center were just beginning to turn. I stood at the window of my corner office on the sixth floor of the RCA Building, gazing at the Time-Life Building to the south, the flower beds of the plaza to the east, and, across Fifth Avenue, the gothic spires of St. Patrick's Cathedral. The streets below me were crowded with busy, fast-moving people who looked as if they knew where they were going. I wished I did.

I had returned to work that morning from a week's trout-fishing holiday in Canada with my wife, Liz, my young son, Trajan, and one of his pals. A peaceful interlude among the lakes and trees. I arrived at my office bright and cheerful, ready to regale people with tales about the trip, and especially about the fish, the size of which had already begun to increase in my memory. But before I could tell any tales, my associates were giving me some bad news.

While I was away, one of the Sarnoffs, either David or his son, Bobby, had fired two of the best men on my staff—Fred Wile, in charge of programming, and George Frey, the head of sales during my first three years at NBC.

I saw the dismissals as the latest in a series of moves to put me in the freezer. In January 1953, David Sarnoff had stripped me of my control over TV and radio and kicked me upstairs by making me vice chairman of NBC, a meaningless job. But he had been forced to undo that maneuver by naming me president in September of that same year, because the network, under other management, was racing rapidly downhill. He had not made that decision gladly, however, as he proved two years later, when he withdrew the presidency and again kicked me upstairs, this time as chairman of the NBC board.

I had fought that move and lost, producing in me a strong temptation to resign. When I finally agreed to stay, it was mostly because I had persuaded at least twenty-five people to leave good jobs elsewhere and join NBC in important executive positions. If I left, they would all be in danger of dismissal. To forestall this probability, I had exacted a promise from Bobby Sarnoff, who was replacing me as president, that none of these key people would be shifted or let go without my express approval. Now someone had fired Wile and Frey while I was out of town, and without a word of discussion, let alone my approval.

I swung around from the window and took a close look—maybe a closer look than I had ever taken—at this huge, polished, deeply carpeted office I had occupied since the day I became president of NBC. I had become so accustomed to the place, and so busy during the countless hours I had spent there, that I had seldom stopped to look at it carefully. It was a long, wide, multiwindowed room featuring my enormous L-shaped desk, which I loved. Liz had designed it and NBC had it made for me when I joined in 1949. It had a battery of phones plus a vidicon screen, which enabled me to talk face to face with my chief aides without summoning them from their offices.

The furniture was sleek and modern, the walls paneled with bleached mahogany. I knew it was mahogany not because I was an expert in identifying woods but because *The*

New Yorker had published a two-part profile of me in the autumn of 1954 that had described it as such—a profile that, incidentally, may have been a factor in my problems with General Sarnoff. *The New Yorker* had never run a profile of him. And from sources close to the General, I had learned that he was quite vexed about it.

Unlike Sarnoff, I was not a publicity seeker. I had never hired a publicist, but when I was at NBC I attracted a lot of public attention. The press kept coming to me for statements on programs and industry trends. I made the cover of *Newsweek*. I was, to a large degree, given credit for the great success of NBC during my tenure—perhaps too large a degree, considering the contributions of the people I had gathered around me. It's true, of course, that some of the publicity coming my way was arranged by the NBC public relations staff, but not at my direction or suggestion.

General Sarnoff, who had always discouraged notice for anyone at RCA except himself, had been from the start aware of all the publicity I was attracting, and, according to people around him, he didn't like it. Despite his cordial exterior, I had the distinct impression he didn't care for me, either, which may have been partly my own fault. I was still a relatively young man at the time, somewhat brash and somewhat presumptuous in my hope that older television executives like Sarnoff would embrace all of my ideas. When they didn't, I could be what you might call irreverent. Privately I would, on occasion, refer to Sarnoff as "General Fangs," and I later learned from his biography that this had gotten back to him. So there were reasons for him to dislike me. But he must also have been of two minds about me, since he could hardly dislike what I had accomplished with his company. In 1949, CBS had been far ahead of NBC, both in ratings and in profits. CBS had eight of the top ten shows on television; NBC had Milton Berle and little else. In less than two years we reversed all that, making NBC number one among the (then) four networks. But more important, by instituting the network as a programmer and owner of its own shows, we had revolutionized television, thus enhancing this important RCA property—which may explain why General Sarnoff had such a hard time deciding what to do with me, even though he might personally have been glad to have seen me gone.

In any case, I decided that morning in September 1956 to make the decision myself. But it wasn't likely to be easy for either me or Sarnoff, because in 1953, when he had "promoted" me to vice chairman, I had signed a contract that stipulated I couldn't quit and Sarnoff couldn't fire me for five years. So we seemed to be shackled to each other for two more years. But now I wanted out.

After consulting my attorneys, Sol and Henry Jaffe, I buzzed one of the secretaries in my outer office and asked her to put in a call to General Sarnoff's office, forty-seven floors above mine in the RCA Building.

When we were both on the line, I wasted no breath in getting to the point. "As you know," I said, "I have a contract which binds both of us for the next two years. I think it's about time we did something about it. I've decided I really want to get out."

He was all business, neither friendly nor unfriendly. "Will it be a peaceful settlement?" he asked.

I responded, "That depends on you."

He said, "I'll have my lawyers get in touch with yours."

And so it was done. I had given up what was at that time the most important job in broadcasting. And I had no idea where I would go from there. But I felt relieved. I felt free.

THE DAY I GOT my first broadcasting job, in 1932, with the Don Lee CBS regional network in California, television was no more than a vision of future wonders—and a very hazy one at best. The Great Depression was plunging toward its depths that year, and while this affected me, as it did everybody, it hardly made me destitute. I had grown up with more advantages than anybody could need. My father was a highly successful roofing manufacturer in Los Angeles. I worked in his factory as a teenager, and also in his Los Angeles sales office and in his New York business office. Not for very long, but long enough to make me realize the roofing business was not for me.

In 1926 he said no to Stanford, where my pals were going, and sent me east to Dartmouth, from which I graduated magna cum laude and Phi Beta Kappa in 1930. I had fun at Dartmouth and made a lot of friends, including Nelson Rockefeller, who apparently thought I was as rich as he was because I drove a better car, a LaSalle Phaeton. I also read almost a book a day and indulged my love of movies, an obsession that had begun when I was ten. In Hanover at the Nugget Theater, a student hangout, the shows changed just about every night, and during my four years at Dartmouth I was there for all of them.

At the end of my first year in college I did my father an inadvertent favor. That summer he took our whole family to Europe—my mother, my two sisters, Sylva and Rosemary, me, and my younger brother, Winstead (who was to become a zany comedian under the name Doodles Weaver). We headquartered in Oxford, where my father had rented a house, but spent weekends in London, where I fell in love with the English theater as I already had with Broadway. We also traveled on the Continent, where I saw Paris, Brussels, Geneva, and some of the most famous battlefields of World War I (which in those days we called simply the Great War or the World War, never dreaming there would be another, even more horrendous one).

During the course of that summer I finally got up the

courage to tell my father I didn't want to join his roofing company. I wanted to be a writer. I'm sure it was a blow to him; he had built a solid, sizable, and highly profitable business, no doubt with the vision of his two sons carrying it on after he retired. Or perhaps only one son: Winstead had already made it apparent that his mind would never be directed toward any business except show business. But I had always been interested when my father talked business. I was fascinated by its workings, and my father must have noticed that. In fact, he had already approved my going to the Harvard Business School for the fall of 1930, after my graduation, three years hence.

When I told him he'd have to cancel his dream, he took it surprisingly well. He must have realized how serious I was, because two years later he sold his company to Johns Manville. That year being 1929, he was selling at the height of his company's value, just before the stock market crash. Which proved, it seems to me, that I had a very good head for business: I had saved my father perhaps a million dollars.

After graduating from Dartmouth in 1930, my pal Jerome Pearre and I took the SS *Statendam* for Plymouth and prowled Land's End up to Ilfracombe, then over tourist terrain to London and the West End theaters. Next we went to Paris. Jerry's older brother was a New York *Herald Tribune* reporter there and knew everyone. I especially recall encountering S. J. Perelman at Le Dôme. I said to him, "I love your woodcuts"—the most famous showed two old-fashioned gentlemen shaking hands at their club with the line, "I have Bright's disease and he has mine"—"but my ambition is to write the funny stuff under the pictures." He informed me that was his job, and he hoped to stop doing woodcuts as soon as possible.

From Paris, Jerry and I went down the Moselle valley to Cologne, then up the Rhine and on to Heidelberg. From there we went to Munich, then on to catch the Passion play at Oberammergau, then to Berchtesgaden, on to Vienna, with its new wine festival and the fun and games on the Kärnterstrasse. In Budapest I rode the waves in the St. Gellert pool, which had an artificial surf. Then on to the main target of the trip—the ancient ruins of Greece. I think we saw most of them, including Mycenae and Olympia, where the games were held. We headed for Italy, because Jerry had to get back, but spent a few days casing Pompeii and Paestum, and a week in Capri. We then went in different directions, with me off by ship to Palermo and a trip around Sicily, seeing the ruins of Segesta, Selinus, Agrigento, Syracuse, Taormina.

Then I took ship to Alexandria and on to Cairo, where I met up with another fraternity brother and friend, Spencer Foster, whose father was treasurer of the Metropolitan Museum of Art in New York and was there to go to work at Luxor, in the Valley of the Kings, where the Met was unearthing the tomb of Queen Hatshepsut. Spen fixed it for me to work on the project, too, and I had a couple of glorious weeks in Luxor before taking a trip down to Aswan to visit the ruins of Philae, which were being submerged by the Aswan Dam. Added to what I had seen of Rome and Greece, these relics of a remote and storied era overwhelmed me. They enlarged my world view, my sense of the importance of history, and offered a fitting climax to a college education in which I majored in philosophy and minored in Classical civilizations.

Unfortunately, some evil germ struck me down, and I woke up on the train back in Cairo, very sick. Next stop, the American Hospital in Paris. I was jaundiced. When I asked the doctor what I had, he told me, "One of several hundred little-known tropical diseases, but we don't know which."

After recovering, I returned to New York, aware that my

boyhood and college years were part of my past. I was eager to get my life started. Though I wanted to be a writer, I realized I couldn't fulfill that ambition overnight, so I planned to look for work in some related field. But this was 1931, and the Depression had begun to paralyze the economy. I was soon adding myself to the hundreds of thousands of New Yorkers looking for jobs. Much to my surprise, I found one—of a sort. I went to work as a salesman for a giveaway advertising weekly. I was supposed to sell store owners on the idea of distributing it to their customers, in exchange for which they could have the name of their store printed on the cover. It sounded better to my boss than it did to the store owners, and in a few weeks I was gone, with a perfect record—no sales. Then I took a job as a writer for a new radio newsweekly called *The March of Time*. Unfortunately, *The March of Time* wasn't yet on the air, and in these hard times it looked as if it might not manage to get there. I decided not to hold my breath. Meanwhile, I was dashing off stories and bombarding magazines with them—*The New Yorker*, the *Saturday Evening Post, Collier's*. I found encouraging notes with my rejection slips, but no sales. I'd have been in a tough spot if I hadn't had a wealthy father. California beckoned, and I responded.

My father set up several interviews for me in Los Angeles. I talked to a number of important men in the film industry, including Louis B. Mayer at MGM, but jobs were scarce in Hollywood, too. Not as scarce as in New York, but there were few enough so that I didn't find one. You might have thought the industry would show more respect to one of its best customers. Since the age of ten, I had seen every movie I could get to, sometimes two or three a day. As a kid, I went to a movie every time I had a dime (which was all it cost in those days).

My father also arranged for interviews at advertising agencies in Los Angeles, but that business didn't take to me any more than the movie industry. Finally, I went to work as a writer and salesman for the Young and McCallister Printing Company, which was engaged in direct-mail advertising. It was at least a toehold, and it turned out to be a lucky one. A few months into the job, someone, I think it was Bruce McCallister, recommended me for the job of editor of the L.A. Advertising Club's house organ, *The Blue Pencil*, which the club still publishes. The first thing I liked about the job was that I didn't receive any more rejection slips. As editor, I decided what to publish, and a lot of it was my own material. Among the things I wrote was funny stuff about advertising, which eventually caught the attention of someone at the Don Lee CBS regional network of eight West Coast radio stations, all either owned by or affiliated with Lee's network. He also had the Cadillac franchise for all of California.

I went to meet him in his eight-story building at Seventh and Bixel, in downtown Los Angeles. On the ground floor was his main local Cadillac showroom. On the second floor was his local radio station, KHJ, which I had already visited a few times. It was remarkably well equipped for an independent local station.

Lee was a short, slender man, expensively dressed. He had a mustache and an aura of self-confidence, perhaps self-importance. He had met my father, he said, though they didn't really know each other. I, on the other hand, had grown up with his son, Tommy, who was a sharp dresser and a sharp dancer. He drove the flashiest automobiles, in which there were always equally flashy girls.

During my pre-college days in the 1920s, the Ambassador Hotel's Cocoanut Grove staged dance contests every Friday. Tommy and I were often there. I won contests with Joan Crawford, Betty Jane Young (Loretta's older sister, who became the actress Sally Blane), and Jane Peters (who eventually changed her name to Carole Lombard). We used to take the girls to Marchetti's on Western Avenue, or the Montmartre, where we could listen to Bing Crosby and the Rhythm Boys.

Joan Crawford was living at that time with Mike Cudahy, a scion of the immensely wealthy Chicago meatpacking family. He had taken up residence in Hollywood for what reason I don't know—maybe to meet girls like Joan Crawford. She had already made two movies and achieved a certain amount of fame. I especially remember the time I won a cup with her as my partner, because Tommy Lee was involved in that. Through the preliminary rounds he danced with Joan, while I was with my most frequent partner, Betty Jane Young. When we had eliminated all the other couples, Tommy came to me and said, "Let's switch partners for the finals." He must have thought Betty Jane was a better dancer than Joan. I can't remember what I thought, but I didn't object, and Joan and I won the cup.

Don Lee and I engaged in small talk about his son and my father, then got down to the purpose of my visit, which was to solicit a job as a comedy writer at his radio station. I was especially eager, not only because KHJ was the Los Angeles CBS outlet, but because it did its own programming. In 1932, though coast-to-coast transmission was possible, it was still a sometime thing, so West Coast stations had to depend largely on themselves for the development of programs. In Los Angeles, with its enormous pool of Hollywood talent, the programming was already quite good, especially at KHJ, which created shows for the entire Don Lee network. It used name performers and maintained a big orchestra. Raymond Paige was the musical director. It seemed to me I could carve out a future for myself here. But when I told Lee what I was hoping for, I discovered that he thought I was there for something else.

"Radio!" he exclaimed. "Why would you want to bother with a little thing like radio? Why don't you join us down here in the car business? Make yourself a real fortune."

My mind was made up, however. "I really want to give radio a try," I said.

So I went to work for KHJ and the Don Lee network, initially as a comedy writer, for $150 a month, which was not bad for a Depression-era salary. A lot of people were raising families on much less.

MY FIRST EXPERIENCE WITH RADIO SHOULD HAVE GIVEN me some sense of its future, and perhaps even of my own.

As a boy in Los Angeles, I had attempted to build a wireless set—a popular pastime of youngsters in those days. I wrapped some wire around an empty Wheatena package; bought a condenser, a crystal, an earphone, and a dial; then connected them as best I could. I was turning the dial one day, listening for Morse code (with which most transmissions were then sent), when I suddenly heard a human voice. I could scarcely believe it. A miracle! No telephone. No wires of any kind. Just a voice coming out of the air.

I was so excited that at first I didn't pay any attention to what the voice was saying. When I had calmed down enough to listen, I realized that what I was hearing was a radio conversation being relayed between the phone company's Los Angeles transmitter and Avalon, on Catalina Island, twenty miles offshore.

The conversation was between a husband and wife—a telephone conversation destined to be repeated a few million times, in one duplicitous form or another, during the years to come. The husband, presumably in his office on the mainland, was trying to explain to his wife why he would be unable to catch the boat to Avalon that night, and why he might also be unable to get home the next day. The wife had apparently heard this story before and didn't believe a word of it. As he talked, she was at first cool to him, then chilly, then downright frigid. Though I was just a boy, I could grasp the nuances.

I should have understood immediately that I was listening to something much more important than a conversation between a philandering husband and a furious wife. I was listening to an emerging development that would soon change the world—a development that would spawn an enormous and influential industry of which I would one day be a part. But at the time, it was to me simply an amazing accomplishment.

Radio, which at first was called "wireless," had been invented in Italy by Guglielmo Marconi in 1895 and patented in England the following year. But not until after its role in reporting the news of the sinking of the *Titanic* on April 14, 1912, did radio become an important worldwide instrument of communication. David Sarnoff had an interesting, though somewhat elusive, involvement in the role radio played in the *Titanic* disaster. At that time, Sarnoff was an employee of the Marconi company's New York branch and had already proven his extraordinary skills in building, repairing, and operating wireless equipment. He was the manager of a wireless station the company had established on the roof of the Wanamaker department store at Eighth Street and Broadway, in lower Manhattan. His official biography, written in 1966 by his cousin, Eugene Lyons, describes his *Titanic* experience as follows:

On April 14, 1912, David Sarnoff was listening casually
to the routine flood of dots and dashes. Suddenly he was
stung to startled attention. The message was dim and
far away and choked by static, but he deciphered it
notwithstanding. It was coming from the S.S. *Olympic*
in the north Atlantic, 1,400 miles away:

S.S. TITANIC RAN INTO ICEBERG. SINKING FAST.

According to Lyons, Sarnoff spread the tragic news (1,517
people died in the sinking of the brand-new British luxury
liner), and soon "the eyes of the world, it seemed, along with
its hopes and fears, were fixed on young Sarnoff and his
earphones." Such huge crowds gathered around the Wanamaker store, Lyons wrote, and so many other wireless stations began jamming the airways in their attempt to get into
the act, that President William Howard Taft ordered all the
others to close down so they wouldn't interfere with Sarnoff's
efforts to gather more information. In Lyons's account, "this
was to be a one-man job," with Sarnoff working every moment for three sleepless days and nights, while "the horrified
world hung on his every word."

A later biography of Sarnoff, *The General*, by Kenneth
Bilby, a longtime employee and admirer, told a more precise
and detailed story. According to Bilby, the *New York Times*,
which "provided the most voluminous coverage of the *Titanic* tragedy," never mentioned the name Sarnoff. On April
15, the *Times* reported that the first distress signal had been
received at 10:25 p.m. on April 14 by the Marconi station at
Cape Race, Newfoundland. The *Times* referred to the Cape
Race station as "the storm center of the great battle for news
of the missing passengers." At no time did the newspaper
mention an order by President Taft silencing other wireless
stations.

The only New York newspaper that even referred to Sarnoff was William Randolph Hearst's *American*. On April 16,

two days after the *Titanic* hit the iceberg, the *American* announced a deal with Wanamaker for the exclusive rights to any *Titanic* information its Marconi station might have to offer. The wireless office, in the newspaper's description, was "converted into a branch office of the New York *American* last night. The office was directed by David Sarnoff, manager of this station, assisted by J. H. Hughes, an expert Marconi operator. . . . With every bit of energy at their command these men stood by their posts all night and fired scores of messages and captured scores concerning the wreck."

So, it is evident that Sarnoff was at least involved in wireless reports of the *Titanic*'s fate, despite the doubts some people have expressed. If, in later years, he exaggerated that involvement, it was no more than many older men do when they review their careers.

BY 1932, WHEN I went to work for KHJ and CBS in Los Angeles, broadcasting had made great strides since its rise to prominence in the *Titanic* tragedy. Though it was not yet an important facet of American life, it was already a robust industry. And on the roof of the KHJ radio studio was a weird-looking contraption that a more prescient person might have recognized as a harbinger of even more marvelous developments ahead.

It was an experimental television transmitter, put together by a clever engineer named Harry Lubcke, who had somehow acquainted himself with the state of television art, such as it was at that time. In addition to the transmitter there were, I think, only three receiving sets, possessed by Don Lee, his son, Tommy, and Lubcke himself. If any of the staff wanted to see the picture being transmitted we had to climb to the roof and look at a monitor there. But we seldom did. Among radio people at that time, the development of television was believed to be countless years in the future. When you looked at the picture on that tiny screen, you might think it would be centuries in the future.

The only thing Lubcke had to telecast were old movies, and old movies in '32 were *really* old movies. I was no more able to envision the future of television from this than I had been able to envision the future of radio from listening to that crude, staticky crystal set I had put together as a boy.

The *World Almanac* for 1932 reported that at the end of that year, 16,809,562 American homes had a radio in the living room, which was where virtually every one of them was placed in those days. Your Philco or Stromberg Carlson or Majestic or Atwater Kent console was the most prominent piece of furniture in the house, and frequently the most expensive. The family would gather around it and stare at it as if it were a glowing fireplace. The 1932 U.S. radio census reported an increase of 4.5 million sets in the previous three years. The American public had spent $1.5 billion buying radios—a staggering figure for the depression days of the early 1930s. California alone boasted 1,067,705 sets; New York, 2,500,723.

In May 1932, Jack Benny made his radio debut, and in October, Fred Allen launched his first show, *The Linit Bath Club Revue*. Jack Pearl introduced his Baron Munchausen character that year, as you might recall if you "vas dere, Charley." And *The Maxwell House Show Boat* began, with Charles Winninger and Lanny Ross.

After only a short delay, Fred Allen started to show his very real contempt for most network vice presidents. Not overly concerned with precise timing, he sometimes let his show run overtime. On one such occasion he was cut off the air, the reason for which he explained in his own terms during his next show. "The main thing on radio is to come out on time," he said. "If people laugh, the program is longer. The thing to do is to get a nice, dull half-hour. Nobody will laugh or applaud. Then you'll always be right on time, and all of the little emaciated radio executives can dance around their desks in interoffice abandon."

Each of these shows originated in New York, which was already established as the capital of radio. The seventy-story RCA Building—the crowning jewel of Rockefeller Center, and still the home of NBC—was then in the process of construction. Meanwhile, the NBC facilities, like those of CBS, were spread out across midtown Manhattan, filling up more and more office space each year for their growing staffs.

On the West Coast, radio facilities were smaller and less dispersed. Our whole KHJ-CBS operation, with a staff of slightly over a hundred, was contained on two floors. The top NBC station, KFI, was owned by Earle C. Anthony, who was also the largest Packard automobile dealer in California. Those were the days when Packard was Cadillac's chief competitor. It was well understood around KHJ that Don Lee did not appreciate any of his employees ever visiting the enemy camp.

Though we could hardly compare ourselves in size to the operations in the East, I think we had more fun and got a better preparation for broadcasting careers than most of the people back there. And this was mostly because of the clock. When it was prime time on the East Coast, it was still afternoon in California. We couldn't just hook into whatever New York happened to be offering—if, in fact, it was offering anything. In those days the menu from New York was pretty skimpy. Even if they did have something we might want to use, we couldn't just record it and then broadcast it in three hours, except under very special circumstances. Because of a prejudice against what was then called "electrical transcription," the big stations did not broadcast recordings. All our shows were live. And we were on the air eighteen hours a day. This meant that we had to do a major share of our own programming.

Since CBS in New York could offer us only enough shows for a few hours daily, a relatively small number of people in Los Angeles had to create programs to fill the rest of the broadcast day. Though we had been hired for specific jobs (I was listed as a comedy writer), most of us actually had to work interchangeably as producers, writers, directors, actors, announcers, reporters, sound-effects inventors, and sometimes even commercial-time salesmen. We also took turns running the hectograph or mimeograph machines to make sure our scripts would be in the hands of the actors when it was time to go on the air. Meanwhile, the actors were standing by, thinking up ad libs to use in case their scripts didn't arrive. Quite often the scripts were delivered a page at a time while the show was already on the air. And since ours was the flagship outlet in Don Lee's network, we had to make our programs available to the seven others, up and down the coast. Fortunately, our staff was capable enough to get all this done, though just barely, sometimes by dint of working eighteen hours a day. There were no unions in radio then to protect us from donating our overtime free.

It was a very inventive time in radio, because there were no preconceptions about what programs were supposed to be. If we thought something might work, we simply tried it. And, as I realized later, every concept that subsequently became part of radio had been done in at least preliminary form during those years of our freewheeling experimentation on the West Coast. This included serious drama and music, as well as comedy of all kinds, audience participation, serials, and every form of news programming, from straight reporting to commentary to the re-creation of actual events in what came to be known as "I Was There" or "You Are There" shows.

All of this was great for me. It gave me experience I would

find immeasurably valuable in years to come. I was allowed to write, direct, announce, and sometimes even act in programs, many of which I conceived and developed. In those days we generated twenty-five or thirty hours of programming a week, and the shows were not provincial amateur hours. The first show on which I worked was *The Merrymakers*, broadcast from eight to nine every Sunday night, before overflow audiences of eight hundred people in our biggest studio auditorium. It was an hour of music and comedy featuring Raymond Paige and his orchestra and chorus, and at least twenty performers in comedy segments. Besides the musical chorus there was also sometimes a "Greek chorus"—my fellow writer Jack Van Nostrand and myself, uttering snide asides. We also hired star singers, leading musical groups, and headliner nightclub comedians.

We were able to take full advantage of the fact that the movie industry had attracted a huge pool of talent to Los Angeles. Paige himself was already well known, though not as famous as he would become in New York as the Radio City Music Hall conductor. He fit perfectly into our jocular style at KHJ. After an outstanding performance we'd call him "Rimsky," but when we didn't think he had been up to his own high standard we'd call him "Ray Fio Paige," in disrespectful reference to the band leader Ted Fio Rito. Paige took it well and gave as good as he got. (I'm not sure how Fio Rito would have taken it.)

Another one of our most popular shows was a police drama created by William N. Robson titled *Calling All Cars*. Robson later became one of the most successful producer-directors in radio, with such shows as *Columbia Workshop* and *Suspense*. The phrase "Calling all cars" has since become a cliché, but at the time it was actually used by the Los Angeles Police Department. The police radio had an announcer named Rosenquist who would pop onto the air in a breathless voice and shout: "Calling all cars! Calling all cars! Man down at Hollywood and LaBrea!" or "Robbery in progress at Fifth and Hill!" with whatever details he had. Then he'd sign off with, "That is all. Rosenquist."

The show was a great success on our CBS western network. Robson continued as producer, but I wrote a few scripts for it, for each of which he paid me an extra ten dollars—a fourth of the forty he received.

At one point, when we couldn't find someone with enough of a voice to satisfy Bill, he asked me to announce the program. All went well for several shows. Then one night, when I got to the final disposition of the case at the end of the show, I signed off by saying, "And today, that man is in San Quison Printon. I mean, San Prenton Quiston." I paused to collect myself. "Anyway," I concluded, "he's safely tucked away in jail someplace."

Years later in New York, when I was helping to put Jack Webb's *Dragnet* on television, I used to think about *Calling All Cars*. *Dragnet* had already been a big hit on radio, and every time I'd heard it I'd been aware of its similarity to *Calling All Cars*. When Jack took the show to television in 1951, he was surrounded by people who kept telling him he'd have to make it more "visual": "You're not on radio now."

"Pay no attention," I warned him. "You've got a good, strong show structure. Don't listen to people who keep trying to change it."

Years after that, Jack told me he had taken my advice. "I shot the first fifty-two TV shows straight from the radio scripts, with no changes whatsoever," he said.

Visuals are unquestionably important in television, but most important of all—whether in radio, on television, or in movies—is the story itself and how it's written.

With all the interchanging of jobs at KHJ, it was inevitable that I would eventually get into selling, especially since my father had been a successful businessman, and I had learned a lot from him. One thing I noticed when I went to KHJ was that automobile companies seldom advertised on radio. If you wanted to find out about the new Hupmobile or Buick or Hudson or LaSalle or Cadillac, you had to spend a nickel on a copy of the *Saturday Evening Post* or *Collier's* or *Liberty* or one of the other national magazines. Here I was working for a radio station and network owned by the biggest Cadillac dealer in the West, yet we had no Cadillac commercials— no other car commercials, either, if I remember correctly. When I asked my colleagues about this, they would explain to me, as if they were reciting a law of nature, that it was impossible to sell cars on radio. Before anyone would buy a car, he had to see it.

That last statement made sense, but it also occurred to me that you couldn't see *any* of the products advertised on radio, yet they must be selling, or the manufacturers and their outlets wouldn't be spending so much money on commercials.

My reasoning did not prevail until, one day, I got together with the manager of Don Lee's used-car lot. Like any secondhand dealer, he had a continuing problem. Some of his cars sold quickly; others hung around the lot as if they had taken up permanent residence. He began calling me every morning to describe two or three cars he was eager to move that day. He'd give me the details on some Dort he was tired of looking at, or some Marmon on which he'd decided to cut the price. I'd type up a commercial, it would be read on the air, and we'd sell his radio specials within a few hours. Even better, the specials would attract so many curious people, he'd also sell a lot of other cars.

Before I knew it, I was involved in selling and management. The salesmen got into the habit of taking me with them when they visited an important prospective sponsor. When we arrived, they'd introduce me, then sit back and shut up, leaving the selling to me. I didn't really mind, because I rather enjoyed the process, even though I had been an outstanding failure in my attempts at selling advertising in New York. Here I had something better to sell—a medium the companies really needed in order to help their sales during the Depression. I would figure out a company's basic marketing problems, find out what kind of customers it was trying to reach, and suggest the type of radio advertising most likely to attract them.

Once in a while I would dream up a show especially suitable for a particular company—though not often, because in those days the broadcaster decided what went on the air, not his clients or the ad agencies. They simply bought time on whatever programs the station had to offer.

I still remember one show I created for a client because of the way it ended. The Western Auto Supply Company, a large Southern California chain, wanted to sponsor a program that would cheer people up in those hard times. I suggested a show called *America Victorious*, and they bought it.

I went back through American history to pick out some of the tough situations the country had faced and how it had overcome each crisis. We dramatized these stories, one crisis at a time, with Raymond Paige's orchestra and a forty-voice chorus in the background.

The show opened and closed with the announcer's voice emerging from the music and crying out in stentorian tones: "America victorious! America unafraid! America unconquered!"

The critics liked the program, and, judging by the mail response, so did the listening public. (We had no rating system at that time.) But after twenty-six weeks, I got a call from an executive at Western Auto.

"America victorious," he said. "America unafraid. America unconquered. America unsponsored."

My first *succès d'estime*, but, alas, not my last.

I had somewhat better luck with my first "spectacular." The Rio Grande Oil Company wanted something unusual to celebrate the octanal power and various other virtues of its brand-new Flying Red Horse gasoline. What was new about it? The name, I guess. And the winged red steed that was its symbol.

What they wanted, they said, was something really big. Huge. Bigger than anything that had ever been done in the radio business. So I suggested they take over KHJ's entire program schedule for a whole broadcast day—eighteen hours. We would pre-empt all of our programs, except for two or three national shows that were protected by contract. Rio Grande Oil could sponsor all the rest, filling the airwaves with Flying Red Horse commercials from 6 a.m. until midnight.

They accepted the notion, and as far as I know they were happy with the result, despite the cost. But I was disappointed personally. I had wanted them to send up a dirigible with a huge inflated Flying Red Horse suspended on a cable from its belly. My plan was to fly it for the whole eighteen hours, covering the entire Los Angeles area, over and over. The oil company, however, refused even to entertain the idea, perhaps because they found out I intended to tout our station by having its call letters emblazoned on the horse's belly.

FROM TIME TO TIME, I also broadcast the news. My biggest story took place on March 10, 1933.

I wasn't at the station when I became aware what was happening. I was at home—not because it was my day off (we didn't get very many of them; we usually worked seven days a week), but because by five o'clock in the afternoon I had thought that particular day's work was done.

I was still living with my parents, but we were no longer in Bel Air. We were back in the Fremont Place house, where I had spent many of my happy boyhood years. It was not as big as the Bel Air house, but it was just as comfortable. My father liked the place so much, he didn't sell it when he decided to build in Bel Air. And we had recently returned to it because, as my father said, "This is no time to own two big homes. We're going back to the old one."

Though my father was hardly destitute, he had suffered losses during the Depression and was concerned about a law that permitted what was called deficiency judgments. In California it meant that even if you owed only $25,000 on a house—which was a small mortgage in Bel Air—and it went up for auction because you couldn't make the monthly payments, you didn't just lose the house; you also owed the new owner $25,000, even if he had bought it at auction for one dollar.

My father did, in fact, owe $25,000 on the Bel Air house, which was why he decided to sell it. He had paid $70,000 to build it, but I doubt if he got more than half that when he sold it. I hated to see it go, because I had some fond memories of the place. I remember coming home from college one summer and looking out the window toward what is now Westwood. There was a lot of construction activity—huge cranes, bulldozers, cement mixers. "What are they doing in Ed Janss's bean fields?" I asked my father. "They're building a Los Angeles campus of the University of California," he said. I was witnessing the birth of UCLA.

That March day in 1933, I had just arrived home when my sister, Sylva, asked me to drive her to the grocery store. I was sitting in the car in front of the store, listening to the radio, when suddenly the vehicle began to sway. I realized we were in the grip of a serious earthquake. Growing up in Los Angeles, I'd experienced a lot of them, but I'd never been in one as loud as this. It roared like a wild animal and screeched like a New York subway train. But I still didn't realize how serious it was, even when I went into the store to look for my sister and found that all the shelves had fallen down.

Sylva was shaken but unharmed. I took her back home, then hurried to the station, where I found Jack Van Nostrand trying to discover where the quake was centered and how much damage it was doing. The aftershocks were still coming, and they were sharp.

We sent out all our short-wave radio cars to report on the most severe areas of damage. (This was before the Cal Tech Seismology Lab could tell you in a few minutes the exact location of the epicenter.) By the time our radio cars had sent in a few hours' worth of damage reports and interviews with survivors, we had decided it must have been centered in Long Beach, about 20 miles straight south from downtown Los Angeles, and there was so much damage in Long Beach that everyone else was arriving at the same conclusion. Since that day, it has been famous as the Long Beach earthquake, even though the nearby suburb of Compton was just as severely hit, and the actual center of the quake was finally determined to have been on the ocean floor some distance offshore from Long Beach. Nor were Long Beach and Compton the only communities seriously hit. The entire Los Angeles basin was badly shaken, and the damage everywhere was increased by the fact that very few buildings in the area then were earthquake-proof. Some still aren't.

After working all night, we learned that at least 120 people had died in the quake, and early estimates put the property damage at $50 million—the equivalent of perhaps $2 billion today. Schools suffered especially alarming damage. Some were wiped out completely, and many were so hard-hit they could never be used again. If the quake had arrived earlier in the day, thousands of children would have been killed.

By 5 a.m., Van Nostrand and I had compiled enough information and interviews about this tragedy for one night. We were about to go home to get some sleep when a call came from New York. CBS wanted a one-hour documentary on the quake, and they wanted it in one hour, to go on the air at 6 a.m. our time, 9 a.m. back east. We made the deadline with about three minutes to spare.

Transcontinental hookups (or TCs, as we called them) had developed gradually, as the popularity of radio increased. The use of wire telephone lines to extend the broadcast range had begun in 1922, when the phone company made a line available between Chicago and New York for a special event.

The regular use of a phone cable between distant radio stations came a few years later, connecting stations WEAF in New York and WCAP in Washington, D.C. Thereafter, the chain of connections kept moving westward and southward as the phone company added more and more stations.

By the early 1930s, monthly cable service was available from coast to coast. The chief obstacle to complete national networking was the three-hour time difference, which complicated scheduling. But even that problem was finally being solved, except in the case of prime-time shows.

While most of the big-name programs aired from New York, more and more of them were originating in California, especially if their stars were in movies as well as radio. In 1933, some of these big Hollywood names began appearing on radio, even though the studios were basically anti-radio. Jack Van Nostrand and I helped write a show featuring Bing Crosby. We did the audition and went over to Bing's house (or maybe Don Ameche's) to celebrate. Also there was Bing's accompanist in those days, Lennie Hayton, who later became one of the great conductors on radio. The report from the client, Woodbury Soap, came soon. Basically, they said, Bing should sing, not talk. We were horrified. Bing rose above it, as usual.

Jack and I were also hired to write a show for Dick Powell, and we thought we were really making the grade as Dick's audience laughed away at our jokes. But afterward Dick said to us, "You don't understand me. I'm not funny, I'm cute. My fans want me to be cute, not funny." End of our relationship with Dick.

The main problem by far in the nighttime emptiness from the east was simple. Radio in 1933 was not yet worth paying the extra money it cost to do live repeats for the West Coast, which would become common in two or three years.

Many of the big radio stars were now appearing in movies. One day Samuel Goldwyn asked me and another KHJ writer, Les Weinrott—who would become the king of soap opera in Chicago a few years later—to write some funny stuff to give more lift to his forthcoming Eddie Cantor picture, *Roman Scandals*. We spent a few hours putting together some scenes. Sam said he would read the material later and let us know, but in the meantime, he had a real treat for us: he was going to let us see the final cut of the new Marx Brothers movie, *Duck Soup*. So we watched the film, just the two of us in the projection room, and we chuckled at it. We also told each other it was funny, but no giant hit like *Animal Crackers*. A week later, we attended the premiere at a big theater with an audience of over a thousand, and although we knew the jokes, we fell out of our chairs along with the rest of the crowd. This was a major learning experience: funny stuff is best done before a large audience, because laughter is contagious.

Another lesson I learned early was the extra power of a joke if it's about a topical issue. On our *Merrymakers* show

the week President Roosevelt ordered all the banks to close
temporarily because of the Depression, one of our stars, Ken
Niles, had a line written by Dick Creedon for his character,
Diddleton D. Wurtle. It worried some of our executives, but
when Niles delivered it before a studio audience, he got one
of the longest laughs ever. The sketch was about money, and
Niles declaimed, "I always say, put your money in the bank.
Then you'll always know where it . . . was."

At least from 1932 onward, the Don Lee network was feed-
ing a few programs to the CBS national network on a regular
basis. It was advantageous to get yourself connected with
such shows because that gave you an opportunity to have
your work, and maybe your name, heard daily or weekly
from coast to coast. I remember the first time it happened
to me. I produced a half-hour show called *California Melody*,
with the Raymond Paige orchestra and most of our major
stars, including Nadine Connor, who later sang with the
Metropolitan Opera in New York; the Rhythm Kings, who
later, with additions, were known as the Pied Pipers; and
Kay Thompson, who was about to become famous as a writer
(*Eloise*), composer, and arranger (for Judy Garland, among
others).

California Melody was successful enough to persuade the
Union Oil Company to do a version of it for the West Coast.
The ad manager, Don Forker, was a good friend of mine,
and he gave me the show to build along the lines of *California
Melody*, but with Arthur Jarrett starring. Lord and Thomas
was the agency, but I even wrote the commercials. In fact,
I ended up not only as writer and producer, but as master
of ceremonies. Along with Jarrett and his orchestra we had
some other stars, including—once and only once—his then-
wife, the swimmer Eleanor Holm, as a vocalist.

Eleanor was a much better swimmer than she was a singer,
but she would also have one difficult time as a swimmer. She

easily qualified for the 1936 Olympics and was expected to win a gold medal, as she had in 1932, but the American athletes in those days were controlled by a stuffy, stodgy man named Avery Brundage, and he threw her off the team because she was seen sipping a glass of champagne. She and Jarrett were eventually divorced, after which she married Billy Rose, who returned her to the place where she belonged, starring her in his highly successful Aquacade at the 1939 New York World's Fair.

As I remember it, *California Melody* was an excellent show, and it was well received across the country, which was not surprising in view of the performing talent that had gone into it. I don't know how much good the show did me, but I do know it made me feel important. I was now a transcontinental CBS producer, and in my imagination, at least, there were network executives in New York who must have been impressed by my work.

3

DURING THE EARLY 1930S, A VIRTUALLY UNPUBLICIZED war broke out between the newspapers and upstart radio stations. Before radio, newspapers—and, to a lesser extent, magazines and outdoor billboards—attracted nearly all the advertising money in the United States. Advertisers, whether wholesale or retail, national or local, had no alternative if they wanted to sell their goods. But radio gave them a choice, and from the late 1920s onward, more and more of them were exercising it.

The newspapers, already pinched economically by the Depression, felt seriously endangered by radio, and they tried various methods of fighting the new medium. Sometimes they threatened to reject ads from manufacturers and department stores that bought radio commercials—especially department stores, which couldn't survive without newspaper ads. They tried to stop stations from broadcasting the news by withholding wire services from radio. (Associated Press was

owned by member newspapers.) Finally, the still-solvent papers (the weaker ones failed during the Depression) began
buying up the most prosperous radio stations in their areas,
thus returning to at least a semblance of their old advertising
monopolies. (By 1940, one-third of the eight hundred licensed
stations in the country were either owned by or connected
in some way to newspapers.)

Despite the continuing growth in the popularity of radio,
this struggle was seriously hurting many stations—the more
so because they, too, were feeling the effects of the Depression.

I don't know to what degree the press-radio war was the
cause of it, but the Don Lee outlet in San Francisco, KFRC,
was one of the stations that felt the pinch. I know that because
in early 1934, I was sent there to take charge of news coverage,
sales, and programming. Apparently, some of Lee's other
stations were also hurting financially, since I was told to do
the job, but to do it "without spending any money."

Why I was chosen to go to San Francisco no one in the
Don Lee organization ever bothered to tell me. Dick Wylie,
who was in charge at KHJ, simply said, "That damned station is slipping. Go up there and do something about it."

I didn't go north to the City (as San Franciscans used to
call it) reluctantly, though I had always been amused by its
defensive stance against that expanding collection of sun-
baked, naive, pushy, and unsophisticated suburbs in southern California. For many years, San Franciscans had been
feeling so threatened by the growth and increasing power of
the monstrous megalopolis down south that they were asking
themselves each morning, "How can I hate Los Angeles even
more today than I did yesterday?" In Los Angeles, the feeling
was not reciprocated, though San Franciscans seemed to
think it was. Southern Californians had no reason to feel
threatened by San Francisco, a city they loved to visit. Every-

one admired its beauty and its charm. Yet when people came to California to live, twice as many of them had been choosing Los Angeles for as long as I can remember.

I was, therefore, a member of a small minority—people from Los Angeles moving to San Francisco. I looked forward to it because I, too, loved the place, even if it was a bit provincial while pretending to be cosmopolitan. I can't say I looked upon my move north as a lifetime commitment. In fact, my first "permanent" residence in San Francisco was a hotel, the glorious Fairmont, on Nob Hill. But if you gather from this the false impression that Don Lee was paying me a lavish salary, I should hasten to add that I had only one room at the Fairmont, and I paid for it with due bills from the station, which cost me about thirty dollars a month. A dollar a day—that same room at the Fairmont would now cost more than $200 a day.

I was also able to keep my car, a Pontiac convertible, in Don Lee's garage at KFRC, on the corner of Van Ness and Geary, and one of the attendants there brought it up to the Fairmont every morning, making me look a lot more prosperous and important than I was.

The KFRC facilities, like those at KHJ in Los Angeles, were quite adequate. And so was our news operation, which was in the very capable hands of Ed Fitzgerald, a battlefront correspondent during World War I, who had come to the station from the Associated Press. But Fitzgerald was talking about moving to New York, where he believed he would find better opportunities, especially in radio. I could hardly argue against this possibility, because he had outstanding and diverse talents. I could only hope he would change his mind and stay.

As for sales, they had fallen off, and it seemed to me the only way to increase them was through programming. The general manager in San Francisco was Harrison Holloway, who also emceed the station's biggest hit, *The Blue Monday Jamboree*. KFRC had a large staff and many strong shows, but as radio began to orient itself to Hollywood, a lot of advertisers had started to shift their emphasis to Los Angeles, which was, I discovered, the main reason KFRC was hurting.

The Blue Monday Jamboree was a two-hour theatrical presentation that took place before great crowds of radio fans in our largest auditorium studio every Monday night after the news. It was a musical-comedy variety show with a full orchestra, several featured singers, and a dozen comedy skits. It was thus similar to our *Merrymakers* show in Los Angeles and had long been a big success.

Another KFRC show, *Hodge Podge Lodge*, was the inspired creation of Jennison Parker, a great writer and a very funny man with a king-sized imagination. It would be impossible to describe his zany collection of stuff and nonsense. Think of something outlandish, and I promise, Parker did it on *Hodge Podge Lodge*.

Ed Fitzgerald and Tom Brennaman (later to star on *Breakfast at Sardi's*) were the emcees of an afternoon musical show called *Feminine Fancies*, a title that sounds quaint and patronizing today. It was a popular concert show, with Claude Sweeten leading the orchestra. He had taken over as musical director when the young and obviously talented Meredith Willson—later the creator of *The Music Man*—left the station to go to NBC.

Our *Happy Go Lucky* show hit the air five days a week, with Al Pierce in charge of the craziness with many comics and singers. It had a comedian who always appeared with a cello, which he never played. He'd cuddle up to the instrument as if it were his pet walrus and rattle off the kind of one-liners that eventually made Henny Youngman famous. But this wasn't Youngman; it was Morey Amsterdam, a comic from vaudeville who was to become well known in television on a show I produced—my first big hit at NBC, *Broadway Open House.*

Besides helping to strengthen the existing shows, I was able to develop and sell several new ones. My fondest memories of the station came from the work I did with John Nesbitt, later known for his *Passing Parade* at MGM and his various radio projects. John came from the celebrated John Drew theatrical family and had a marvelous voice. He also had brains. I hired him to do a strip of nightly shows called *Headlines of the Past*, but we also did special-coverage shows. For instance, we covered the celebration of the Jumping Frog of Calaveras County, which Mark Twain had made a part of American literature; Leo Carillo was our main actor. We did a CBS transcontinental show that was very well received.

Not so well received was *If Radio Had Been Invented*, on which we did a broadcast of the 1906 San Francisco earthquake and fire as if it were happening right then. I put in lots of "shields"—warnings to the listener that this was only a re-enactment. But, of course, a lot of people didn't hear the warnings and thought it was a new disaster, so we had to cancel the show. (Several years later, the thought crossed my mind that Orson Welles might have known about our broadcast.)

Many versions of this kind of program have since been produced. *You Are There* is probably the best known, but an earlier version we did in Hollywood was called *I Was There*. This show took a historical event, re-enacted it, and then brought in someone who said, "I was there." The live audition for the sponsor was set up to re-create the Battle of Gettysburg. The producer found a Civil War vet whose record showed that he had been at Gettysburg. The audition proceeded with sound and fury. At the end, the announcer said, "You have just heard a re-enactment of the Battle of Gettysburg. Here to tell you in his own words, 'I was there,' is Staff Sergeant Charles Smith."

Sergeant Smith, looking as old as he was, which was at least ninety, tottered up to the mike and said, "Oh, Gettysburg. That day I was posted north with my squadron. When we got back it was all over. Yep. I missed Gettysburg."

The series did not sell.

Most of these programs were heavy on comedy. I had come to a conclusion I never forgot: comedy will always be the key ingredient of successful programming, whether on radio or on television. The smart thing to do is to build your schedule around well-placed laughter. And it's not so dumb to use comedy in commercials, either. If you associate a product with something that caused you to laugh, you'll be well disposed toward it when you're faced with making a selection. And that includes a product like a radio program or a radio station. If people have a choice between a lot of sober, serious stations and one that's likely to make them laugh, they'll choose the latter.

It wasn't long before we began to see that happening at KFRC. The signs of the station's resurgence were evident as advertisers showed increasing interest in us. San Franciscans were once again talking about what they had heard on KFRC the previous evening. After a hectic first few months of long hours and hard work, we were finally able to relax a bit. And San Francisco, as everyone knows, is a great town in which to relax.

For the people at KFRC, this often meant Taki's place, on Van Ness, where Tommy's Joint is now. We regarded it as our own restaurant and bar. When we were there, the phone operator at the station would put our calls through to us.

Taki, who was waiter, bartender, manager, and maybe even owner, would take the calls sounding like a male secretary.

"Mr. Weaver will be with you in a moment," he'd say.

And I'd pick up the phone as if I were sitting at my desk. If the caller wondered about all the noise in the background, I'd simply say, "You know how it is at a radio station." Then I'd shout, "Turn that set down." And the gang at the bar would lower their voices for me.

The end of Prohibition was not the only big story of the time. The continuing depression was the biggest, of course, and there were a lot of others. In 1933, Franklin D. Roosevelt had become president of the United States, and Adolf Hitler chancellor of Germany. Roosevelt was now attacking economic problems with his National Recovery Administration (NRA), Public Works Administration (PWA), Agricultural Adjustment Administration (AAA), and a long list of other alphabetical measures. Hitler had quickly eliminated democracy in Germany after the Reichstag fire by suspending all constitutional guarantees of individual freedom. The United States had officially recognized the Communist government of the Soviet Union for the first time. And in September 1934, a carpenter named Bruno Richard Hauptmann was arrested as a suspect in the kidnap-murder of Charles Lindbergh's 20-month-old son, Charles Jr., in 1932.

At KFRC, everything was running smoothly, except for one problem that arose in the latter months of 1934. Ed Fitzgerald and his wife, Pegeen, decided to move to New York, where they hosted a successful radio show for several decades. So I had nobody qualified to broadcast the news. Among those I considered unqualified was myself, but since there were no other prospects on the horizon, I decided to take Fitzgerald's place while looking for someone else.

It was during this period that I saw a chance to get a free plug for the station while enjoying a pleasant experience myself. The 785-foot-long navy dirigible *Macon*—the most celebrated, and at that time I think the largest, airship in the world—was based at Sunnyvale, across the bay and about 50 miles southeast of San Francisco. We learned from a navy press release that this monster of the sky (whose sister ship, *Akron*, had crashed in the Atlantic, off Barnegat lightship, in 1933) would be visiting San Francisco on February 12, 1935, and hovering over the city long enough to give everyone an opportunity to get a good look at it. Having lost the *Akron*, the navy was eager to prove the continuing viability of dirigibles by displaying the majestic *Macon* in flight.

I saw a different opportunity. Having failed in my Los Angeles attempt to talk the Rio Grande Oil Company into plugging KHJ on the belly of an inflated Flying Red Horse, I decided I'd try another scheme—this time to get the U.S. Navy to promote KFRC.

I called the *Macon* commander in Sunnyvale and said, "If you're going to be cruising around over San Francisco that day, how about me doing our news broadcasts from the gondola of the ship? I'll be happy to promote the navy in any way I can. You tell me what you want me to include in the broadcasts." It sounded good to him, so we settled on it.

On the morning of the flight, however, they called and canceled. The *Macon* would be flying elsewhere that day. I was annoyed when I got the call, but by evening I was glad the navy had cut me out of its plans. That afternoon, the upper fin structure of the *Macon* malfunctioned above the Pacific, several miles off Point Sur. The enormous vessel settled slowly into the sea and sank. Eighty-three crew members were rescued; two drowned. I probably would have survived, because I was a good swimmer. Of course, if I'd been broadcasting from the *Macon*, CBS nationwide would have picked it up the minute we got in trouble. There went my chance to be the next Lowell Thomas.

A week or two later, while I was still doing the news show, I had a call from the manager of the CBS station in Honolulu.

He had spent several days in San Francisco and caught my newscast. He was prepared to offer me $50 a week more than the $250 or so I was then making, and all I would have to do was broadcast the news—no other responsibilities whatsoever.

Visions of Waikiki floated through my head. I was so enchanted by the prospect of being a surfer again that I accepted immediately. I had accomplished everything I could in San Francisco, and there was nothing more for me to do on the Don Lee network in Los Angeles. Besides, my friends in programming at KHJ were complaining that the local advertising agencies were moving in on them, buying time and providing their own shows.

From what I could gather, the radio business in Los Angeles was not as much fun as it had been only a year earlier. If that was true in Southern California, it would soon be happening in San Francisco. So I resigned from my job at KFRC and began reading everything I could find about Hawaii.

At the same time, however, I was also getting good reactions from people like Ed Fitzgerald in New York. Some network executives there had heard about me. One had even referred to me as the number-one CBS producer on the Coast.

I had also done some more thinking about Hawaii. It was just too perfect, too easy. If I took the job there, with nothing more strenuous than a newscast or two a day, five days a week, how would I spend all my leisure time? I was accustomed to long hours of work, but only when there was work to be done. I loved to goof off whenever I got the chance. And I liked a few drinks whenever the occasion arose, which was more often than I needed. I thought of myself as a potentially weak vessel. Given the opportunity, I might soon become a broken one. Waikiki was just too convenient for a beach-born addict like me.

THE BEST SEAT IN THE HOUSE

So instead of calling the Matson Line and booking passage on the *Matsonia* or the *Lurline*, I called Panama Pacific and took a cabin on a ship whose name I don't remember. I spent two glorious weeks on that ship, with stops at Mazatlán, Panama, Havana, and finally New York. Ed Fitzgerald was there to meet me at the dock. He took me home and gave me a bed for my first few nights.

It was exciting to be back in New York, especially for a young man who believed, like so many others, that you hadn't really made it in America until you made it there. I also loved the theater, and among the great new Broadway shows waiting for me in 1935 were Clifford Odets's *Waiting for Lefty*, Sidney Kingsley's *Dead End*, Lillian Hellman's *Children's Hour*, Sam and Bella Spewack's *Boy Meets Girl*, and a revival of Ibsen's *Ghosts* directed by and starring Nazimova.

But the first thing I wanted to do was to rush over to CBS as soon as their offices opened on Monday morning and let them know I was in town. Every day I delayed I might be missing out on a chance to produce a big comedy show for them. Comedy was what I wanted to do more than anything. Names like Fred Allen, Jack Benny, Eddie Cantor, Ed Wynn, Bob Hope, and Burns and Allen kept dancing through my mind. If I was as well known at CBS as I had convinced myself, it would put a big-name show in my hands. Hadn't someone at CBS said I was the network's number-one producer on the West Coast?

Fate seemed to be running in my direction. Before Monday came, I lucked out in my quest for a place to live, so that I could stop freeloading on the Fitzgeralds. I ran into some Dartmouth friends who were sharing a large apartment on East Seventy-third Street, between Second and Third avenues. They had an empty room, so I moved right in with them. Fortunately, we were on one of the upper floors of a tall building, high enough to escape the train noises from the old Second and Third Avenue Els.

I had already decided to begin at CBS at the programming department. The people there would know what shows the network was planning, since they would be the very people doing the planning. Besides, if they weren't creating any shows at the moment that looked suitable for me, I could take a job in programming. I had proven that I was pretty good at it. There was a long list of shows I had created and produced, both in Los Angeles and in San Francisco. And if I was working in programming, I'd be among the first to know when something good came along.

I went to the CBS offices at 485 Madison Avenue and into what looked like the main office. I asked a man there to direct me to the commercial programming department.

"We don't have a commercial programming department," he said.

"I beg your pardon?" I looked around. "This is CBS, is it not?"

"You've got that right."

"The Columbia Broadcasting System?"

"The very same."

"Well, as we both know, you've got a lot of programs on the air. And they change from time to time. So you must have a department that plans those changes. A programming department."

"You might think so," he conceded. "But, surprisingly enough, we don't program our shows. We don't even own them, except for the few sustaining [no advertising] shows we run—culture, public service, that sort of thing. The advertising agencies put the commercial shows together and bring them to us. And they own those shows."

I was astonished. Though I had realized this sort of thing had begun to happen in L.A., I could hardly believe it was true in New York, right up and down the street from men like William S. Paley, who owned and ran CBS.

"What you're telling me," I said, "is that CBS is not really a network. It's merely a technical facility for the convenience of the ad agencies."

The man smiled indulgently. "Not exactly the way we would put it," he said, "but that's about the size of it."

"Well, then," I said in disgust, "I guess I'd better go see the people at NBC or ABC."

"If I were you, I wouldn't bother," he said. "They work the same way we do. The agencies produce and own their shows, too."

4

PERHAPS I SHOULDN'T HAVE BEEN SURPRISED BY WHAT
the man at CBS had told me, but it was hard to believe the
networks didn't control the programs they were broadcasting. This was not the way it had been done during my years
in California, where the CBS Don Lee regional network, and
even the independent stations, owned just about everything
they put on the air. But I was aware that in Los Angeles
some of the agencies had begun to horn in on programming,
and New York radio people who came to the West Coast had
told me the agencies were becoming more and more powerful
back east. When Jack Benny had moved his show west earlier
that year, I talked to his producer, Tom Harrington, who
filled me in to some degree, but I hadn't suspected that things
had gone this far in New York.

I called on two CBS men I had met during their trips to
California. "You'd better look into what they're telling people downstairs," I said. "If I can believe the fellow who talked

to me, CBS doesn't even own its own shows. You're just a facility, selling airtime to ad agencies for shows they own."

"Welcome to New York," one of them said. "You were expecting, perhaps, something else?"

"I was hoping," I confessed, "to get into production with the network here—more or less the same thing I was doing on the coast."

"And doing it pretty well, according to what we hear."

"Thanks," I said. "But what good does that do me if the networks aren't in production?"

"From what we know about you, you didn't come to the big city to produce public-service, sustaining shows, the kind we do. You want to get into big-time production—Eddie Cantor, Ed Wynn, Fred Allen."

"That wouldn't exactly displease me," I admitted.

"Then you shouldn't be talking to the networks. Talk to the agencies. If you can't beat 'em, join 'em. They own the shows. They've got the power."

"Fine. But how?" I knew few if any people at New York ad agencies.

"It won't be easy to get a big show. But with your record on the coast, our CBS Artists' Bureau ought to be able to get an ad agency to hire you in some capacity. We'll introduce you to Ralph Wonder and Herb Rosenthal. They run the bureau."

I was taken to the Artists' Bureau, which was actually a talent agency within the network. Wonder and Rosenthal knew about shows I had done on the coast. They told me I'd hear from them in a few days—and they meant it. They called me to tell me they had set up an appointment with Thomas A. McAvity, head of radio at Lord and Thomas, a large ad agency presided over by Albert Lasker, one of the giants of the advertising business.

McAvity, a Canadian by birth and a graduate of McGill

University, was a friendly and forthcoming man. He had been filled in on my background, and he had a problem he wondered if I could solve. The agency was interested in a French singer named Odette Myrtil, who had enjoyed some success in Paris. She was a talented chanteuse, though not exactly of star quality. But they had a client, Bourjois Toiletries, whose executives—or, at least, whose chief executive—wanted to make her a star. Bourjois had ordered a radio show built around her. Could I do it?

I put together the outline of a show about a nightclub high in the air, atop a skyscraper. At least, it was a skyscraper in my mind. The program was to be called *Evening in Paris Roof*. I'm not sure why, and I'm not sure what made me think of a skyscraper. As I well knew, there were no skyscrapers at the time in Paris. One thing I must have had in mind was the fact that the sponsor was Bourjois, and I could hardly call it *Evening in New York Roof* when the star was a Parisian chanteuse. It may even be that Bourjois was pushing a perfume called Evening in Paris, but I don't remember. I'm sure they weren't pushing a perfume called Evening in New York. So it was *Evening in Paris Roof*, whatever that might mean.

We did the show from the stage of NBC studio 8G—as far from a Paris roof as your imagination could take you. Odette, a charming, sophisticated lady, was backed up by Mark Warnow's orchestra and the Pickens Sisters, who later earned much more fame than this show brought them. The agency produced the show, and I was the writer—if you could call it writing. Surprisingly, the program was a modest success, though too modest to make Odette a star. Within a year, she was back in Paris.

Fortunately for me, something more interesting came up a few weeks after *Evening in Paris Roof* went on the air. When the CBS Artists' Bureau asked me if my new job was keeping me busy, I replied, quite honestly, "About one day a week." There wasn't much for me to do on the show except to write that little story line and pick up my paycheck, which, as I recall, was $200 a week, enough at New York prices to keep me in the black.

The Artists' Bureau took me to meet the board of directors of United Cigar Stores and Whelan Drug Stores, which had combined. United-Whelan wanted to get into radio but didn't know how to go about it, because its advertising was handled by a house agency that had no experience in the medium.

Ralph Wonder was aware of my selling experience in California and hoped I was the man to advise them. Part of my advice to them, he advised me, should be to create a show around the Isham Jones orchestra, a good, well-known band that the bureau was handling. Jones had an eighteen-piece group and an arranger named Gordon Jenkins, who was to become one of the greatest arranger-composers of his time. Eddie Stone played the violin; Woody Herman played the clarinet and saxophone, and both also sang.

I felt at home with the United-Whelan directors. I was doing what I had often done in California—selling a show to a possible sponsor. It was a show I hadn't yet put together, but I didn't worry about that. I discussed with the directors all the obvious questions: what was their marketing setup, what kind of audience did they hope to reach, how much money were they were willing to spend—subjects about which I was able to talk from past experience. They seemed to think my marketing advice made sense, so I recommended that they buy a musical-variety program, twice weekly, with the title *Good Evening Serenade*, and with a name band. Whose band would that be? I dropped a hint that Isham Jones might be available. They went for it.

Jones and I then put the show together. It was easy to work with Isham. Not only was he an excellent music man, but he didn't have the aggressive or abrasive personality of some musicians I've known. Of all the band leaders I've met—and I've met most of them—Isham displayed the least temperament. He was never "on." He just led the band.

Jimmy Saphier, a young fellow who was then getting started as a talent agent, talked me into hiring a female vocalist he was handling named Loretta Lee, and I'm happy he did—not only because she worked out quite well, but because it gave me a chance to know Jimmy, who became a good friend, as well as an immensely prosperous agent, handling Bob Hope and other important clients. I found some additional acts, and we soon put together *Good Evening Serenade*, with Harry Von Zell as the announcer. (Harry was already announcing the Fred Allen program *Town Hall Tonight* on NBC.)

The only person we didn't have was a master of ceremonies. We came up with a long list of acceptable personalities, but they were all either busy, uninterested, or too expensive. Finally, the United-Whelan board chairman said to me, "Why don't you do it?"

"That's very flattering," I responded, "but no. I hate going on the air. Makes me nervous."

"Didn't you tell us you used to broadcast the news in San Francisco?" one of the directors asked.

"Yes, but that was because there was no one else."

"And did't you do a transcontinental show with John Nesbitt?"

"Yes, but I didn't enjoy it."

"Would you enjoy it," the chairman asked, "if we paid you an extra hundred and fifty a week for it?"

"Well, I guess I'd enjoy that part of it," I admitted.

So I became the producer, writer, and emcee of *Good Evening Serenade*. Along with Harry Von Zell, I also did the audience warmup before the show.

We broadcast it for the Mutual Network, from the New Amsterdam Roof Garden on Forty-second Street, a spacious and popular spot, where Bob Hope, some years later, had his first television show. We did two half-hours a week in front of a live audience, which meant that I now had two "roof" shows—*Evening in Paris Roof*, a musical that pretended to come from a roof but was done in a studio, and *Good Evening Serenade*, a musical that could have come from a studio but was done on a roof. I also had my picture, in white tie and tails, displayed in two thousand United Cigar stores, and I was making $700 a week—$500 for the Isham Jones show plus $200 for the Odette Myrtil program.

Within a few weeks I began to get tired of *Evening in Paris Roof*, because I had so little to do on it. My weekly story line had become even more meager as the demands of the music reduced the words to nothing more than short title gags. With what I was getting from United-Whelan, I didn't need the $200 from Bourjois, so I jumped off the Paris "roof," and as far as I could tell, they hardly noticed I was gone.

On the salary from United-Whelan I could afford to live a pretty decent life, and I took full advantage of the opportunity. The waiters at 21, Le Pavillon, Chambord, and Louis and Armand's began to recognize me, as did the bartenders at the Oak Room of the Plaza and the bars at the Biltmore, Ritz, and Waldorf. At night I got acquainted with the Stork Club, El Morocco, and some of the Fifty-second Street hot spots.

My favorite of these was Club 18, across the street from 21. It was a saloon–comedy club with Jack White as emcee, Frank Hires as the headliner, and, among other comedians, a young Jackie Gleason. Every night, it seemed, at some point, a waiter would walk through the room with a garbage can on his shoulder.

Jack White would stop him and ask, "Where you going?"

To which the waiter would reply, "Across the street with another load of garbage for Twenty-one."

At the other end of Fifty-second Street, near Sixth Avenue, there was an intimate boîte where Louis Prima and his troupe entertained. I used to take Kay Thompson, her boyfriend, Don Forker, and her younger sister, Blanch, to hear Prima. Sometimes I took Jeri Jones. She and Blanch were both members of Kay's all-girl chorus on the Chesterfield program.

I could now afford an apartment of my own, but I continued to see the Dartmouth friends who had taken me in when I arrived in New York. Another buddy was George Russell, one of a family of seven brothers and sisters from Waterbury, Connecticut. The first thing you noticed about the family was that all the girls were stunningly beautiful. One of them, Rosalind, was an actress, Hollywood bound, hoping to break into movies. Though I knew how many stunningly beautiful women were already there trying in vain to do likewise, I didn't tell her how impossible her quest was likely to be—she would find that out for herself. She seemed to have her feet planted firmly on the ground, and she had a great sense of humor, especially about herself. If she failed in the movies, she would still maintain her equilibrium. I took her out several times, though not as often as I dated her sister, Mary Jane.

Another of the lovely Russell girls, Clara, had married a prominent man in the advertising business, Chester LaRoche, president of the prestigious Young & Rubicam agency. The LaRoches maintained an active social life, and, thanks to George Russell, I began getting invitations to their splendid country house just outside Fairfield, Connecticut. It was surrounded by ten acres of green farmland and had a huge pool. The large house had I don't know how many guest rooms, most of which seemed to be full whenever I was there. Weekends with the LaRoches were always enjoyable.

Both Clara and her husband were unfailingly friendly and hospitable. Chester, who soon invited me to call him Chet, was an easy man to get to know, and he seemed to take an interest in me, perhaps because I was in radio and advertising, though hardly at his level. I assumed he was attentive because he wanted to know what the young people in the business were thinking. He was a man with an open mind and a wide range of concerns. He had been a quarterback at Yale, which led some people to think he was just a football player, capitalizing on the celebrity it earned him, but, in fact, he had also been a serious student. When you talked to him you quickly realized how intelligent and perceptive he was.

We often discussed advertising, and especially the effectiveness of radio sponsorship for big corporations—the companies that made up most of Young & Rubicam's clientele. He was particularly concerned about how to measure the effectiveness of radio as opposed to, say, magazines and newspapers. I gave him my frank impressions, always stipulating the limits of my experience.

Though I wasn't yet acquainted with all the inner workings and politics of an ad agency, I was well aware of a dichotomy that existed within the industry between radio people and almost everyone else. Radio was still the upstart, Johnny-come-lately in the business, and most of the veteran ad men hated it, because they had come from print and graphics backgrounds. They believed in the printed word and the eye-catching illustration, neither of which could be used on radio. Yet radio was siphoning off more and more revenue each year from the magazine, newspaper, and billboard ads on which they had always worked.

Chet LaRoche didn't share these feelings. While he might not have known much about radio, never having worked in it, he realized how popular it was already and how big it seemed destined to become. He wanted to be ready for it—to know how to take advantage of the opportunities it offered.

One weekend that summer, while everyone else was partying, Chet took me for a stroll. I supposed he was simply eager to get out of the house so we could breathe some fresh country air, away from all the cigarette smoke in his living room. But he had something else in mind.

"What's your impression of Fred Allen?" he asked me.

"Well," I said, "a lot of American boys grow up wishing they could be Babe Ruth. I don't give a damn about Babe Ruth. I wish I were Fred Allen."

"How would you like to work on his show?"

"Even as an usher I'd be glad to work on his show, provided I could get to know him."

"Well, then, you may be the man we're looking for."

I was even more puzzled than I was astounded. "I thought Benton and Bowles had the Bristol-Myers account," I said. Ipana toothpaste and Sal Hepatica laxative, both Bristol-Myers products, sponsored the Allen show on NBC.

"Benton and Bowles is losing the account," Chet informed me. "Bristol-Myers is coming with us, and we're looking for a new producer for Fred Allen. Would you be interested?"

"Would I! I listen to him every week. I went to see him on Broadway every time I had the chance. I even tried to write some comedy material for him once, while I was riding the Super Chief on my way home to California. I think he's the best we have."

The following Monday morning I was at the Young & Rubicam office, at 285 Madison Avenue, where Chet introduced me to Bill Stuhler, vice president in charge of the agency's radio division, and Don Stauffer, his second in command.

Apparently, Chet had at least talked to them about me. They seemed well acquainted with my California background and with my Isham Jones show, which was still on the air in New York. Unfortunately, Stauffer didn't seem to think much of it. Though he was polite enough in discussing the program with me, I got the impression he didn't consider it exactly first-rate.

That impression was confirmed nineteen years later, when *The New Yorker* quoted him in the profile they did of me: "As I recall it, Pat as an M.C. wasn't so hot," Stauffer told the reporter, Thomas Whiteside. "As a matter of fact, he had a pretty miserable show, and we felt we had to take him off as a performer. That wasn't any blow to us or to him, though. He was so damned smart, he was just being wasted in front of a microphone."

So my uneasy feeling during my meeting with Stauffer had been more than justified. He must have had some serious doubts about me, since the Isham Jones show was basically my creation. Yet when we talked about shows I had done in California, he seemed more enthusiastic. I knew the limitations of the Isham Jones program. It wasn't a big, expensive production—the kind in which Stauffer himself might be involved.

We also talked about Allen, whom everyone in advertising and broadcasting seemed to consider a serious problem. Stauffer obviously felt that way about him. I don't remember his exact words, but they closely resembled another of his *New Yorker* quotes. "We knew we had to have a guy smart as hell to cope with Fred's vagaries," he told Whiteside. "Fred as usual was being hard to handle. Complete disgust at the thought of any contact with agency, client or network. Utter loathing of vice presidents of any description."

When Stauffer said essentially the same thing to me that first day, I could understand his attitude. Yet Allen was my show-business hero, and I didn't like to hear anyone talk that way about him. I also wondered if he was really as difficult as Stauffer seemed to believe. If I got the job, would I be stepping into a mess I couldn't handle? Why was the Bristol-Myers account moving to Young & Rubicam? Was Benton and Bowles eager to get rid of Allen? Or was Allen eager to get rid of Benton and Bowles? Why was he changing producers? What was wrong with the one he had? These were lively questions in my mind, but they didn't make me want the job any less.

Finally, after considerable discussion, Stauffer looked over at Stuhler, then turned to me and said, "Well, it looks as if you've got the job."

It couldn't be that simple, I thought. Surely they'd want to know more about me than they could learn in one interview.

"You mean, just like that, I'm hired?" I asked.

"Unless you decide to turn it down."

"I hope you're not hiring me because the president of the agency brought me to you," I said.

Stauffer smiled tolerantly. "We don't do business that way around here."

Another question arose in my mind. If Fred Allen was really that hard to get along with, could it be that they were offering the job to me, an outsider, because no one in the agency would take it? I decided I'd better not ask. Instead, I said, "Don't you want to look more into my background?"

"We know your record," Stauffer replied, "and we think you'll do all right. At least, we hope so."

"But I've never even met Fred Allen."

"Go meet him. Go to one of his shows. He has three or four more to do before he breaks for the summer."

"What if we don't hit it off? If he's as difficult as you say, he may not like me."

"That's part of your job," Stauffer said. "You've got to make him like you."

BEFORE I MET FRED ALLEN, I THOUGHT IT MIGHT BE WISE
and politic to pay a friendly visit to Benton and Bowles, whose
man I hoped to be replacing. I met both Bill Benton, later a
U.S. senator, and Chester Bowles, later governor of Connecticut, and was surprised to find them cordial, even though
I was taking one of their most popular shows away from
them. Again, I couldn't help wondering if they were relieved
to be getting rid of Allen.

If so, they didn't say. They filled me in on everything they
thought I'd need to know about the show and answered
whatever questions I had. But they didn't give me any personal information about the star, and I didn't have the guts
to ask whether Allen was as bad as everyone seemed to think,
or why they had either lost or dropped the account.

I asked them whether they minded if I went to one of the
rehearsals as an observer. While they were still in charge,
they might not want me snooping around. But they told me

that I really ought to go and familiarize myself with the show. They'd even arrange for one of their people to introduce me to Allen. So I was now about to meet my hero, a fearsome beast who might bite my head off before I got a chance even to say hello.

The one-hour Fred Allen show, *Town Hall Tonight*, was on NBC every Wednesday at nine, an hour that millions of Americans put aside each week to make sure they didn't miss him. The first rehearsal for the show was on Monday. Assuming he wouldn't be quite as busy that day, I showed up the following Monday at NBC. There was Allen and his cast doing their first run-through. I found the Benton and Bowles man, introduced myself, then sat down to watch the proceedings.

In person, on the stage in front of me, Allen didn't look or act like the ogre he was supposed to be. He was a man of medium height with a prominent nose, frowning eyes, and a slightly rumpled pompadour. He made a lot of irreverent remarks to his cast and crew, but they were always funny. Several were mildly sarcastic, but I saw no indication of the slightest bit of cruelty. No one seemed to be afraid of him.

There was a break in the rehearsal, and the Benton and Bowles man beckoned me up onto the stage where Allen was finishing up with one of his people. The Benton and Bowles man, whom I didn't know (he may have been the soon-to-be ex-producer), stepped up to Allen and said, "Fred, this is Mr. Pat Weaver of Young and Rubicam."

I presumed that no further explanation was necessary. Allen had to be well aware of the coming changes, and he might even have been told something about me, his putative new producer. Needless to say, I would not be his new producer unless he was able at least to tolerate me.

He looked me over fairly carefully, assessing my business suit, which was regulation Madison Avenue—dark gray and expensive—then raised his eyes to my face, which was considerably higher than his own, since I am six feet, four inches tall.

"Ah, yes, Mr. Weaver," he said. "I presume you're a vice president at Young and Rubicam."

"No, sir."

"Oh? What's the matter over there? None of the vice presidents want to talk to me? Tell me, Mr. Weaver, how many vice presidents do you have at Young and Rubicam? More than there are janitors, I suppose."

"I don't know," I said. "I'm brand-new there myself." In fact, I wasn't even there yet, but I'd be joining the agency if I got this job.

"Brand-new, you say? Then what agency did you come from? I presume you were a vice president there. You're dressed like a vice president."

I was feeling uncomfortable already but was determined not to show it. "I wasn't with any agency," I said.

"You mean they had to go out on the highways and byways to find someone willing to produce my little show?"

At this, everyone within earshot laughed, and Allen himself almost smiled, making it clear that he was simply having fun. He shook my hand and said, "Welcome in off the street, Mr. Weaver. We hope you like it here."

We had only a short time to talk seriously that day. I sketched in my background, and he told me about the way he liked things done. Before we were through, I had the impression he was at least willing to give me a chance.

He also introduced me to his wife, Portland Hoffa, who was his costar; Harry Tugend, his chief writer; and Everard Meade, the show's publicist, who was helpful to me in all possible ways from that day forward. He knew every aspect of the show, and he set about filling me in as quickly as possible. He also tried to allay the fears he assumed I had about Allen. "If you're any good," he said, "you're going to like him." But that, of course, had to mean if Allen thought I was any good.

I went to the broadcast that Wednesday night, and to all the rehearsals and broadcasts during the next three weeks, before the summer break. In the meantime, I had to make a decision about the Isham Jones show, which I was pretty sure Y&R would expect me to drop, since Don Stauffer didn't seem to hold it in very high regard. I had agreed to do the twenty-six programs already set for the Mutual Network, and we still had about half of those to go.

I asked Chet LaRoche if I could do the rest of them (especially since United-Whelan was paying me more than the starting salary I would be getting at Y&R), and he said yes.

I then went to the United-Whelan board of directors and broke the news that I'd be moving on to Y&R as producer of the Allen show. It was a program I dearly loved, I explained, and an excellent opportunity for me. It was the chance of a lifetime. I had enjoyed working for them, and I was sorry I'd have to be leaving, but I wouldn't leave them stranded. Young & Rubicam had agreed that I could finish out our twenty-six-week contract.

Their reaction surprised me. The chairman of the board asked, "Does this mean you'll be joining Young and Rubicam?"

"Yes," I responded. "I'll be working for them, but my basic job will be to produce the Allen show."

"Young and Rubicam, that's a very good agency," he said. "One of the best."

"All we have is our house agency, and it's really not equipped for our needs. Why don't we go with you to Young and Rubicam?"

I was hardly prepared for this. As far as I knew, Y&R handled only big, national companies, and United-Whelan was a regional concern. I doubted that Y&R would accept them as a client, but I didn't want to say that.

"I don't think Young and Rubicam is the kind of agency that would do you people the most good," I said. "They handle companies like General Foods, Bristol-Myers, Packard Motor Cars. Companies whose products sell nationally, and even internationally. I'm not sure they'd be very effective at the hard-hitting merchandising you fellows do. I don't know that they're set up for that."

"But they could be, couldn't they?"

"Well, I suppose so."

"Good. Because we want to go with you."

I was flattered, but also uneasy for fear that Y&R would turn them down. All I could do was shrug.

With some trepidation, I went to Chet LaRoche bearing this news. But he didn't even hesitate. "Fine," he said. "Whatever they need, we'll set it up for them."

As I soon learned, Y&R had an excellent merchandising department. They handled Borden Dairy and other blue-chip companies. To me, United-Whelan was pretty big, but not to them. Regional retailing is hardly what a major agency goes after, so I was pleased that Chet was willing to take them on. United-Whelan became a Y&R client, and I finished out my obligation to the Isham Jones show. Since it went off the air after its twenty-six-week stint, I was fortunate, even financially, despite my cut in salary, to be able to fall back on the Allen program. There wasn't much danger of it being canceled.

During one of my first private conversations with Fred after he returned to New York from his summer home in Maine, he confided to me that he wasn't completely satisfied with *Town Hall Tonight*. "Benton and Bowles kind of imposed it on me because of *Show Boat*"—a big radio hit, based on the 1927 Broadway smash. "I don't want to have the trouble with you that I had with some of those guys. They kept trying to shove an eggbeater up my ass and make a floating faux pas like *Show Boat* out of me."

I said, "As far as I'm concerned, what you've got is a marvelous format." And as soon as I said it, I decided I had made a mistake. He says he doesn't like his show, so I jump in and tell him it's marvelous. I'm not sure what you should say to someone when he knocks his own creation, but I think you should be careful about praising what he has just condemned. I hastened to change the subject.

"I want you to know," I said, "I saw you in the first *Little Show* on Broadway, and in *Three's a Crowd*. I saw each of them two or three times. I couldn't get enough. I've been hooked ever since."

As I said this, it suddenly occurred to me I was making another mistake. I waited for him to tell me he hated both of those shows, too, but he just passed over my remark and explained to me, as he later explained in his book, *Treadmill to Oblivion*, how the hated format of *Town Hall Tonight* had come into being.

He had been doing a half-hour show, from 9:30 to 10 p.m., sponsored by Sal Hepatica. From 9 to 9:30, Ipana toothpaste was sponsoring a musical program, which drew a much smaller audience than the Allen half-hour. Since both Ipana and Sal Hepatica were Bristol-Myers products, someone at Benton and Bowles (Allen assumed the villain was a vice president, inasmuch as most villains to him were vice presidents) convinced Bristol-Myers that it should drop the Ipana musical, thus saving the expense of an orchestra, and make Allen fill the whole hour with his comedy.

"Anyone who knows how hard it is to be funny for a half-hour," he said to me, "will realize it's three times as hard to be funny for a whole hour." But he agreed to try. During the rehearsal, there was only one hitch. The new Sal Hepatica commercial was supposed to feature the sound of the laxative fizzing in a glass of water, but the sound man hadn't been able to make it fizz. At the rehearsal, however, the fizzing sound was bright and clear. Afterward, Allen asked him how he had been able to bring forth this miracle. "It was easy," the sound man said. "I used Bromo Seltzer." So much for truth in advertising in those days.

Perhaps lulled by the effervescence of the commercial, the Bristol-Myers people bought the idea, whereupon Allen had a whole hour to fill. The Bristol-Myers slogan, "Ipana for the smile of beauty—Sal Hepatica for the smile of health," prompted someone at Benton and Bowles—presumably another vice president—to name the show *The Hour of Smiles.*

Allen finally put his foot down. *Hour of Smiles* reminded him of all the sugary sweetness and light he disliked about the currently popular *Show Boat.* It was at this point, apparently, that he decided they weren't going to make a "floating faux pas" out of him. He changed the title to *Town Hall Tonight,* but he was still somewhat unhappy about the matter.

In the fall of 1935 I became the producer of *Town Hall Tonight.* Each weekly show had four parts. The first was the Town Hall news, Allen's sendup of whatever current events, important or trivial, attracted his sardonic sense of humor.

Part two was Portland Hoffa's segment. She would bring in a guest, usually a fictitious person she wanted Fred to meet. He would then do his best to make some sense out of whatever weird ideas she and her guest would propose to him.

One day she produced two men who were supposedly eager to help the Allens decide whether to vacation in the mountains or at the seashore. They were both, in fact, accomplished professional comedians. One, Ed Brown, was touting his Catskill resort, Chez Katz, while the other, Jack Smart, was extolling the convenience and luxury of his Sea Gull Manor, on the New Jersey shore.

For two or three minutes, each belittled the other's resort. Smart observed, in a comic Yiddish accent, that Chez Katz was actually a tacky place where the riff met the raff. Brown insisted that Sea Gull Manor was not an idyllic place to bask in the sun but a disaster getting ready to happen. When the tide came in, he said, the rooms were flooded.

Portland feigned astonishment and alarm. "You don't mean to tell us the tide comes right into the rooms?"

Brown assured her that the situation at his rival's resort was even worse. "You have to be treading water to get undressed," he said. "It's so wet, the chambermaids have webbed feet."

Part three consisted of a big sketch by the Mighty Allen Art Players, a comedy group whose members remained fairly anonymous on *Town Hall Tonight* but several of whom became almost legendary some years later, when Allen changed his format to create *Allen's Alley.*

And part four was the amateur segment, in which Allen would interview a person who purported to have some usually outlandish talent, whereupon this person would perform whatever it was he claimed he could do. These were real people, chosen from among three or four hundred who applied each week. I was soon to find myself involved in their selection.

Preparations for the first show that fall seemed frantic to me—because, in fact, they were frantic—and by the time we got on the air I was fairly nervous. As I stood in the control booth behind the technicians, watching the performers on the stage and listening to their routines, I could think of all kinds of things that might go wrong. Suddenly I realized there were two men in the booth I didn't know. They were chatting and joking amiably, making it difficult for me to concentrate.

Finally, at the first commercial break, I turned to them and said, "I'm sorry, gentlemen, but if you will, I'd like you to leave the booth. This is my first show, and you're bothering me."

They left without argument, and the show continued with no further complications. When it was finished and we were off the air, one of the technicians turned to me and said, "Do you know who those fellows were who you kicked out of the booth?"

"No," I said.

"One of them was Deke Aylesworth, the president of NBC. The other was Lee Bristol, the president of Bristol-Myers, your sponsor."

How could I repair a goof like that? I decided I'd better let Fred Allen know, before Aylesworth or Bristol told him. Allen was the only person who might be able to save me from getting fired. But why should he care about me?

I hurried backstage and found him outside his dressing room. I congratulated him on the show, which I thought had been very funny, and then told him, rather sheepishly, how I had kicked the presidents of NBC and Bristol-Myers out of the control booth.

For a moment he stared at me in disbelief, but then he burst out laughing as if it were the funniest thing he had ever heard. He started telling everybody on the staff about it, and I suddenly found myself a hero instead of a goat. In an article written about Allen some years later, he indicated to the author that what had cemented our relations was the time I threw out the presidents of the network and the sponsor.

Reassured about my relationship with Allen, I moved into my new office at Young & Rubicam, which I was to share for some time with Harry Von Zell, Allen's announcer, who was so good and in such demand that Y&R had hired him full-time to make sure he was available for their shows. I already knew him and liked him from the Isham Jones show. I must admit he led an enviable life. For a few minutes of airtime per week easy minutes for someone as smooth as he was—he lived luxuriously with his wife in a country home where I was destined to spend many a happy hour.

Also coming with us to Y&R, and into an office near ours, was Everard Meade, the show's publicist, a gentlemanly Virginian, who still lives in Charlottesville. Whoever made the decisions about agency personnel was apparently adept at spotting good people and grabbing them. Maybe that accounted for the success of the agency, which had been founded only ten or so years earlier.

One of my first assignments at Y&R had nothing to do with Fred Allen. Jack Benny, whose show the agency also owned, was touring various cities in the east, though he had recently moved to California. He was all set to do a broadcast in Boston, about Boston, when Don Wilson, his longtime announcer, had to fly back west because of a family emergency. Knowing I had had some experience on the air (I was still doing the Isham Jones show at this time), the agency sent me to Boston to fill in for Wilson. I don't know why they didn't choose Harry Von Zell; he may have been busy on something else.

I had met Benny in California but didn't really know him. I did, however, know his producer, Tom Harrington. When I was reintroduced to Benny, he acted as if he remembered having met me before, though I'm not so sure he did. Thereafter, whenever he saw me he would call me "kid," even after we really got to know each other. I assumed he had trouble remembering names, because he called lots of people "kid."

I announced the show for Benny and then returned to New York, where I found Allen gleefully awaiting me. A critic for one of the Boston papers had disliked the program because he thought Benny was taking his fair city too lightly, or some such thing. Allen had clipped the review and was laughing about it when he gave it to me. He never let me forget how I had been "panned in Boston," a play on the expression "Banned in Boston" which lampooned the prim theater and book censorship there in those days. It was Benny, of course, who had actually been "panned in Boston." I doubt if any Bostonian was even aware of my presence—or of my existence, for that matter—but Fred was so involved with language and so nimble in its uses that he could hardly resist an inviting play on words.

I was now beginning to settle comfortably into Allen's weekly routine. After the Wednesday-night show, we had to wait two hours until midnight, when we did a live repeat of the whole thing for the West Coast. By this time there was so much demand around the country for New York programs, and so much money to be made on them, that all the big ones were doing live repeats, which meant that the entire self-contained radio production situation I had known in California was falling apart. I had come east at the right time. Allen was now so popular that as soon as the capacity crowd of twelve hundred people vacated studio 8H after the nine o'clock show, another twelve hundred pushed their way in for the midnight repeat.

Town Hall Tonight was an endless grind for Allen. When he and Portland arrived home at their apartment in the Dorset Hotel some time after 1 a.m. Thursday morning, he would get just a few hours of sleep before he had to begin work on the next week's show. Because he did almost all of the writing, he never had much time to himself. He had to come up with more than fifty pages of dialogue before the following Sunday night, when I took the script to the NBC censor. (Network censorship then was much stricter than it is now. It's never called censorship today, because the word is unpopular; it's called "continuity acceptance," or some such euphemism. But the practice persists.)

With all the deadlines, the censorship, and the length of the show, "You just lived in a fog," as Allen once put it. "A bedlam."

He did have three writers, good ones, but that didn't much help a man as meticulous as Fred Allen. His chief writer, Harry Tugend, fashioned the Mighty Allen Art Players segment after Allen had outlined the basic theme. Tugend would put together ten pages or so, often quite funny, then Allen would read it carefully and rewrite it, even if he liked it. Sometimes he would use none of Tugend's material, because a completely different idea would pop into his head, and he would compose the whole thing from scratch.

His other two writers were young men just out of Columbia University and both destined for fame, though not through the Allen show. One was Herman Wouk, now renowned as the author of such works as *The Caine Mutiny* and *The Winds of War*. The other was Arnold Auerbach, who became a highly successful Broadway producer. He and Wouk were less successful with Allen—not because they lacked talent, but because his demands were so exacting. They would submit material, and he would throw it out. He would take lines from them once in a while, but I don't recall him ever using one of their scripts while I was there.

I remember one occasion when he told the cast to perform a scene Wouk and Auerbach had written while they listened. Afterward, he said, "Well, boys, do you understand now why I have to do what I do?" They said they did.

The fact is, Allen wrote the whole show himself, except for the amateur segment, which was left unscripted, so as to

challenge his ability to ad-lib on the air—a challenge he had
no trouble meeting.

This segment was prepared by me, Harry Von Zell, and
"Uncle" Jim Harkins, a longtime Allen friend and associate.
Each week we would audition an endless number of hopefuls,
and would usually choose the most unlikely. We looked for
people with a far-out talent or occupation that would lend
itself to a funny interview. We'd put some ridiculous clue on
a card for Allen, and this would be all he'd know about the
guest.

Once, our card said, "Don't be surprised if God, who's
coming in to play the French horn, is very, very tall."

When this tall young man entered with his round, coiled
instrument, Fred said to him, "Son, I hope you realize you
have there a very dangerous horn."

The fellow didn't realize any such thing. "What do you
mean?" he asked.

"I had an uncle down in Texas," Fred explained, "and he
played the French horn. One day a wind came up, a big
wind, maybe a tornado, while he was playing the horn in his
back yard. This wind hit his horn and spun him thirty feet
into the ground . . . so deep he struck oil."

Fred would labor over the script from Thursday until Sunday evening, printing it in tiny letters with a pencil. Meanwhile, to relieve him of routine work, I would write the
continuity—the opening of the show and the lead-ins to each
segment. Sometimes my memory of comedy writing in California, and my old ambition to write for Allen, would get
the better of me, and I'd insert bits of my own. But I had
no more luck than Wouk and Auerbach. Years later, he told
The New Yorker that the only difficulty he had had with me
was my persistent desire to write for him: "Pat was always
batting out scripts and trying to get me to use them on my
show. I remember one of them. It was a comedy sketch about
the Foreign Legion. I suggested to Pat that he join it."

Late Sunday afternoon, I would go to Allen's apartment in the Dorset with the continuity sections, which were to be blended in with what he had written—or, in most instances, what he was still writing. Usually he'd be alone in his study at the rear of the apartment, pencil and script in hand. He would also be chewing tobacco, which horrified me. Trying to develop some funny phrase in his mind, he would push back his chair, get up, and pace the room, spitting tobacco juice out the rear window when he passed it. I often wondered what he was hitting down below, but I never went to the window to look, for fear some angry person with a splattered head would be staring up and shaking a fist at me. I'm happy to say that Fred broke that tobacco-chewing habit early on in our relationship. He had enough health problems as it was.

I would sit with him until he finished writing, after which we'd put the script together. Then, unless I was going out to dinner with him and Portland, I'd take the script over to Miss McCrory, the NBC censor. I don't remember her first name. I'm not sure I ever knew it, as I spent as little time as possible with her. Theoretically, we had to deal with three censors—the network's, the sponsor's, and the ad agency's. Being the agency's representative, I was also its censor, and Fred's scripts never had any trouble getting past me. Bristol-Myers had long since made it clear they wouldn't appreciate, to quote *The New Yorker*, "gags about doctors, who might be considering prescribing Sal Hepatica, or about druggists, who sold it and Ipana, or about dentists, who might recommend it."

I don't remember any censorship issues with Bristol-Myers, perhaps because Fred was accustomed to avoiding their taboos. Sometimes we had trouble with Miss McCrory, and I'd battle it out with her, winning some and losing some. I must have won often enough, because Allen frequently expressed his appreciation of my efforts. Once he even pinned a medal on me, which he said was for valor above and beyond the call of duty in my duels with Miss McCrory and her deadly sharp blue pencil.

On those Sunday nights, when our work was done and Fred and I would be gossiping or joking, Portland would sometimes appear, obviously to get rid of me. She monitored Fred closely because he had heart trouble, eye trouble, and I don't know what else. She was determined to make sure he got enough rest. A devoted wife as well as a congenial companion, she seemed to have great fun trading jokes with him, but one thing she didn't joke about was his health.

When Fred was feeling well, the three of us would go out to dinner together. I always enjoyed that, because both of them were so entertaining, even though, unlike other comedians, neither was ever "on"—they saved their performances for their shows. Yet they were so intelligent and so well informed, their observations about everything were worth hearing. And whatever Fred said was bound to have some humor in it, because he had his own way of looking at the world. His sarcasm, for which he was famous, was always present, but it was gentle, while his use of language was so sharp and original, I think he was the greatest wordsmith of his time. Only S. J. Perelman came close.

Much as I enjoyed the company of Fred and Portland, I can't say I enjoyed the restaurants he chose. He'd never take us to 21 or Le Pavillon or any of the really great ones. We'd go to places I considered dumps—hash houses and storefront cafes. I don't know why he picked such places, when he could afford to eat wherever he pleased. Maybe these were the kinds of joints he remembered fondly from his early days in vaudeville, when he didn't have much money. He was born poor in a slum section of Cambridge, Massachusetts, the son of an impoverished Irish bookbinder. His real name was John Sullivan, and he went into vaudeville as a teenager, not so much because he was stagestruck but because he saw it as one of the few ways he might escape poverty. Despite his celebrated, extravagant, and sometimes foolish generosity to panhandlers and down-on-their-luck show people, he became a fairly wealthy man, though not until after years of hard work and deprivation.

On Mondays, when rehearsals began with a preliminary run-through, Allen would still be tinkering with the script. His fertile mind was a gusher of ideas that he kept pouring out on paper. He wouldn't finish adding and subtracting until Wednesday, when the final rehearsal began, and even then he wouldn't hesitate to make more changes.

We staged several rehearsals that day, culminating in the dress late in the afternoon. Joe Allen, the Bristol-Myers advertising manager, was there to represent the sponsor, and so was Ed Grimm, the Y&R account executive.

After this final rehearsal, eight or nine of us would sit around a table deciding on timesaving cuts that might be necessary and sharpening any segment that seemed to lag. Fred and his three writers would dominate this discussion, and he would make the final decisions. Then we would all take a dinner break before airtime.

Once the program began, it seldom lagged. Fred's sense of timing was as good as Jack Benny's, though it wasn't Fred's style to milk a gag, which was a routine Benny could perform better than anyone. Fred capped each gag with dispatch and hurried on to the next, as if he were afraid the audience might leave before he finished. Actually, he was the best at holding an audience—better than Benny. Fred had so much stage experience and was so adept, he could make an audience laugh just by standing there and glowering at them. And if that was what he felt like doing, he would do it.

One night, he was annoyed at the audience. (He never did

have a high regard for the crowds—mostly tourists, who, he felt, came not to hear the show but simply to gawk at celebrities. He once wrote to a friend, "Most of them look as if somebody turned over a pool table and they crept out of the pockets.") During a musical number between comedy segments, he picked up a phone on the stage and called me in the control booth. "What are you doing with the tickets to this show? I could reach down in my toilet and pick up a better class of people than this." As he spoke on the phone, he kept scowling at the audience, and before he was through they were laughing as if he had just said something hilarious. Thank God they couldn't hear what he was saying.

Fifteen or more years later, when his health was deteriorating, Fred did some ill-conceived television shows, which weren't well received. I remember one critic writing that Allen was "failing in television" because he didn't have the necessary stage presence. "He's too used to radio." That critic couldn't have been more wrong. It was on the stage that Fred Allen had become a star, long before he made his radio debut. And he could have been a gigantic television star if his health had held up and he had found the right format. If I had been able to put him on the *Tonight* show at NBC, for instance, his ability to ad lib would have made him even more legendary than he is.

The story of Mr. Ramshaw, the eagle, typified Allen's knack of maintaining audience control and finding the humor even in difficult situations. One of the amateur guests was an Englishman named Captain Knight who had a trained eagle named Mr. Ramshaw. This happened when I was no longer producing the program but still supervising it. Portland introduced the captain as "the world's foremost authority on eagles," of which one, very large and threatening, was perched on his leather-clad wrist.

Captain Knight introduced Mr. Ramshaw and assured Fred the bird wouldn't hurt him.

Fred looked unconvinced. "Aren't they supposed to be ferocious?" he asked.

"They're not only supposed to be," the captain assured him, "they are. I've seen two young golden eagles kill each other in a fight." The talons, he explained, had "a deadly grip," and when Mr. Ramshaw went into a tantrum he would sometimes "nip me right through the glove." Captain Knight was sure no such thing would happen on the show. At Fred's suggestion he even agreed to have the eagle fly around the stage and land on the bandstand.

Fred had every reason to feel confident about this flight, because Mr. Ramshaw had performed it perfectly in the empty auditorium during several practice runs. This time, however, when the bird took off from the captain's wrist and saw more than a thousand people staring up at him, he decided to alter the script. He kept flying back and forth above the multitude, causing people to scream and duck. The audience began shoving and elbowing each other in their frantic haste to reach the exits.

Finally, Mr. Ramshaw landed on a perch high above the stage, from which he ignored every effort by Captain Knight, including the offer of a severed chicken head, to come down and resume his rightful wrist perch. The place was in an uproar, with Captain Knight shouting English imprecations at his eagle.

At this point, Allen turned the discord into laughter by remarking that while it wasn't unusual for a comedian's script to get the bird, this was a first on radio. The eagle was getting the script, and changing it to suit itself, but the show had to continue. Standing almost directly under the loftily perched Mr. Ramshaw, Allen segued to his next segment with only occasional jokes about the problem hanging over his head.

Fred soon had everyone laughing, but the eagle had the last laugh. Shortly before the end of the hour, Mr. Ramshaw, a true critic, showed what he thought of the whole program by dropping a whopping deposit, which just missed Allen and a college student who was giving him some kind of award.

The executives at NBC were not amused. Though Captain Knight eventually coaxed Mr. Ramshaw back down onto his wrist by waving a huge raw beefsteak at him, the soaring star of this nine o'clock performance was scratched from the midnight live repeat. And the next day, Allen received a letter from someone in the NBC hierarchy (I think it was Deke Aylesworth, the president, but I'm not sure), castigating him for the aerial maneuvers and the high-altitude bombing over which he had presided. A few days later, Allen wrote in reply:

> . . . I thought I had seen about everything in radio but the eagle had a trick up his feathered colon that was new to me. . . . Toscanini, your house man [Toscanini conducted the NBC Symphony Orchestra], has foisted some movements on studio audiences in 8H, but when Radio City is torn down, to make room for another parking lot, the one movement that will be remembered will be the eagle's movement on Wednesday last.

Three or four times a year, Allen would put me on the program, usually as a villain when he dreamed up ideas lampooning advertising agencies, his favorite target. I would be presented as Mr. Weaver of Young & Rubicam.

"You'd better be careful of him," Allen would warn his staff from the microphone, as if to alert them, and the audience, that I was there to foist some Madison Avenue outrage upon them. Then, pretending to be respectful and obsequious, Fred would launch into a straight-faced satire on the agencies, with special attention to their vice presidents.

On one occasion, when he was having great fun at the

expense of the agencies, I remember saying (I'm not sure whether it was in the script or off the top of my head), "You'd better straighten up and fly right, Mr. Allen, because we can find plenty of comics to replace you."

"Oh? Name one."

"Phil Baker, for instance," I said. Baker was a middle-echelon comedian whose program Young & Rubicam handled.

"Ah yes, Phil Baker," Allen repeated after me. "The Punchinello without the punch."

When Allen made sport of the agencies and the networks on the air, it wasn't all spoof—he was usually expressing in comic terms some deep-seated feelings. He took a gently satirical view of everything, an anti-authoritarian slant that strongly appealed to me, because I often felt the same way about the powers in control. Everybody knew he was joking, but we also knew that there was a deeper meaning beneath the jokes. The agency spoofs he wrote for the Mighty Allen Art Players were among the most profound, as well as the funniest, of all his skits.

Hollywood was another of Allen's favorite targets. There was his famous line, "Hollywood is a great place to live if you're an orange," and he really believed it. Long after the other big comedians had moved their shows to the West Coast, Allen remained in New York. He was lured out there by Jack Benny in 1940 to make a movie, Love Thy Neighbor, and in a letter to me from Hollywood he wrote: "we are hoping for the best but wish that we were in maine" (he eschewed the use of the capital letters on his typewriter). He concluded, "portland sends her sunkist regards. we had her regards out on the patio until they started to blister. we brought them in to send them off red hot to you."

He liked to tease me about Hollywood because I had come from California. While I was still connected with his program he did a takeoff on California beauty contests and starlets in which he offered a prize for Miss Low Tide of San Pedro (the location of the Los Angeles harbor), mostly, I thought, to needle me about the Los Angeles way of life, which, I argued, was not as bizarre as he pictured it.

During Fred's annual summer hiatus I had to produce his replacement program, as well as Jack Benny's, whose sponsor, General Foods, the maker of Jell-O, was another Young & Rubicam account. Though Benny was based in California, his replacement show one year, starring Tim and Irene Ryan, originated with us in New York. The Ryans were a good comedy team, somewhat like Burns and Allen (also with Young & Rubicam), and quite funny, though they never became as successful as George and Gracie. Irene gained considerable fame in the 1960s, however, as Granny on the long-running television comedy *Beverly Hillbillies*.

Doing the summer replacement for Allen gave me special pleasure because it was so easy, it allowed me two or three free days a week. One year it starred Chase Taylor and Budd Hulick, better known as Colonel Stoopnagle and Budd, whose antics on and off the air kept me laughing. They used to come into my office and, while we talked, lick my supply of stamps, one after another, and flip them up to stick on the ceiling. There was a knack to it that I never mastered, but they carried it off with amazing success. By the end of summer my ceiling was virtually papered with stamps.

Chase introduced me to a friend of his named Jack Peacock Green, who was to become a lifelong friend of mine. Jack owned the Coral Island Club in Bermuda, where I often went for a few days' rest when I wasn't skiing or sailing. On most weekends from December to April, a small group of us, led by Lowell Thomas, would meet at Grand Central Station and take the ski train to Stowe or Mad River or North Conway or the Laurentians—wherever the snow forecast was most promising.

Having grown up in Los Angeles, I had never seen snow, except on distant mountains, until I went to Dartmouth. As soon as the first snow fell in Hanover, I bought ski equipment and found out that skiing is very much like body surfing, which I had done throughout my California boyhood. Like the ocean waves, the ski slopes provide the momentum; you had only to control the speed and direction. This was so much my kind of sport, I made a pledge that I would never embrace any other in which I would have to do the work.

My love of sailing fitted neatly into that pattern—the wind did the work. I joined the Manhasset Bay Yacht Club and raced with a friend, Phil Tomlinson, on his boat in the 28-foot class. Together we bought a 56-foot yawl, the *Andot*, which we sailed all over Long Island Sound as well as up and down the Atlantic coast. I found out that there's a world of difference between the Atlantic and the Pacific. On the West Coast you can fairly well count on the prevailing winds, which are almost always dependable. On the East Coast, especially around New York, you can encounter a sudden squall, a 180-degree wind shift, and a total calm, all within twenty-four hours.

I had learned to sail as a boy, with a friend whose father owned a 50-foot yawl. The two of us were the crew. We sailed to Catalina, San Clemente, or one of the Mexican ports, and I don't remember running into any big problems. The Atlantic, though, was a constant challenge, and I loved it.

Fred Allen, something of a landlubber, used to rib me about my enthusiasm for sailing. I still have a letter he wrote me in August 1936, while he and Portland were vacationing at their house in Old Orchard Beach, Maine:

> portland and i have kept our eyes glued to the sea expecting to see you luff past in your trim sloop one of these days but either you haven't luffed past or you have been too quick for us. . . .

we thought we had you sighted one day, a man passed using an old ipana commercial for a jib but upon close inspection it proved to be a catboat trying to get away from a school of dogfish. another day, we saw a small sailboat skimming along when there was obviously no breeze. i thought it could be you but raising the glasses again i recognized a clerk from mr. brentano's [bookstore] who was sailing along holding a copy of that bestseller, "gone with the wind" up in the stern. . . .

In 1937 I took on enlarged responsibilities at Young & Rubicam, which meant that I had to give up producing the Allen show. Jack Van Nostrand, my friend from the Don Lee network days in Los Angeles, replaced me as producer, but I retained full responsibility for the program as its supervisor. It was now one of several I had to supervise, but to me it wasn't just another show. *Town Hall Tonight* took precedence over all the others I had to oversee. I kept up with it on an almost daily basis—which led to another adventure with another NBC president.

Deke Aylesworth had recently resigned, and General Sarnoff had brought in a man from Chicago named Lennox Lohr to replace him. I didn't know Lohr, but I soon would.

Whoever handled the network's rehearsal bookings was so imprecise about it, we would often arrive and find our assigned studio full of people rehearsing another show. It always embarrassed me, because I was ultimately responsible for making the operation run smoothly. I couldn't lay it all on Jack Van Nostrand, who was still new on the job.

One day, when we had finally gotten into our studio after another long delay, I went to the microphone and said, "I understand you people here at NBC have so little to do that you monitor the conversations in your rehearsal studios. If so, please listen to this, because I want you to know that I've decided to start moving some of our Young and Rubicam programs to CBS, just because you keep screwing up here. This is Pat Weaver being monitored. Good day to you."

Shortly thereafter I received a call from Lohr summoning me to his office. "I'm told you're a very bright, able young man, destined to go a long way," he said to me, "but it's a terrible mistake for you to get into trouble with giant corporations like NBC. It can do you a lot of harm but no good."

What ensued from this conversation was a perfect illustration of the ad agencies' power over the networks. I went back to Young & Rubicam, to Chet LaRoche's office, and told him exactly what had happened. He picked up the phone, called Lohr, and told him he was no doubt a very bright, able man, but it was a terrible mistake for him to get into trouble with Young & Rubicam. Then Chet reiterated my threat to move some of our programs to CBS, and in the weeks to come, we actually did so. The Colonel Stoopnagle and Budd show was one of them.

While this demonstration of the naked power of advertising agencies impressed me, it also made me uncomfortable after I had time to reflect upon it. Was it healthy for the agencies to have that much power over the networks? The question was beginning to grow in my mind.

Fred Allen was the one person I knew who was neither impressed nor frightened by the power of the agencies. Though Young & Rubicam was as important to him as it was to NBC, I don't remember him ever coming to our office in all my years at the agency. It was not because he was afraid of anybody there. He had earned so much admiration that people everywhere fawned over him, and all of us in the advertising business had the highest respect for him. Yet that never stopped Fred from making ad men, myself especially, the butts of his jokes. I became his target with increasing frequency as our professional relationship grew into friendship.

I now had so much work that I needed a rest every so

often. On one occasion I flew to Bermuda and spent a couple of weeks at Jack Green's Coral Island Club. While I was there I grew a mustache, which I was sporting when I returned to New York.

The Allen show was in rehearsal as I walked into the studio on my first day back, but Fred, from the stage, spotted me and my new facial feature immediately. He stopped in the middle of a skit and peered more closely at the hair on my upper lip.

"Look at our Mr. Weaver!" he cried out to the people around him. "It just goes to show that puberty has no sense of direction."

Allen's most famous stunt during my years with him was his "feud" with Jack Benny, a long-running caper I played a small role in launching. One day, when Jim Harkins, Harry Von Zell, and I were auditioning applicants for the amateur segment, we came upon a little boy named Stewart Canin, who was a pretty good violinist. As everyone knew, Jack Benny played the violin—not often, but not very well, either—and he also listened to Allen every Wednesday. Here was an opportunity we couldn't resist.

The following Wednesday on *Town Hall Tonight*, little Stewart Canin played "The Flight of the Bumble Bee," and played it remarkably well. When he finished, Fred said to him, "Gosh, that was beautiful. How old are you, Stewart?"

"I'm ten."

After a few more questions, Fred said, "I suppose you know that Jack Benny also plays the violin. It's amazing that a ten-year-old boy like you can play a difficult number like 'The Flight of the Bumble Bee' so magnificently, and yet Mr. Benny, who's been practicing all his life, couldn't stumble through the first ten bars."

After that nudge, we sat back and awaited the reaction. We didn't expect Jack to contact Fred about it; he was too subtle for that. We figured he would respond on his show, and he did. On the next Benny program he praised the little boy's skill and announced that "The Flight of the Bumble Bee" was also a part of his repertoire. "I played 'The Bee' so often," he said, "I got the hives." He added that he would be glad to play it again on the air if any music lover requested it.

Allen, on our next program, said that he was a music lover, but in spite of that he would like to hear Jack Benny play "The Bee."

As Fred later wrote in *Treadmill to Oblivion*, the battle had begun: "Jack and I didn't plan anything. I didn't want to explain that I thought it would be good for us. The Jack Benny program was the highest-rated show in radio at the time. . . . To ask Jack to participate in a feud with me . . . would be like hitching my gaggin' to a star. All I could do was to hope that Jack would have some fun with the idea."

Before they were through, they had both had great fun. During the first three or four months of the feud, from December 1936 to March 1937, they attracted almost enough national attention to make people forget the Depression.

Allen said that Benny was so cheap, if he ever got his hands on all the nickels in the country buffaloes would become extinct. And he was so anemic that "when a mosquito lands on him, all he gets is practice."

Benny said that Allen was so weak, he had to starch his legs so they wouldn't wobble.

Allen replied that he had seen better legs than Benny's on a bridge table. "At a cannibal dinner, Benny wouldn't even get on the menu."

Eventually they arranged to meet on the Benny show and fight it out. By that time the feud had so captured the public's imagination, no radio studio was large enough to accommodate the number of people begging for tickets. The long-awaited showdown was held on March 14, 1937, before an overflow crowd in the largest ballroom of the Pierre Hotel. Benny brought his troupe all the way from California for just the one night, but it was worth the trip. That show attracted one of the largest audiences in the history of radio, even though Benny didn't play "The Flight of the Bumble Bee," and, needless to say, he and Allen didn't punch each other in the nose. The only jabs they traded were verbal, and Benny, it seemed to me, landed the funniest thrust by making fun of his own preference of working from a script rather than ad-libbing. He waited patiently while Fred excoriated him with ad libs, whereupon he said, "You wouldn't dare talk to me that way if I had my writers with me."

They finished the show as the best of friends, reminiscing about their old days in vaudeville. But that didn't mean the feud had come to an end. They were still trading insults on the air well into the 1940s. They were, I think, the most talented comedians radio has ever produced.

6

THE ENLARGEMENT OF MY RESPONSIBILITIES AT YOUNG
& Rubicam included the supervision of several other programs. Then, as the Allen show was winding down toward
its summer hiatus in 1937, I started to oversee all the agency's
radio shows.

This came about because of another man's misfortune.
When Bill Stuhler, head of the radio division, became ill and
had to retire, Don Stauffer took his job. I was now Stauffer's
number-two man, which meant I would have to give up
producing for Allen, because I would be too busy supervising
his show and all of the others, plus their commercials.
Though this was a significant promotion, I accepted it with
some reluctance, because I cherished my relationship with
Allen. I would still be seeing him frequently, but I would no
longer be an integral part of his program.

Until then, I had considered myself a radio man, even
though I worked for an advertising agency. From now on, I

would have to regard myself primarily as an advertising executive, even though I was involved in more radio production than ever. I can't pretend I regretted this change. Though in some circles, including Fred Allen's, advertising men were coming under criticism as manipulators of public habits and attitudes, most of us in the business thought of ourselves simply as salesmen, and no one had ever told me that salesmanship was a dishonorable occupation. Without it, our entire economic system would collapse.

I had found out in California, during my early months in radio, that while the entertainment aspect of the medium—the structuring of programs—was creative and really a lot of fun, the challenge of marketing was equally stimulating. Whom did the advertiser want to attract? Which people were potential users of his product? What did he hope to say to them? Which others could be ignored because they would never use the product? How could he make sure his commercial message would reach the most potentially receptive ears? The whole problem of marketing had excited me in those early days in Los Angeles, and here I was, about to get more involved in it.

This didn't mean I considered the advertising business to be above criticism. I knew then, as I know now, that it is suffused with hype. Many products are sold solely on the basis of clever slogans or exaggerated claims. And as a profession, it can be very taxing. The stress is such that a study conducted many years ago indicated that the average advertising man died at the age of sixty-one, from six to ten years younger than executives in other fields. I would guess that a similar ratio applies today. Advertising is an exceedingly challenging profession. In addition to the persuasiveness of a salesman, it demands the skill of a writer, the imagination of an artist, and the business acumen to cope with some very tough and sophisticated corporate executives.

You have to live with the constant awareness that if you can't produce and can't cope, you may be out on the sidewalk tomorrow, with few if any doors open to you.

None of that bothered me, perhaps because I was not quite twenty-nine. When you're that young, it's impossible to imagine you'll ever be old, let alone dead. I welcomed the challenge that was opening up for me. The advertising business, even with all of its pitfalls and shortcomings, fascinated me. During the two years of my association with Young & Rubicam I had begun to see from the inside the industry's opportunities, as well as its limitations.

I had also learned some things about one aspect of advertising that I was to find especially useful in the years to come. Bristol-Myers wanted research done on the Allen show's ratings and what these numbers meant to them. Who were they reaching with their commercials, and who should they be reaching but weren't?

George Gallup was then in charge of Young & Rubicam's research department. (This was while he was also launching his own public-opinion polling company.) I was so interested in his methods and findings, I began to work closely with him, and he taught me some lessons about radio listeners that I later applied to television viewers.

Two examples stand out in my mind. The Crossley ratings, which the networks used at that time, reckoned that the Allen and Benny shows were reaching somewhere in the mid-twenties each week, indicating that about one-fourth of the radio audience was listening to each of them. But Gallup saw a fallacy in the survey. It implied that the same people listened to a show every week, in which case 75 percent of the nation's radio audience never heard Fred Allen or Jack Benny. Gallup had done samplings that proved this supposition to be absurd. In response, he conceived what has come to be known as the cumulative audience—the percentage of homes a program reaches over a period of one month. When this research was pursued, it was discovered that about 75 percent of the potential audience listened to Allen and Benny, though most people did not hear them every week. This meant that Bristol-Myers and General Foods were getting more than their money's worth: they were reaching three out of every four homes in the nation.

I was so impressed by the commercial importance of this discovery that I never let myself forget it. Twelve years later, when I went to NBC, I made the Nielsen rating people include cumulative calculations in their reports to us on all of our programs. The "cumes," as they are called, are much more important to the advertiser than the bare ratings, because the cumes show the reach. And they're just as important to the network manager, because they tell him who his programs are not reaching. You have to identify a segment of the population before you can figure out how to attract it.

The second important lesson I learned from Dr. Gallup was that research had to be used with a lot of caution. (Gallup and most of the other pollsters had that lesson forced upon them in 1948, when they unanimously predicted that Thomas E. Dewey would defeat Harry S Truman in the presidential election.) The research staff had provided pushbutton machinery for the audience at one of the Jack Benny shows. The button panel offered each viewer a selection of reactions, from "Very Enthusiastic" down to "Don't Like," to each personality and segment the show featured. The result of this polling indicated that the most popular personality on Benny's program was Kenny Baker, the regular tenor before Benny hired Dennis Day. Yet everyone knows that musical numbers on a comedy show are nothing but punctuation—rest periods when the comedians can catch their breath. If you really believed that poll, you would throw Jack Benny off the air and call it *The Kenny Baker Show*.

My work as supervisor of radio programs at Young &

Rubicam would entail frequent trips to Hollywood, where several of our stars were now broadcasting. In addition to Benny, these included Burns and Allen, Fred Astaire, and Charley Butterworth. But the bulk of my work was in New York, which was still the nation's radio capital.

Fred Allen remained my chief concern, though I also had to deal with Kate Smith, Phil Baker, Colonel Stoopnagle and Budd, Goodman and Jane Ace, and *The Aldrich Family*, to name a few. These shows were in the hands of competent producers who were selected by Stuhler and Stauffer, so I wasn't presented with any serious problems. The biggest difficulty I encountered in that job was the occasional need to replace a lost sponsor. The sponsor is the ultimate judge of a radio or television program. He's the one putting up the money for it. If you can't make him like it, you may have trouble making the public like it. Replacing sponsors was not the producer's responsibility, and may not have been mine, but since it involved salesmanship, I was ready to give it a try.

One of my colleagues, unnamed, made some comments to *The New Yorker* about my selling methods. "I never saw such enthusiasm, even in the advertising business," this anonymous informant said. "Pat just breathed confidence. He would grab a client and get him so excited over a show—even a dog of a show—that he would hardly know what he was doing. Of course, a lot of clients were out-of-town businessmen who were stunned by New York advertising people, but Pat, with his six-feet-four, his wisecracks and his fast talk, could stun them more effectively than anybody else."

I can't deny my height, or my enthusiasm, but I don't think I ever conned anyone into anything. If I were to fast-talk someone into buying a program that wouldn't profit his company, I'd be doing no favor to him, to the program, to my agency, or to myself.

By 1937, we had entered the golden age of radio in America,

when almost every home, poor as well as rich, had at least one set. Only the movies offered another choice of mass entertainment, and they cost money. While the Depression was slowly abating, money was still scarce, and many people couldn't afford the twenty-five- or thirty-cent price of admission to a movie theater. Radio was free and offered music, news, sports, drama, and above all comedy, both day and night.

Our business was booming. The popular radio shows were major attractions, especially comedies. The great radio comedy era of the thirties and early forties established audience-percentage records that even television has not approached —and probably never will, with so many other attractions and distractions available at present. Jack Benny, Fred Allen, Edgar Bergen and Charlie McCarthy, Burns and Allen, Fibber McGee and Molly, and Bob Hope were better known to the public than even the most celebrated movie stars. Only a few million people at best would see a Clark Gable, Bette Davis, Spencer Tracy, or Shirley Temple picture, while upwards of 50 million heard the great comedians—perhaps not every week, but at least once a month. In 1937 there were 37.6 million radio sets distributed among the population of 120 million, with more than two-thirds of these sets in homes. And in those days, unlike today, radio listening was not a solitary habit but family entertainment. Today, one or maybe two people listen to a radio, usually in a bedroom, a kitchen, or a car. During the thirties, the whole family gathered around the set in the living room.

MY APPOINTMENT AS the number-two man in the Young & Rubicam radio division did not come as a complete surprise. As the Fred Allen producer, I was interested in everything that might have even the slightest effect on the program, including advertising policies and other aspects over which I had no control.

Occasionally, some facet of the Allen show would come under discussion by the Young & Rubicam plans board, a committee of the agency's top executives, who made all the important decisions. Allen and I always received notice when such discussions were to take place. Needless to say, he never bothered to attend, regarding the whole process as meddlesome and ludicrous. He ran the show as he saw fit, and if they didn't like it, he could always go elsewhere. His idea of nothing to do was to listen to a bunch of ad men talk boring nonsense for an hour or two.

I, on the other hand, considered the plans board meetings important, not only to the Allen show but to myself. I couldn't pass up a chance to hear people at that level of the advertising industry talk, whether they were discussing the Allen show or anything else. I attended each time I was invited, and sometimes when I wasn't, in which case George Gallup would take me.

Whatever the subject—production costs, advertising policies, economic trends, client acquisition, merchandising, research—I listened carefully, offering my opinions only when they seemed to add something important. In matters concerning radio my contributions became increasingly frequent, because most of these executives, having come from the print and graphic media, knew only as much about radio as they may have heard from people like me, who were in the midst of it. Even in the radio division, nobody else had experience as broad as mine, because I had done so much writing, planning, soliciting of sponsors, even coming up with ideas for commercials and writing them. In matters other than radio I had a lot to learn, but as a result of listening to the plans board members, I was picking it up rapidly.

When I became the supervisor of all the Young & Rubicam

radio programs, my involvement with the plans board increased commensurately, until I was attending just about every meeting. Before I knew it—I think it was sometime in the latter months of 1937—I was notified that I had been appointed to the board. It must have been when Don Stauffer was given the new title of director of the radio division and I became the manager of the division, which sounded more impressive than supervisor, although it entailed only a slight enlargement of what I was already doing.

Because I had shows to oversee on the West Coast, I had begun traveling back and forth between New York and Los Angeles. In those days this was quite adventuresome, because commercial aviation was still fairly new, and not nearly as safe as it is today. The Douglas DC3, one of the most dependable airplanes ever manufactured (some of them are still flying regular routes in South America, although Douglas produced the last one in the mid-1940s), had just recently been put into commercial service. But reliable as it was, the DC3 couldn't manage high altitudes—partly because the engines necessary for high-altitude flight were only then being developed, but, even more important, because there was no such thing then as a pressurized cabin. At altitudes above ten or twelve thousand feet, every passenger would have to wear an oxygen mask, a requirement that was in no way feasible.

None of this created problems east of the Rockies, where the highest "mountains" were four thousand feet or less, but from the Rockies west, planes had to fly between the peaks or just above them. In dense clouds or stormy weather, a pilot couldn't always be absolutely certain he was between or above. From the mid-thirties until at least the early forties, plane crashes into Rocky mountainsides were alarmingly common. For example, on October 17, 1937, according to the 1938 *World Almanac*, a United Airlines plane enroute to Salt

Lake City with nineteen people aboard "crashed at 10,000 feet altitude into Chalk Mountain in the Uinta Range south of Knight, Wyoming. It was 15 miles south of its regular course, in a rain-snow storm. All were killed."

Since no airliners then carried more than twenty or so passengers, these tragedies were less horrendous than modern-day air crashes (except, of course, to the people on the planes). Though I was fortunately never involved in one of those sudden encounters between plane and mountain, I was a frequent flier on that coast-to-coast route, and the dire possibilities were never far from my mind. Yet I couldn't ignore the fact that it took less than twenty-four hours, including stopovers, to fly between New York and Los Angeles, whereas a train ride consumed five days. The amount of work I had to do on this job wouldn't allow me to spend ten days going back and forth between the coasts when I could go both ways in less than two. I did, however, steal some time occasionally during the ski seasons by getting off the plane at Salt Lake City and hurrying up to Alta, which had only recently opened, for a glorious day or two on the slopes. Then I'd get back on the next available DC3 for the last leg to Los Angeles, with nobody the wiser.

There were, of course, no nonstop flights from coast to coast in those days. Whichever airline you took, you would have four stops. On United, you landed in Chicago, Omaha, Denver, and Salt Lake City. On American, it was Washington, D.C., Nashville, Dallas, and Tucson. This southern route was less mountainous, to be sure, and therefore safer, but it didn't offer many skiing opportunities, so I usually chose the trip through the Rockies. As I said, I was young at the time.

I took special pleasure in those trips to Los Angeles because my family was there and it still felt like home. My only regret was that I didn't get to see as much of them as I would have liked, since all of them were occupied and I was so busy that I barely got everything done before having to return to New York.

My father was still in good health, but my mother was not so well. In fact, she died in 1938, and my father moved into the Jonathan Club, of which I believe he had been one of the founders (the club referred to him as Member Number One). The Jonathan originally occupied the upper floors of the Pacific Electric Subway Terminal Building, the Big Red Car station at Fifth and Hill streets in downtown Los Angeles, but built a beautiful clubhouse on Figueroa in the early twenties.

Both of my sisters had married by this time. Sylva married Edgar Tevis Smith, whom she divorced. Later, she married John Roland, of Pasadena. My other sister, Rosemary, was also married twice, first to Hilton McCabe, an attorney who became a judge, then to Paul Fritz, also an attorney, in Los Angeles.

My brother Doodles was still at Stanford in 1937, when I began these trips west. Though he had been expelled several times for his outrageous (and legendary) pranks, my father always managed to get him reinstated. By 1938, he was through school and performing in nightclubs. He was also in *Meet the People* on Broadway about that time, so I saw him more often in New York than in Los Angeles. It was never easy to get the whole family together, yet when I was in L.A., however busy we all were, I usually managed to arrange at least one family dinner.

I stayed at the Beverly Hills Hotel or the Bel Air, except when I drove down to Palm Springs, during the winter, where I was partial to Charley Farrell's Racquet Club. Many of the radio stars and their writers maintained homes in the desert and would drive up to Los Angeles only one day a week, for their broadcast. The rest of the time they'd be at Palm

Springs, working two or three hours and spending the rest of their time playing golf or pursuing some other kind of game.

One man I used to watch quite closely in Palm Springs was Charley Butterworth, who was teamed with Fred Astaire on a new show for Packard automobiles. For several years, Packard had sponsored a musical program with the opera singer Lawrence Tibbett, and when it went off the air, they were sold on the unlikely combination of the suave, debonair Astaire and the comic, unpredictable Butterworth.

Astaire gave me no cause for concern. He was as charming in person as he was in films and on the air, a fascinating man, having been everyplace and done everything, which may have accounted for the fact that he was also wonderfully resourceful. He knew, for instance, that he didn't have much of a singing voice, so he had compensated by developing a unique style. What he did best of all, his dancing, was superb, as everyone knows, but no one has ever figured out how to watch a man dance on radio. Astaire came closer to solving that puzzle than anybody else. The tap routines he designed to be listened to on radio were so good, everyone was talking about them. He was a true renaissance man—an amazingly creative artist.

Strange as it seems, his sophistication blended well on radio with Butterworth's comedy routines, but Charley needed a little more watching than Fred, because he was inordinately fond of the sauce. Once in Palm Springs I apparently got there too early for my morning appointment—about noon—and he was just getting out of bed.

"Come have breakfast with me," he suggested, and I agreed, as it was time for my lunch.

When we arrived at the restaurant at the Racquet Club, he said, "I must tell you, I never have orange juice for breakfast."

"That's all right with me," I said. "I won't have any, either, because I never have it for lunch."

"I don't mean to insult a born-and-bred Californian like you," he continued, "but I can't stand orange juice, especially at breakfast time. If you don't mind, why don't we have a Dubonnet cocktail instead? I find it does wonders in waking me up."

Since I had already been up for several hours, I thought myself equal to it. "I don't mind a bit," I said. I had one cocktail, but Charley seldom settled for just one of anything. He was still drinking his breakfast when I finally had to excuse myself and retire to my room.

Even on the day of his broadcast Charley was always looking for the nearest bar, and I often went along to make sure he returned to the studio. I may have been worrying too much. He always came back, on time and ready to perform. He was always sober on the air—or, at least, he looked and acted that way. His timing was so perfect, I used to think he must be sober, yet I was never certain of it. Perhaps those perfect pauses at which he was so adept wouldn't have been as effective if he had been abstemious.

I remember one example of his flawless technique during a Broadway show. An impeccably proper straight man—one rather like Fred Astaire—said to him, "I say, sir, do you happen to have the right time?"

Charley said, "Yes, I do." Then he looked at his watch. "Let's see, now. Eight-fifteen plus one hour is nine-fifteen, plus seven minutes, which means the correct time is exactly nine-twenty-two."

The straight man was puzzled. "Why is your watch an hour and seven minutes slow?"

"Well," said Charley, "that's the way it was when I bought it."

"But why don't you reset it?"

Charley stared at the man as if he had just said something unthinkable. Finally he replied, righteously, "I am not one to tinker."

One of the pleasures of my Hollywood trips was the opportunity to hook up again with people I knew and liked. Tom Harrington, who had produced the Jack Benny program for some time—perhaps since its inception—was now also the manager of Young & Rubicam's Hollywood office. And Everard Meade was producing the Burns and Allen program.

I never worked closely with George Burns and Gracie Allen, but I was around them enough to notice how funny both of them were and what a natural comic genius she was. In daily life she was almost as funny as she was on the air, and apparently without effort, as if those lines just popped into her head on their way out of her mouth. George was, as everybody knows, the mastermind behind their act. His brain was, and still is, an encyclopedia of comedy, and he knows on a moment's notice exactly where to find the joke he needs.

Benny and Burns were close friends, and I would sometimes see them together at restaurants in Beverly Hills, where they both lived. George would greet me with "Hello, Pat," whereas Jack would say, "Hi, kid." I had assumed he simply couldn't remember my name, but now I suspected it was his way of being friendly. By this time our paths had crossed so often, and we had worked out so many program decisions together, there could be no doubt that he knew me. I guess I should have been flattered. Alas, nobody calls me kid anymore.

The boom in radio that had swept the country was especially evident in Hollywood. So many New York shows were moving to California, where more and more of the stars had chosen to live, that NBC had put up new studios on Melrose Avenue, near Paramount, and CBS was planning to build on Sunset Boulevard. Eventually, both networks would have new studios on Sunset, NBC at Vine Street and CBS a few blocks east. Radio program production in Los Angeles had developed enormously since my days at the Don Lee studio downtown, where we had to broadcast with auto mechanics below our windows honking horns outside the Cadillac repair shop.

When I was at KHJ, Prohibition was still in force, and we used to buy our drinks at Herman's Drug Store down the street, where we would sit at the soda fountain and order Cokes, and Herman, by prearrangement, would slip a shot of bootleg booze into the bottom of the glass. At NBC in 1937, we were close to the Melrose Grotto, which, in these happier days, was wide open and flourishing. If we wanted to walk a little farther, there was Lucey's Restaurant across the street. The Brown Derby on Vine, Musso and Frank's on Hollywood Boulevard, and the Polo Lounge in the Beverly Hills Hotel were also welcoming the thirsty and the hungry.

The days of the Hollywood guest star had begun, and we used a lot of big-name movie actors and actresses on our radio shows. Some were forbidden by their film contracts to appear on the air, because the major studios still regarded radio as competition, but even this silly restriction was breaking down. We had a drama program called *Silver Theater*, which featured film stars every week. One of them was my friend Rosalind Russell, who had already proven herself a skillful and intelligent actress. Within a year after her arrival in Hollywood she starred in the movie version of *Craig's Wife*, a Broadway stage hit that had won a Pulitzer Prize for its author, George Kelly. At least one prominent critic, Deems Taylor, attributed the film's success to "an uncompromisingly honest performance by Rosalind Russell." The following year, she starred with Robert Montgomery in the big box-office thriller *Night Must Fall*. Roz was already an important star when I began making those trips to Hollywood for Young

& Rubicam, but she hadn't forgotten our friendship in New York. In fact, we renewed it every time she returned east to see her family. We resumed seeing each other in Hollywood, and I found that her great success hadn't changed her a bit. She still refused to take herself seriously, and her puckish sense of humor was sharper than ever.

I arrived one night when she was trying to write an article for *Vanity Fair*. She was having trouble because she thought the piece they wanted would be embarrassing drivel, but her agent had promised she would do it. When she told me what it was supposed to be, I agreed it would be drivel. They wanted her to do a two-part article—first, things she loved; then, things she hated. Unfortunately for the article, she wasn't the hating type, so she had no idea what to include.

I offered the most perverse idea I could come up with. "Why don't you start with, 'I hate the American flag.' Then you can go on to list motherhood, apple pie, the Fourth of July. . . ."

"That's a start," she said. "Maybe we should also include Christmas, the Ten Commandments, 'The Star-Spangled Banner.' . . ." I can't recall what else she listed, but she got right into the spirit of the jest.

"And for the list of things you love," I said, "you've got to start with communism, then atheism. . . ."

It didn't take us long to reduce the article's whole premise to its true value. I don't know what she eventually did about the piece, though I'm quite sure it never appeared in *Vanity Fair*—at least not in the version we composed that night.

Roz Russell's career included an endless number of excellent films—*The Women, His Girl Friday, No Time for Comedy, Sister Kenny, Auntie Mame*, and many others. She remained a good friend right up until her death, in 1976. I still miss her.

The only thing I disliked about those trips was the backlog

of work that piled up in New York while I was away. Now that I was manager of the radio division I had to find the right people to hire, motivate the staff to work harder than it was reasonable to demand, protect the creative people from interference by the non-show-business executives, and figure out strategies that would sell products.

One product that was causing a problem was Minute tapioca. A lot of people were using it, but not often enough. A box of the stuff lasted so long, the stock in the grocery stores was moving too slowly, which meant the stores were reluctant to display it. I thought of reducing the amount of tapioca in each package, but that wasn't deemed practical. Finally, I came up with a gimmick. The commercials would begin and end with with the ticktock of a clock, to remind the housewife that she should be in the kitchen using up her Minute tapioca. I can't say my idea revolutionized the ad industry, but I guess it didn't hurt the product—it can still be found in supermarkets.

Besides all these day-to-day chores, I had to find time for more and more activity on the plans board, because I was now the resident authority on radio. Whenever we picked up a new client, the first question was which medium would best serve his products' needs. By this time, radio was always a possibility and often a probability, which meant I had to suggest the right kind of program, and maybe even the right kind of commercials for it.

The Kate Smith daytime hour on CBS demanded more of my attention than any of the other programs. Kate was a pleasant, amiable woman, always cooperative, but her manager, Ted Collins, also her seemingly constant companion, could be difficult. He watched over her as if she were a helpless child, which she certainly was not. I never figured out their relationship. It was hard to believe there was anything romantic about it. Kate weighed about 250 pounds, and she never struck me as irresistible, but it's impossible to predict what might appeal to other people. Her broadcast ratings were always good, and her sponsors were happy. We found the show useful for testing new personalities. Though Kate had a good voice, she couldn't sing away the entire hour. She needed guest performers and new ideas, and we did our best to supply them. It was Kate Smith who gave Bud Abbott and Lou Costello their first break on the air. Several years later, when I brought her show to NBC, she was still willing to experiment with new people and new ideas.

The one disadvantage of the increased workload was the restrictions it placed on my friendship with Fred Allen. Though I still supervised his program, I didn't get to spend as much time with him as I wished. I did, however, attend most of his rehearsals, as well as the broadcast, and Jack Van Nostrand was doing an excellent job of producing the show, so I had very little supervising to do. On the other hand, I was seeing more of Fred and Portland socially, and I enjoyed that.

By this time I was quite well acquainted with every aspect of Young & Rubicam's business. The client I found most interesting was the American Tobacco Company, for whom we handled only the Half-and-Half pipe tobacco and Pall Mall cigarette accounts. Lord and Thomas advertised the company's most important account, Lucky Strike cigarettes. As I became more absorbed in the workings of our agency, and of the industry in general, I became convinced that many big corporations were wasting their money because of misguided advertising policies. American Tobacco seemed to me the prime example. Though it was spending more money than any other tobacco company, Lucky Strike had fallen to third place in sales among the big four cigarettes at the time—Camel, Chesterfield, Lucky, and Old Gold. They had to be doing something wrong, and I thought I knew what it was.

7

ONE OF THE MORE SATISFYING EXPERIENCES OF MY
early career had been my 1934 success in San Francisco,
where I had helped to boost the declining fortunes of radio
station KFRC. It had shown me how much pleasure there
could be in reviving a drooping organization. Perhaps this
was partly why I was so fascinated by what I perceived to
be a sorry situation at American Tobacco Company. The
dramatic drop in Lucky Strike sales during the 1930s, despite
the truckloads of money spent on advertising, was a subject
of concern as well as gossip on Madison Avenue. Was advertising really as effective as we claimed it to be?

I didn't think advertising as such was the root of the Lucky
Strike problem. Camels and Chesterfields, both of which had
surpassed Luckys in sales, were advertised heavily, though
less extensively and expensively than Luckys. In my opinion,
the dramatic decline of Luckys was due to the wrong kind
of advertising and media selection.

Under the leadership of the American Tobacco Company's president, the extraordinary, even legendary, George Washington Hill, Lucky Strike advertising included what he called the "back cover" policy, according to which he might take out one ad in *Life* and one in the *Saturday Evening Post*, and every back cover of the less important magazines. He saw back covers as little billboards in the home, which was modestly true, but to get this value he lost the selling power of all but two or three of the huge-circulation weeklies, few of whose back covers were, or were likely to become, available.

Hill also insisted that Lucky Strike launch a new ad campaign every six months, because he was convinced that people soon tired of hearing the same message. When a new promotion opened, he bought full-page ads in every English-language daily newspaper in the country, plus billboard space from coast to coast. The only medium he used sparingly was radio. He sponsored the very popular *Your Hit Parade* and a couple of lesser shows, but that was it.

Lucky Strike advertising was costing American Tobacco an estimated $20 million yearly—more money than any company spent on any product in the entire world—yet however many dollars Hill kept throwing at his problem, he couldn't find the solution.

I thought I knew the solution, but I wasn't entertaining grandiose dreams of taking over the company and returning Lucky Strike to the premier position it had held only a few years earlier. I had never met the flamboyant and rambunctious George Washington Hill, who controlled that company absolutely. But I was more than casually concerned, as well as fascinated, with the company's problems, because I had charge of its radio activities for the Pall Mall account, which Young & Rubicam handled. And while I didn't know Hill, I was acquainted with his son, George junior, a company vice president. During our dealings in regard to the Pall Mall account I may have had some short discussions with him about those problems, yet I can't remember making any suggestions to him concerning products other than Pall Mall. Though it had never been one of the top brands, it was more than holding its share of the market, and there were no complaints about the way we were handling its ad campaigns.

Perhaps this was the reason I began getting phone calls from Jack Latham, a pal from Young & Rubicam who was now an executive at American Tobacco. He wasn't calling me about Pall Malls; he was calling me about myself. I don't remember why he had moved from Y&R to American—I suppose it was to take on a more important job or for more money. In any case, he wanted me to know he was very happy there. He assured me it was a solid organization and an excellent place to work. Why didn't I consider the possibility of joining him there? As for its problems with Lucky Strike, I should see them not as a drawback but a challenge.

"Challenge" was a green-light word to me, with my dreams of reviving moribund companies, but I didn't take Latham's arguments seriously. Nobody at American had ever made me an offer. Then one day George Hill, Jr., called, and gave me the same pitch as Latham, but much more specifically. He had talked to his father about me, and they wanted me to become the company's advertising manager. I went down to their headquarters at III Fifth Avenue for a chat with George junior, then returned to my own office and began thinking about his proposal.

I wondered if I could actually manage to accomplish what I thought should be done at American. I still hadn't met the senior Mr. Hill, but I knew his reputation. Would I ever be able to persuade a man as willful and strong-minded as he was reputed to be that he was pursuing the wrong policies?

It would be a tricky thing to accomplish, but in my youthful optimism, I felt sure I could do it.

I also had to consider my situation at Young & Rubicam. Even today, I must say it was the best place I ever worked. I was scheduled to become the thirty-eighth stockholder at Christmas 1938, which was only a few months away. I wasn't making a fortune, but Chet LaRoche had promised me a vice presidency soon, and said that within a year after that, I'd be making $50,000 a year, which was a considerable sum in those days. American Tobacco was offering me $20,000 to start, then $30,000 within a year, plus a $10,000 annual expense account, which wasn't bad, either. And I wasn't yet thirty.

In the end, it wasn't the money that made up my mind for me; it was the challenge. If I could bring Lucky Strike back to the top of the cigarette market, I would become a major force in the advertising world. So I accepted the American Tobacco Company offer, even though I still hadn't met George Washington Hill and had heard all kinds of strange, daunting stories about him.

Everyone admitted that though he was eccentric, he was also sometimes brilliant. It was he who made cigarettes universally popular in the 1920s with women as well as men, by coining such slogans as "Lucky Strike means fine tobacco," "It's toasted," and "Reach for a Lucky instead of a sweet." That last slogan had prompted thousands of weight-conscious American women to switch from candy to cigarettes, even though it had been socially unacceptable until then for women to smoke.

If Hill had made a name for himself in the history of tobacco, it was not only for his accomplishments. His modus operandi was unique. I had heard that he always wore a hat, even indoors—a broad-brimmed felt one in winter, a Panama in summer, and always with a fishing fly stuck in the

band. His suits featured huge patch pockets filled with packages of Luckys, which he handed out to everyone he met.
He was reputed to be loud and self-dramatizing, especially
at company meetings, where his executives sat at a long table,
agreeing with him. It was obvious that he lacked patience
with employees who had the temerity to disagree with him.

When I stopped to think about all this, I realized that the
revival of the Lucky Strike brand wasn't the only challenge
I faced at American Tobacco. But I had thought of a strategy
I hoped would work. With the approach of winter 1938, I
resigned from Young & Rubicam, cleared out my desk, and
moved my personal belongings down to lower Fifth Avenue,
where I had been assigned the third-most-sumptuous office
at American Tobacco. The senior Mr. Hill occupied the enormous corner suite. George junior was next door to the father,
and I was next door to the son. My office was at least 50 feet
square, with two huge desks facing each other and a big
leather chair between them, so that I could swivel from one
to the other. For visitors there were plush sofas and lounge
chairs with coffee tables. As in all of the company's offices,
there was also a big brass cuspidor. For those readers too
young ever to have heard the word, a cuspidor is a spittoon.
They've gone out of style in recent years, except in the U.S.
Congress, where they don't keep up very well with the changing times. I don't remember what kind of pictures were on
the walls, but I do recall a framed slogan that graced everybody's office: "Quality of Product Is Essential to Continuing
Success."

The first thing I did as an executive at American Tobacco
was to switch from my usual three daily packages of Parlia-
ments to three packages, and maybe more, of Lucky Strikes.
When I recall how much I used to smoke, I realize it's a
miracle I'm still alive. But, of course, in those innocent days
of the 1930s and forties, almost everybody smoked.

The importance of tobacco to our young nation in its pioneer days was impressive. So, too, was the romance of the business—the auctions, the methods of curing, the variations in manufacture. To me the smell of good cigarette tobacco was delicious. My father smoked cigars, which I didn't like, though I was to deal with them at American, which owned major interests in cigar production and sales. Of course, even then, any intelligent person knew the dangers of heavy smoking. My attitude, then and now, was that tobacco, like food and alcohol, was meant to be used for pleasure, but not to excess. I learned to my sorrow that I fell into that segment of the population which developed the "motor-habit" fixation with cigarettes. If the phone rang, I'd light up; if I wanted to write, I'd light up.

My recommendation to doctors during my volunteer work throughout my life (American Heart Association, fifteen years, last three as chairman; Muscular Dystrophy Association, twenty-six years as president, chairman, and vice chairman of the executive committee, now president emeritus) has been to make studies of young people to determine if they are prone to addictions. Alcoholics are a small percentage of drinkers; obesity is not common, though everybody eats. If a person is analyzed as being likely to overdo one thing, he or she will probably overdo others. The famous 1964 Surgeon General's report on smoking and health did not find nonsmokers to be the healthiest segment of the population, but rather light smokers. Tobacco can be dangerous to many, and people should be warned to forgo its great pleasure if they can't control their habit.

I remember only vaguely my first meeting with Hill. I was invited into his corner office by his male secretary, Doc Bowden (I never knew his full name, since everyone always called him Doc), with a summons to which I soon became accustomed, because it was always worded the same way: "Could you give Mr. Hill a minute?"

Hill was at his desk with his hat on, just as I had been led to expect. He was polite—even enthusiastic, it seemed—in welcoming me to American Tobacco, but if we discussed company business that day, I have no recollection of it. I think it was simply a pro-forma introduction.

I do vividly remember the way he conducted meetings. As I described them for *The New Yorker*, those meetings were arranged dramatically, almost like scenes in a play. The stage would be set beforehand in the spacious company board-room, the central feature of which was a long table with a thick glass top. It felt strange to sit at that table and see everybody's legs and feet sprawled out beneath it. As the weeks passed, I began breaking this pattern by putting my feet on the table, which was a shock to my more proper colleagues.

Before each session, all the pertinent materials—reports, charts, layouts, and, most important, ashtrays—were arranged on the table, one each per person. For outsized exhibits there was an easel near the head of the table. A few feet away was a phonograph, to play recordings of proposed new commercials.

When everyone was seated and, in my view, looking nervously expectant, several minutes of uncomfortable silence would ensue. Then the door would burst open and this human storm would enter. His stern face was oval-shaped; his features were regular, though not exactly handsome. He was of average height but seemed taller, because of the way he loomed over his seated executives. His complexion was reddish; his hair—or, at least, what you could see of it from under his hat—was black as shoe polish, leading me to suspect it might be dyed, since he was in his mid-fifties.

He would glower down at everyone but say nothing as he walked the length of the table and took his place at the head. Sitting there, erect and steely-eyed, he would fix his stare on one man after another, down the right side of the table and up the left, looking each of us in the eye. With a sudden move he would pull a pack of Lucky Strikes from one of his patch pockets and slam it down on the table with real force (which explained why the glass top had to be so thick). Almost invariably he would begin, in a loud, clear voice: "Tobacco, gentlemen, is what it's all about."

Opening the package, he would light up a Lucky and inhale so deeply, he would draw the flame at least a half inch down the length of the cigarette. Since by his own estimate he smoked four packs a day, he must have had prodigious lung power, though he was not destined, unfortunately, to retain it.

He would begin the meeting by asking each man, down the line, what project he was working on and what proposal he could offer to improve the product or increase its sales. I was never sure whether he was actually soliciting ideas or simply scaring his executives into thinking harder about their jobs. He seemed to listen to what they said but didn't often react to their ideas. Usually he let out a noncommittal grunt, which would relieve its recipient, because it meant that at least the boss wasn't angry. When an executive made what Hill considered a stupid suggestion, he would erupt in fury and throw ashtrays on the floor, or kick the nearest cuspidor. One day he smashed a potted plant, spreading soil all over the rug. When confronted with a reasonable suggestion that he nevertheless intended to veto, he would say, "We shall forgo that course of action for the following reasons," of which he would list maybe a dozen, even though one would have been sufficient.

Finally, when he was tired of listening to everyone else's ideas, he would start launching his own. And as soon as he suggested something, however impractical it might be, heads would eagerly nod, and the rush to agree would begin.

"Great idea, sir."

"A sure-fire winner."

"Wonderful."

"Why didn't one of us think of that?"

I don't believe he paid any more attention to his executives' praise than he did to their proposals, but he was an actor and they were his audience. He was the star of the show, and he liked that role, especially if he thought he was scaring his audience. Anyone who was easily frightened should not have been working for him; yet if everyone had lived by that rule, there wouldn't have been many people in the boardroom with him. I soon decided that if I hoped to get anything accomplished, I had better not conduct myself like most of these other fellows.

My first noticeable project at American Tobacco was a twenty-four-page, single-spaced memorandum that I'm embarrassed about now but apparently meant a lot to George Washington Hill at the time. Though it purported to be a treatise on his company's advertising policies, it was basically the story of the history of advertising, expounding the theory that it had been practiced since the dawn of civilization. I argued that advertising was nothing but selling, which had always been with us, and I traced the development of selling techniques from ancient Egypt to the present day.

Hill loved every word of it. In fact, he was so smitten, he insisted I take it to my former colleagues on the plans board at Young & Rubicam and read it to them aloud. Silly as I knew this to be, I was still so new on the job, I could hardly refuse to do it, and since Y&R still handled two significant American Tobacco accounts, my old friends there could hardly refuse to listen. They must have become increasingly impatient as I droned on, as rapidly as I could. They were busy men, with more important things to do. But instead of telling me to knock it off, they simply smiled, and sometimes almost snickered, as I wore out my voice reading them what they already knew. It was an embarrassing and uncomfortable experience for me, but by a stroke of luck I was able, in the end, to take the curse off it with a touch of humor.

When I finished, there was an awkward pause while they perhaps tried to think of something polite to say. One of them, completely ignoring the tedious thesis I had just inflicted upon them, finally said, with a slightly cynical smile, "How're you getting along with Mr. Hill down there, Pat?"

On a sudden impulse I pulled my right hand up into the sleeve of my jacket, out of sight, so I looked like an amputee, waved my arm, and said, "I've got him eating out of my hand."

Thanks to Hill's enthusiasm for my memo, I soon found there was some figurative truth in that jest. The man who had been fearsome to so many advertising managers now began treating me like a favored son, tolerating the liberties I took.

The New Yorker quoted a remark from one unnamed American Tobacco Company executive that startled me when I first read it, though I suppose there was some truth in it. "Pat handled Hill with an insouciance that amazed us all," the man said. "He would turn up late for those meetings in the board room, lean back in his chair with his feet on the table right under Hill's nose, and argue with him on matters the old man had already made up his mind on." The magazine also quoted George Hill, Jr., several years after I had left the company: "Father's relationship with Pat was never that of boss with servant. Father saw that Pat needed a freer rein than other men."

If so, it must have been partly because I happened to get off on the right foot with him by writing that long-winded memo, but the fact that he seemed to like me didn't lead me into the dangerous impression that he would accept my opinions about how to run his company. He was so opinionated himself, he would have to be convinced that my ideas were actually his own.

I was sure we could turn around the slump in Lucky Strike sales if we made a few major changes. First, I thought we should take twenty-six full-page color ads—back covers or not—in the few really big weekly magazines (*Life, Look, Time, Newsweek,* the *Saturday Evening Post, Collier's,* and *The New Yorker*), which blanketed 90 percent of the people who bought magazines. Second, we should drop all those expensive newspaper ads, because most newspaper readers bought at least one of the major magazines. Third, we should stick to one overriding theme in our advertising message— the fine quality of Lucky Strike tobacco—creating variations on that theme but never wandering from the basic message. And fourth, we should take some of the millions of dollars we'd save and pump it into prime-time radio programs.

I did not, however, argue for these changes at the frequent boardroom meetings, as the unnamed informant seemed to suggest to *The New Yorker.* If I argued with the old man at those meetings it was mostly about details. I took up important matters with him privately, making sure that if my insinuations and subtle suggestions got through to him, he could announce them to his other executives fully convinced they were his own ideas.

I emphasized to him, supported by research data from George Gallup, that the six or seven top weekly magazines combined were reaching nine-tenths of our market. I used his own slogan, emblazoned on all of our office walls, "Quality of Product Is Essential to Continuing Success," plus another of his slogans, "Lucky Strike means fine tobacco," to convince him that this was the one and only message that would actually impress prospective smokers. I also reached into my own experiences to educate him about the phenomenal influence of commercials during those golden days of radio.

Softly but persistently, I kept suggesting concentrating on
the tremendous power of the big weekly magazines and radio
in the evening hours. In less time than I had dared to hope,
he went for this concentration theory, and Lucky Strike advertising policies began to take a new direction. But Lucky
sales had fallen to 38 billion cigarettes a year, which represented a headlong plunge into third place. We faced a tough
climb.

Because Lord and Thomas handled Lucky advertising, I
soon began working with its account representatives—Bill
Griffin, Boge Carlau, and Emerson Foote—and found them
as efficient as they were imaginative. This amazed me, because they weren't showing good results. I soon decided this
was not their fault but that of Albert Lasker, the big chief
at Lord and Thomas. He advocated and fostered the enormously expensive scatter-money policy in Lucky Strike advertising, and I suspected his motive was simple greed. The
more money American spent on Lucky campaigns, the more
commissions his agency collected (I won't say "earned," because they weren't earning it, despite the diligence of their
men on the account). Lasker was not the only disadvantage
with which the account representatives had to work. Lord
and Thomas simply didn't have the basic internal structure—experts in research, marketing, media, art, copy-
writing—to which I had been accustomed at Young &
Rubicam. I realized that this, too, was Lasker's responsibility, and gradually developed a rather low opinion of his work,
despite his prestige as a giant of the advertising industry.

One day in 1939, eight or nine months after I had gone to
American Tobacco, I walked into a restaurant where ad men
gathered and saw an old friend from California, Don Francisco, with whom I had worked on several Don Lee network
programs. He had been in charge of the Lord and Thomas
Los Angeles office and had just arrived in New York to take
over management of the agency's main office. He invited me

to sit down with him at a table where he was having a drink with Lasker.

I accepted Francisco's invitation, welcomed him to New York, then said, "I think you're arriving just in time. I came to work for American from Young and Rubicam several months ago, and I'm appalled at the treatment Lucky Strike gets from Lord and Thomas, compared to what Y&R does for its clients. Maybe you can turn things around, Don, because you ran the best agency in Los Angeles."

I don't recall that Lasker said anything to refute me that day. Maybe he was too surprised at the impertinence of a young upstart. But I soon learned that Lasker had come in person to Hill's office the following day with a fanciful version of what I had said. According to Lasker, I had accused not only him but George Washington Hill of using their advertising policies to siphon off money that should have gone to the company's stockholders. He strongly urged Hill to get rid of me forthwith.

Apparently, Hill knew me well enough by this time to decide I would never say anything quite that stupid. According to his son, he simply listened to Lasker's accusations. But Hill obviously did want to know what I had said, so he sent George junior to ask me. I related the incident exactly as I remembered, and that was the last I ever heard about it inside the company. Hill never mentioned the incident to me, but Lasker made pointed references to it on several occasions when we were thrown together at meetings. He would say as he proposed some course of action, "I don't have to ask Mr. Weaver's opinion. I already know what he thinks of me and my ideas."

I, in turn, would smile and say nothing, which must have infuriated him, because it tacitly confirmed my low opinion of him. His son, Ed Lasker, whom I knew and liked, told me later how deeply I had offended his father. "My old man says nobody in his whole life ever spoke to him the way you did. He'll never get over it."

Ten years later, I was to learn that Albert Lasker never did get over it.

IT TOOK ME A WHILE to convert George Washington Hill to my ideas about the use of radio. He was never anti-radio, but he simply didn't seem to think he needed more of it than he already had. Since 1935 he had been sponsoring *Your Hit Parade*, the opening of which I had happened to attend, because Meredith Willson, my friend from California days, believed the idea of the show had been stolen from him. I couldn't disagree with Willson. For several years, he had conducted a San Francisco program of his creation called *Big Ten*, in which he featured each week the ten most popular tunes as listed in the industry journal *Billboard*. Willson often talked about suing American Tobacco for stealing his format, so finally, when I went to work for American, I mentioned it to Hill.

"Talk to the agency," he said. "They brought it to me. I don't know anything about how it was put together." Needless to say, I got no satisfaction from Lord and Thomas, and eventually the whole issue evaporated.

By this time, the Lucky Strike *Hit Parade* on CBS had become one of radio's top shows. When it began it had Lennie Hayton and a big orchestra with many stars, including my pal from the coast Kay Thompson, Gogo de Lyss, and others. Later, MCA took over and scheduled a different band each week. I remember traveling to El Paso for the show with Orrin Tucker's orchestra and wee Bonnie Baker—and it was hard to get there in those days. Later, when I could exert stronger influence, I persuaded Hill that Mark Warnow on a regular basis would be better for the show, and so it proved.

Mark's brother, Raymond Scott, also came aboard, with his marvelous quintet.

Kay Kyser's Kollege of Musical Knowledge, featuring Ginny Simms, was about to begin on NBC when I arrived at American Tobacco, so I had nothing to do with putting it together, but I did make some changes, which seemed to work. While I liked both of those shows, I didn't think they gave us enough exposure, especially among educated, affluent people. I soon found a solution to that problem, when a program called *Information Please* became available. It was a high-class quiz show, but without prizes or audience participation. It featured a panel of extremely intelligent people—the Shakespearean scholar and *New York Times* sports columnist John Kieran, the classical pianist Oscar Levant, and the humorist Franklin P. Adams—answering very difficult and complicated questions put to them by emcee Clifton Fadiman. When I persuaded Hill to buy the show, he didn't seem enthusiastic about it. But he soon saw its worth. One night, the first half of the show's hour was preempted on NBC station WJZ for a political speech by Thomas E. Dewey, who was then running for governor of New York. When listeners realized they were hearing Dewey instead of *Information Please,* the WJZ switchboard lit up. The audience verdict was 8 calls favoring Dewey, who was destined to win the governorship, and 920 demanding an immediate return to *Information Please.*

When I persuaded Hill to sponsor the show, my reasoning was that it would be like advertising in *The New Yorker.* We wouldn't reach a mass audience, but we would get to quality listeners. I was only half right—we reached both quality and mass. *Information Please* was a big hit for several years.

I was convinced we needed still more radio exposure, and in 1940 I tried to get Jack Benny, who had been one of our clients at Young & Rubicam. Don Stauffer and I had negotiated Benny's latest General Foods renewal. The contract tied him up until 1942, but it included a provision that would eventually result in his personally controlling his NBC 7 p.m. Sunday time slot if General Foods did not renew him. In 1942, General Foods did not renew him, and Benny was bought by American Tobacco. I was already on leave from the company, in the war effort.

It was on his Lucky Strike program, which continued for many years, that Benny came up with what some people consider the funniest line of his entire career.

On one of his shows he was being robbed by a man who put a gun to his head and said, "Your money or your life."

In his penny-pinching radio persona, Benny faced a tough decision. "Hmm?" he said, after which there was an almost interminable pause. He was indeed the all-time master at milking a gag.

Eventually the impatient robber shouted, "Come on! You heard me! Your money or your life!"

Finally Benny said, with equal impatience, "I'm thinking it over!"

ADDING JACK BENNY to the other programs really powered our business on up. Whether the policy of giving artists free cigarettes helped is less sure. Fred wrote me a thank-you letter I still have. He sent it from Hollywood, where he was making a movie. But the main purpose of the letter was to thank me, in Allen's inimitable way, for a consignment of cigarettes and cigars I had sent him when he and Portland and their entourage were boarding their train in New York en route to Los Angeles:

> dear sylvester
>   . . . i have been mulling over a variety of ways to thank you for your kindness in bestowing your american tobacco company's free samples on our little company

as we departed your city. . . . everyone was put to work on your products. women and children were smoking luckies in the club car, the porters were puffing coronas in the aisles, the brakemen were lighting up pall mall after pall mall, using the lighted ends instead of lanterns. i was perched out on the observation car tacking and spitting and spitting and tacking as the winds changed coming across the country. we arrived here a nicotine infested little band. how to thank you for contributing to the curtailment of our life spans has bothered me since I saw the newly baked depot in los angeles. . . . mr. benny is relaxing in honolulu and will return in two weeks ready to creep into action. . . .

We should all have been as wise as Fred Allen. He knew, even before the scientists and doctors, that tobacco could be the death of some of us, but he always joked about health, perhaps because he himself never enjoyed the best of it. He had sent me another letter, shortly after I went to American Tobacco, congratulating me, if you could call it that, on my new job:

dear p sylvester;
   gone the halcyon, devil-may-care day when we were expected to hail you as "weaver," "dear pat," "p.w." and "sir!" now that you have moved from the agency to become a client, all fraternal salutations must give over to greetings that smack of the dignity accorded the man who sports the furrowed brow, the "tums" packet peeping out of his upper waistcoat pocket and the look of neurotic importance and other vestiges we associate with clients. . . .

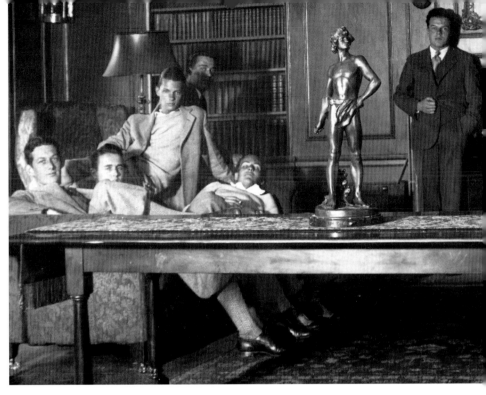

Pat Weaver (far left) in the sitting room of Phi Kappa Psi
fraternity house at Dartmouth, circa 1928

With (from
left to right)
Fred Allen, Bill
Rousseau, and
Tom Lewis,
circa 1935

LEFT: George Washington Hill, 1935
(AP/Wide World Photos)

BELOW: With his wife, Elizabeth, on their
honeymoon in New Hampshire's White
Mountains, 1942 *(Bray Photo)*

From left to right: Pat's father, sister-in-law Rita, and brother
Doodles, circa 1942 *(Ralph Morris)*

Producing *Command Performance* with Rita Hayworth, Charles
Boyer, and Jack Benny, 1945

LEFT: David Sarnoff with a transistor radio, 1955 *(UPI/Bettmann)*

BELOW: Signing a contract with Sid Caesar, circa 1956 *(NBC/Globe Photos)*

With Dave
Garroway
*(NBC/Globe
Photos)*

With J. Fred Muggs *(NBC/Globe Photos)*

Robert Sarnoff, 1970
(AP/Wide World Photos)

Elizabeth with Norma Shearer at Sun Valley, circa 1970

With Elizabeth and Sigourney at home

With Trajan Weaver (left)

At the Television Academy Hall of Fame with (from left) Sid
Caesar, Carol Burnett, and Walter Cronkite, 1985
(AP/Wide World Photos)

At the Smithsonian Institution

Later in the same letter he had some "healthful" advice for me, now that I was an executive with furrowed brow:

. . . never attempt to quaff your phenobarbital from a dixie cup. the sodium salicylate works havoc with the glue in dixie cups. surer than hell the bottom of your dixie cup will fly open and you will have to sit around the office with an effervescing lap . . . also am enclosing one special client cork swivel guard. the guard, sewed into your drawers prevents swivel-piercing, a great menace to most clients. sitting in a chair day upon day, the swivel is apt to run through the wood and enter the lower colon without so much as a "touche." chet bowles of benton & bowles once found himself impaled in a naked swivel and spun around in his chair for several hours before being unswiveled and medicated.

Allen was only one of many celebrities, especially film and radio stars, to whom I sent free cigarettes. I had inherited this practice from my predecessor, and I continued it because I knew enough stars to realize that many of them were susceptible to the simplest kind of flattery. Each of them received a free carton a week in the mail. It cost us virtually nothing, and would have cost them only a dollar and a quarter in a store, but I was amazed at the effusive letters of gratitude I received even from wealthy celebrities like Clark Gable and Leslie Howard. Fred Allen didn't fit into that category. There was nothing effusive or even grateful about his "gratitude." He simply couldn't resist an opportunity to have some fun with me. As I knew, he didn't smoke.

In late 1939, after my first year at American Tobacco, George Washington Hill honored me with a new title. Instead of advertising manager I was now advertising director. I don't yet know the difference between the two titles, but I appreciated the change in salary.

By that time I think I was really earning my wages. Hill was spending several million dollars less a year on advertising, yet Lucky Strike sales had begun to climb. He was dangling in front of me the possibility that I might one day be a vice president at the colossal salary of $200,000 a year. He himself was taking home $420,000 a year, which even some of the people on his staff considered a bit too much. In March 1940, several disenchanted stockholders tried to whittle that down but failed, because the American Tobacco board members were all creatures of Hill. He appointed no outside directors. Was he worth $420,000 a year? That's difficult to measure, but it was he who had made American the giant company it was.

I gradually became involved not only in Lucky Strike advertising but in other aspects of sales as well. Hill had developed a corps of five hundred salesmen who traveled from town to town, store to store, making in-person pitches, especially for Lucky Strike. I didn't understand the need for such an expensive army of salesmen, since it had been well established that advertising was the prime factor in selling tobacco. The cigarette business was basically an advertising business, not a door-to-door operation.

With this in mind, I asked Hill one day why he continued to maintain such a large sales force. His answer was interesting, because it helped me define and understand the man.

"Look here," he said. "We're a great big company. We make lots of money, and our labor costs are only two or three percent by volume. But I don't want people to think we're just a bunch of rich guys sitting in fancy offices on Fifth Avenue in New York. When people think of us, I want them to think of an average-looking guy, like themselves, walking into stores everywhere, working hard and getting paid to do his job. The personal approach to selling keeps this company at a common-denominator level, makes the public think of us as just another company, like Sears Roebuck or Montgomery Ward, with common people working for us, which is what we ourselves are. They can also tell us if anybody's cutting prices."

By Hill's edict, the salesmen were required to memorize their pitch and rehearse it in front of a mirror. They were also equipped with portable phonographs and recordings that told the tobacco story, complete with the voices of the auctioneers who were featured in the Lucky Strike commercials. There were two of them, F. E. Boone and Steve "Speed" Riggs, who actually were tobacco auctioneers. During the commercials they rattled indecipherable but real auction babble, which ended with two clearly spoken words, "Sold American!"—thus providing one more enforcement of our central message: Lucky Strike meant fine tobacco, because American bought only the finest.

Though I considered the five-hundred-man sales force virtually superfluous, it remained. I had to write the ever-changing sales pitch for these men, and I also regularly went out on the road to make sure they were delivering the message forcefully and accurately. I did enjoy some of my travels with them. We made field trips to attend tobacco auctions and visits to cigarette factories. The value of the sales call jumped after the war, because we switched to little movie setups the salesmen carried into the stores. In these, before television, you could see Jack Benny and his cast of characters doing funny stuff, watch the tobacco auctions, and see filmed commercials. I also aimed this presentation at heavy smokers, because we knew from research that they were an important factor in overall sales. I tried to convince them Luckys offered them better tobacco with lighter smoke, meaning less nicotine. Our work for the sales calls also gave rise to early TV commercial ideas, including the dancing cigarettes that were featured in one of our campaigns.

Early in my regime, I brought Everard Meade aboard as my right-hand man. Since the days we began working together on the Fred Allen show, Ev had gained enough experience to know as much about the advertising business as most of the top people in it. He had produced the Al Jolson show in Hollywood and the Burns and Allen program. I had always wanted to get him back with me, and now that he was, we had a lot of fun together. He would stride into his office next to mine with almost regal bearing, sit down, reach back behind his head, and make pulling motions as if he were extracting his spine. Then he'd crumple forward as if he were without backbone, look up at me, and say, "Ready, chief." At tedious meetings he passed me "urgent" notes that, when opened, would turn out to be "German Bombing Targets" or other insanities. In our spare time, Ev and I would try to develop formats for comedy stars we liked who had not quite made it in radio—Bert Lahr and Wheeler and Woolsey, and later Don Adams, Mike Nichols, and Jackie Gleason, to name a few.

From the beginning at American Tobacco, I plotted ways to improve the Lucky Strike package, but I was afraid it would be like stamping on the flag if I were even to suggest it. One side of the package, with the Lucky Strike bull's-eye logo, looked good and was recognizable. But the other side was so undistinguished, it made no impression at all, which meant that half the time, depending on which side was facing you, it offered no real Lucky Strike identification. Despite my fears, I mentioned this to Hill, and he, surprisingly, allowed me to put the celebrated industrial designer Raymond Loewy to work on a new package. In due time Loewy brought me two samples, one basically green, the other basically white, with a much-improved bull's-eye symbol on each side and no superfluous wording. I liked both designs but preferred the white.

Hill chose the green, whereby hangs a tale. Time passed, the United States finally entered the war, and in 1942 I was in the Navy on a ship in the Atlantic Ocean when I heard on the radio a commercial with a new slogan: "Lucky Strike Green has gone to war."

In those days there was a lot of talk about doing without items that would be needed for the war effort. I don't think green pigment was one of those items, but that sly fox George Washington Hill had obviously decided that he, too, preferred Loewy's white package, and he was using the war-shortage theme to get rid of the green and, in the process, garner some free publicity for his product. As far as I know, only "Lucky Strike Green" is still fighting the Germans and the Japanese. It has never come back from the war.

In early 1941, before we entered the war, while the British were still struggling alone against the apparently unbeatable Germans, I, too, thought of a way to use the war, in devising what was to become a famous Pall Mall commercial. By that time the Ruthrauff and Ryan agency was handling the Pall Mall account, and they sent me a proposal for a commercial with a war motif. I liked the idea of a war symbol but didn't like their commercial, so I called in R&R's director of radio, Merritt Barnum, and asked him, "What kind of sounds do you associate with land warfare?"

He replied, "Gunfire, artillery, tanks, bugles . . ."

"Air war?" I asked.

"Bombs, planes, dive-bombers . . ."

"And sea war?"

"I don't know. Big guns, foghorns, alarm bells . . ."

"Did you ever hear a British destroyer whistle?" I asked. "Whoop! Whoop! Whoop!" It was a very distinctive sound with which most people were familiar, because on newsreels at the time one often saw destroyers in action against U-boats.

Barnum caught my suggestion immediately.

"All right, you take it from there," I said, and he did. The result was a Pall Mall commercial that everyone was soon echoing: "*On land* [bugle sound], *in the air* [dive-bomber sound], *and on the sea* [a British destroyer's Whoop! Whoop! Whoop!]. *Modern design* makes the difference."

George Washington Hill liked it so much, he raised his hat to us three times.

I also had a small, almost accidental role in the creation of king-size Pall Malls. With the possibility of war approaching, the government raised the levy on cigarettes, which were taxed so much per thousand units. I went into Hill's office and said, "What if we doubled the length of Lucky Strikes, or maybe just one of our off-brands, like Pall Mall, to begin? We could raise the price without paying the extra tax."

"We can't do that," he said. "I'm sure Congress wasn't so stupid as to leave such a big loophole in the law."

I wasn't so sure of that. "Are you telling me that cigarette lengths were set by the government and we can't change them even a fraction of an inch?"

A faraway look came over his face, and he said, "I'll see you later."

I was rather miffed about being thus dismissed but soon forgot it. Then one day, maybe two months later, while I was engrossed in some other problem, Hill's secretary, Doc Bowden, came into my office with his usual polite summons: "Could you give Mr. Hill a minute?"

When I entered Hill's office, I noticed immediately that something was different. He was sitting there bareheaded, with his hat on the desk in front of him.

"Something wrong?" I asked.

"On the contrary, something's right—great. Sit down and I'll show it to you. Remember the day you asked me how long a cigarette could be and still remain within legal limits? Take a look at the new king-size Pall Mall."

He picked up his hat to reveal a mockup package of Pall Walls at least a half-inch longer than the regulars. That time he had done more than tip his hat to me. He had actually removed it.

Throughout my two and a half years at American Tobacco, I kept getting bids to "come back home" to Young & Rubicam. Though I didn't intend to do so, I continued my close friendship with all the Y&R people, including Chet LaRoche.

In May 1941, I met my wife-to-be: Elizabeth Inglis, who had just returned from Hollywood. I was staying with Chet and Clara LaRoche at their home in Fairfield, Connecticut, and Liz had come out to play in a tennis tournament and attend the local Hunt Ball, where Chet LaRoche was Master of Hounds. Her date was Carleton Palmer, who, it turned out, was separated from his wife. Having been unaware of the separation and of the fact that Carleton's wife would not be in residence, Liz had insisted on returning to New York. Carleton prevailed upon her to wait while he made a telephone call. This call—which was to the LaRoches—changed my life and Liz's. Instead of driving her to the railroad station, Carleton took her to the LaRoches', where Clara welcomed her with open arms and showed her to a guest room. She suggested that Liz meet them downstairs for cocktails at seven o'clock. The very British Liz was downstairs at 7:05 p.m.; I was the only one around. The LaRoches didn't appear for at least half an hour.

We all went that evening to the Hunt Ball, but I had had Liz to myself for quite a while. I found out that she was from a large family, that her father was a retired lawyer, and that four of her five brothers were serving in various branches of the armed services. Liz had performed in several plays in London's West End. She had gone to the Royal Academy of Dramatic Art in London, and had had a season at the Northampton Repertory Theatre and one at the prestigious Liverpool Playhouse. I was able to look her up in *Who's Who in the Theatre* (English) and was suitably impressed. Just as well that I found the listing, because she did not much want to talk about herself and instead was always asking about me.

The morning after the ball I was up early. (I was doing the Fred Allen show and had to return to New York.) I went down to the swimming pool, thinking that no one else was up and that I would swim and have breakfast. Liz was by the pool, and we had breakfast together. After this meeting, we saw each other frequently.

Liz had come to the United States to play her original role in *Gaslight*. This play had been a great success in London, and she was being fitted for her wardrobe and was due to start filming in her original role, when war was declared. Theaters and studios closed down immediately. The Shuberts had the rights to *Gaslight* and wanted to do the play in New York. They had cabled Liz to find out if she would be interested in playing her original part. At the time, she was committed to do the film, so she had not thought much about the Shuberts. The war changed everything. Eventually the Shuberts lost their rights to the play, but they had another play up their sleeves—*Tony Draws a Horse*. In the tryout at the Liverpool Playhouse they saw that Elizabeth Inglis had played the ingenue role. They changed the name of the play to *Billy Draws a Horse*. Liz accepted the role. The play opened in New York and ran ten days, and Liz signed a Hollywood contract with Warner Brothers. At the end of six months her option was dropped. Warners put Liz in a western—in which, she says, she was pretty bad—and then in *The Letter*, with Bette Davis, which she enjoyed working on. They changed her name to Elizabeth Earl. She changed it back to Elizabeth Inglis and left Hollywood.

WHILE I STILL had no intention of accepting the invitations to return to Young & Rubicam, I had decided by the spring of 1941 that I wouldn't be remaining at American Tobacco, either. Since Lucky Strike was back at the top of the sales charts, ahead of Camels and Chesterfields, I felt I had done the job I had come to do. And though I was one of the few who felt a genuine admiration for George Washington Hill, I was facing the realization that something much bigger loomed on the horizon—the country's participation in the war. I didn't think we could keep out of it much longer, and I felt such contempt for Adolf Hitler and his gang, I didn't think we should stay out of it.

The German war machine had already overrun virtually all of Europe, as far east as the Russian border, and it was beginning to look as if Russia would be next—unless Hitler decided to take England first. Few people believed England could resist an invasion. German submarines were sinking British ships at the rate of almost 100,000 tons a month, and it was becoming apparent, at least to me, that only a full-scale American entry into the war could stop Hitler.

All of this kept weighing so heavily on my mind that I went to the Naval Intelligence Office in lower Manhattan and said to the officer who interviewed me, "I'm a sailor by avocation. I have a fifty-six-foot yawl which I've sailed up and down the Atlantic coast from Canada to the Caribbean. I know that stretch of the ocean well, and I know something about seamanship. I want to apply for a commission as a reserve officer, to be called to active duty whenever the navy needs me."

My application was accepted, and I began preparing myself for a complete turnaround in my life. But before the navy was through processing my application, I received a surprising telephone call from Nelson Rockefeller.

MY FRIENDSHIP WITH NELSON ROCKEFELLER FROM OUR
student days at Dartmouth had never lapsed. By the time I
was producing the Fred Allen show at NBC, his family had
placed him in charge of the RCA Building, which was—and
is—the centerpiece of Rockefeller Center, as well as the NBC
headquarters. We ran into each other frequently and often
had lunch together, so I was not surprised to receive a call
from him. I was, however, surprised at what he had to say.

"You know, I've got this job in Washington," he said.

I did know it. The previous summer, he had been appointed by President Roosevelt to direct a newly created
organization with a fancy title—Coordinator of Inter-
American Affairs. I didn't know exactly what that meant.

"I'm conducting a whole new operation for the government," he continued. "I want you to join me, because I know
you speak Spanish, and this organization has to do with Latin
America. You also know radio, which will be one of our main

concerns. I want you to manage whatever we do in radio."

"Wait a minute," I said. "I think you should know that I've applied for a commission in the navy. I can't get out of that. It's too late for me to be talking about anything else."

"No, it isn't," he insisted. "The job I have in mind will make you untouchable in the draft. Even if you're already signed up for the navy, we can get that canceled."

"Are you suggesting," I asked, "that this project of yours will have something to do with the war in case we get into it?"

"It has something to do with the war," he said, "even if we don't get into it."

As I knew, he hated Hitler and favored our entry into the war as much as I did. He also believed that it would happen eventually. When we were together we talked about all kinds of things, including politics, war, and world conditions. He was exceptionally well informed, intelligent, and, it seemed to me, ambitious, but I always felt that regardless of his family's vast financial interests, he wanted to do what was right for the world. He never mentioned selfish or family concerns, never talked like a man of enormous wealth. He must have thought I, too, was wealthy, perhaps because at Dartmouth I drove a better car than his. In later life, whenever he ran for public office he asked me to be his media advisor. This was a big job, but while he was generous with his other campaign workers, he never offered me a penny. When I began adding up all the Rockefeller campaigns on which I worked, I decided I had paid dearly for driving my LaSalle Phaeton in college.

The purpose of his organization, as I learned, was to counteract pro-Axis propaganda in Latin America by making sure the people there would also get at least equal doses of more convincing pro-Allied propaganda. Radio was only one aspect of Rockefeller's plans. He had already engaged Don

Francisco of Lord and Thomas as head of general communications, Jock Whitney to handle movie projects, and a
whole cast of other people for purposes—perhaps some
secret—that were never explained to me.

When I agreed to take part in Nelson's project, he asked
me to move to Washington and join the nucleus he had
gathered there. After taking a friendly leave of absence from
the American Tobacco Company, I did so, and stayed until
I realized that if I wanted to accomplish anything for his
radio division, Washington was not the place to be. Socially,
it was fascinating. Nelson knew everyone of importance, and
when you were drawn into his sphere you soon ceased to be
surprised at the people you might meet—cabinet members,
senators, congressmen, ambassadors, royalty, industrialists
from all over the country. I never met President Roosevelt,
but Nelson, of course, knew him, since they both came from
extremely powerful New York families. The whole CIAA organization had grown out of one of FDR's urgent ideas. He
realized that if Hitler conquered England, South America
would probably be his next steppingstone on his way to the
United States. With Japan posing a serious threat in the
Pacific, the U.S. Navy would find it almost impossible to
defend the entire Atlantic coastline of South and North America at the same time, especially if Germany could manage to
capture any significant part of the British navy to supplement
its own small but modern fleet, plus its growing pack of U-
boats. If, in addition, the people and governments of Latin
America proved sympathetic to Hitler, he would have a hospitable base from which to isolate North America while he
prepared to invade us. With Germany so totally ascendant
in Europe, that scenario was not only possible but likely,
and Roosevelt felt constrained to do whatever he could to
forestall it. Since American isolationists were powerful
enough to prevent him from taking an active role by entering

the war, he was determined to do everything possible short of that. His "lend-lease" to Britain of fifty destroyers and other resources was one step in that direction. Creation of the Coordinator of Inter-American Affairs was another.

Why did he choose Nelson Rockefeller, a Republican, to run the agency? I can't say for sure, but the Rockefellers controlled such vast resources in Latin America and exerted so much influence there that anyone bearing the Rockefeller name was assured of instant recognition and respect.

Despite the blandishments of the Washington social scene and the fun of being on the inside, I knew I was wasting my time there. New York was the nation's radio capital. The people and resources I needed were there, and that was where I belonged.

"The only way we can do this job," I said to Nelson, "is to set up a radio operation out of New York, where I can find the right people to write, produce, and perform in the kinds of programs we want. We'll need dozens of Spanish-speaking announcers, actors, singers, and commentators with accents acceptable to all the different kinds of Spanish speakers down there. For Mexico, Cuba, and Argentina, you'll have to have voices with different accents for each of them. And then there's Brazil, where they speak Portuguese. We'll have to have a full complement of Portuguese speakers. Brazil is too big a country to ignore."

Knowing very little about radio production and its complications, Nelson simply said, "Fine. Do it. Go back to New York and open an office. Hire whomever you need."

My plan was to develop an informal Latin American network that would feed programs carrying our message to any stations down there willing to use them. Since I was aware of the political climate of many South American countries, especially those governed by fascist-type dictators, I wasn't sure how successful we would be. But the only way to find out was to try.

I was happy to return to New York—not just because it was the only place from which to operate, but because most of my friends were there, and in particular, Elizabeth Inglis, for whom my feelings had deepened. I can't say I had been smitten by her the first time we met at the LaRoches'; not since I was a teenager had I fallen in love at first sight. But I had been immediately impressed by her, and I had continued seeing her whenever I could.

I rented two floors of the Newsweek building in mid-Manhattan and opened an office with a small staff. We rattled around in all that space for a while, but it soon began to fill up with people. In a remarkably short time we hired more than a hundred.

My first priority was to assemble a staff of experienced radio writers, and since I had little familiarity with Spanish-language writers, most of the people I hired wrote in English. I then had to hire equally competent translators. This promised to create a coordinating problem, until I found Mucio Delgado, a Mexican-American Arizona native who was totally at home in both languages and exceptionally well qualified in every other way. When I finally succeeded in talking him into trading the good life out west for a hectic existence in New York, he proved to be just the man we needed to assure cooperation between Spanish and Portugese translators and our veteran radio writers who knew only English.

We got our Portuguese translators and performers directly from Brazil, thanks to the fact that the ruling dictator at the time, President Getúlio Vargas, found it expedient to court the favor of the United States. He had the usual Latin American *caudillo*'s attitude about civil liberties and political freedom, and he ran a pretty tight ship. But he had apparently decided to bet on the big northern uncle against Hitler and company, so we were able to persuade him to send several members of his own propaganda organization to New York. They turned out to be rather casual and fun-loving, not very diligent but willing to cooperate with us. Every evening they broadcast to Brazil what was supposedly a news report. Some of it was not quite what we would call news, but as long as they included our messages and didn't get too far out of line, we left them alone. We did, however, always monitor them closely.

While we were putting together our staff—including technicians as well as Spanish- and Portuguese-speaking actors, announcers, commentators, musicians, and even comedians—we were also in the process of building our Latin American radio network. We found that the best approach was through large American companies that already sold their products in Central and South America, and therefore advertised extensively on stations down there. Most of these companies proved willing, even eager, to cooperate, because we didn't try to conceal from them our real purpose, and they, too, feared the rise of fascism. We promised that both our news and entertainment programs would be of professional quality, and that our messages would be subtle enough to make sure listeners wouldn't accuse them, as sponsors, of being U.S. propagandists. That was important, because anti-U.S. feeling was so widespread in Latin America, our efforts would be counterproductive if too many people realized what we were doing.

Within a short time we had a big network. Stations in just about every capital and large city in Central and South America accepted what we sent them—partly, I think, because we were turning out pretty good programs, most of which became popular, but also because they were getting these programs free. The U.S. government was financing the whole operation, though the commercials may have brought in some revenue to defray a small part of the cost.

Our best program, *Americanos Todos* (Americans All), was a big success. A half-hour show five nights a week, it was a combination of news and entertainment with the underlying theme that all Americans, North and South, were united in their love of freedom and individualism, as opposed to totalitarianism, which we defined as fascism—German, Italian, and Japanese. I think we gave Latin Americans their first glimpse of German and Japanese villains committing all kinds of atrocities, which was a staple of Hollywood war movies at the time. In our programs, the German and Japanese evildoers were hissing their threats in pidgin Spanish or Portuguese instead of pidgin English. By the time we were in full swing I had an office in Hollywood, because that was where most of the "villainous" German and Japanese actors were to be found.

Our Hollywood office also had another noteworthy function. There we put together a program like *Americanos Todos* for broadcast in the United States, especially in the Southwest, where there were large Hispanic populations. On this show we included all kinds of features publicizing Hispanic ideas, culture, and accomplishments, but not just to flatter Hispanic audiences. We tried to make other Americans appreciate Hispanic traditions. Unfortunately, we didn't dare emphasize the history of Hispanic people in North America, because our message was one of peace and understanding between people, and we Anglo-Americans couldn't boast a very commendable record in the treatment of Hispanics. The program proved so worthwhile, we also broadcast it in Latin America, hoping to convince people down there that the United States was not as prejudiced against them as they had been led to believe.

We launched our share of successful shows—news, commentary, and entertainment. We even had programs starring famous Latin American stage and film comedians. The trickiest to control were the commentaries, because we had to hire prominent Latin American news analysts and we weren't always certain of their loyalty to our cause. The one I remember with the most ambivalent feelings was Alejandro Sux, a big name in Argentina, whom we had to watch carefully. He was clever in his inflections and his on-the-other-hands.

Some Latin Americans realized exactly what we were doing and let us know that they didn't like it. We got our share of hate mail, though less than I had expected. If there were any serious problems with South American fascists or communists, I'm not aware of it. Such difficulties would have been handled at the local level by CIAA offices Nelson had opened in the principal cities.

By the autumn of 1941, our radio operation was running so smoothly I had some time on my hands, most of which I was happily spending with Elizabeth Inglis. I was more certain than ever that America had to get into the war, though I sometimes wondered if it would actually happen. In October, the German armies had advanced so far into the Soviet Union that Hitler, after visiting the Ukraine battlefront, told the German people Russia was already broken and would never rise again. His troops were advancing eastward so fast, it was hard to doubt him. In November, he denied Roosevelt's charge that he planned to convert Central and South American countries into vassal German states. The U.S. Congress finally amended the Neutrality Act, but only to allow American merchant ships to carry arms and other supplies into British ports. And in Tokyo, the Japanese foreign minister declared that Japan must establish a new order in Asia. Despite the power of the isolationists and their leading organization, America First, it was hard to believe the United States could continue to ignore all the dire developments in the rest of the world.

Meanwhile, Liz Inglis had opened in a play on Broadway, *Anne of England*, starring Flora Robson and featuring Jessica

Tandy. It was a big, expensive production that had only a short run, but during that time I got acquainted with Hume Cronyn, since both of us were stage-door Johnnys every night while he waited for Jessica, whom he was courting, and I waited for Liz. Was I courting her? I guess so, though I wasn't really aware of it at the time. All I knew was that I wanted to be with her whenever possible. Hume and I got along well from our first meeting at the stage door, and we've been friends ever since.

On the afternoon of December 7, Liz and I were in her top-floor apartment on Fifty-sixth Street, trying to decide where to go to dinner that evening. Her radio was playing, though I don't recall that we were actually listening to it, until, just before three o'clock, a breathless announcer broke in with an urgent news bulletin. The White House had announced that Japanese warplanes had attacked our naval base at Pearl Harbor, and might even be attacking it still. There were few immediate details.

We sat by her radio the rest of that afternoon, except for when I was pacing back and forth in front of it, listening for more details, but without learning very much. It sounded preposterous. Japan was several thousand miles from Hawaii. How could its warplanes get close enough to attack it? Presumably by aircraft carrier, but it would take a whole fleet of carriers, plus their support ships. Such a huge armada could hardly approach the islands without our navy spotting them. Yet they had obviously managed it somehow. By seven o'clock, the radio hadn't yet told us how it had happened, but we could no longer doubt that it was true. The suspense was over. We were finally at war. Liz and I did go out to dinner that night, though I don't remember where. Our minds, certainly, were not on food.

9

I'LL NEVER FORGET THE BEWILDERING UNCERTAINTY OF those first days and weeks after Pearl Harbor. It was quickly evident that the attack on Hawaii was not just a superficial foray launched by a token number of planes. The Japanese claimed they had sunk two U.S. battleships and severely damaged two others, plus four large cruisers. President Roosevelt admitted severe damage to our naval and military forces, plus the deaths of many Americans. Within a few days, the government conceded that more than two thousand sailors had died.

In addition, the Japanese (or "Japs," as they were then derisively called) had enough reserve strength to attack almost simultaneously our bases at Wake Island, Midway, and the Philippines, plus the British-held Malay Peninsula and Hong Kong. They had taken the whole of Siam. The U.S. Army announced that on December 8, two squadrons of enemy planes had flown over San Jose, California, twice, though they had dropped no bombs. The army report was erroneous, but no one knew that until much later. A few weeks after that, a Japanese submarine actually did surface off the Pacific coast, near Santa Barbara, to shell oil installations there.

By this time, nothing seemed unbelievable. Were the Japanese preparing for an immediate invasion of California, where my whole family lived? There were few facts available, because our government had quickly imposed wartime censorship, but there were so many rumors, no one needed facts. Those were worrisome days for every American. I guess the only people who felt good about all this (aside from the Japanese) were the British. At last they had an ally—presumably a very powerful one. But our first weeks in the war made us look more ridiculous than formidable.

Liz Inglis was, I think, even more concerned than I, and with good reason. She now had five brothers involved in the fighting. Shortly after December 7, I renewed my application for a navy commission. Then I said to Liz one day, "I think maybe we should get married."

She didn't say yes, but neither did she say no. She said, "Let's talk about it."

At that time, many young men were suddenly deciding to get married, some of them in the hope of escaping military service. She knew I didn't fall into that category. I had put in my original application for a navy commission nine or ten months earlier, and if I wanted to back down now that it was time to fight, I could do so without resorting to such an extreme measure as matrimony—I had only to keep my draft-exempt government job with the Coordinator of Inter-American Affairs. But, after notifying Nelson Rockefeller, I had reapplied.

That gave Liz an even more serious worry. If I joined the navy, wouldn't I be courting the fate of those two thousand sailors who the government admitted had already gone to the bottom of Pearl Harbor? A clear-thinking man jumped off a sinking ship, not onto it, and the U.S. Navy at that time seemed destined soon to be a whole sinking fleet. If its early performance against the Japanese was any indication, it wouldn't take many more engagements to eliminate it. I'm sure she didn't need a marriage that would soon end at the bottom of the ocean.

Liz had no urgent need to get married. She was doing well as an actress. After *Anne of England* closed she went into another play, also destined for a short run, but she often worked in radio. She was on many of the Sherlock Holmes shows with Basil Rathbone and Nigel Bruce. She was making more money than I was. The CIAA paid me $6,000 a year, which was about as much as I could hope to make as a lieutenant in the navy. If money had been a consideration she would never have begun seeing me. She was so beautiful, there were plenty of men in New York she could have married. She had enough offers. But she must have loved me, because she eventually said yes to my proposal.

That was in early January, about a month after Pearl Harbor, and we were at Charles' Restaurant, in Greenwich Village. I know that only because Liz recently reminded me of it. So much was happening those days, I've forgotten half the details. I remember, though, our discussion about how, where, and when to do it. If we were to tell our friends, especially the LaRoches, they'd insist on making a big event of it, which seemed to both of us inappropriate at such a critical time. We took a look at her work schedule and mine, then chose January 23.

On the morning of the twenty-third we simply got into my car and drove out to Port Washington, on the North Shore of Long Island, mainly because I knew the Nassau County treasurer, Robert Kerr, who was also a jeweler in that town.

I figured he could sell me a ring. After buying the ring, and a license, we returned to the car and headed for a church I had noticed. It was an imposing stone-and-brick building with an impressive rectory. We were welcomed by a clergyman in a black suit, showed him our license, and asked if he could marry us right away.

He looked us over carefully and asked, "Is this your parish?"

"Parish?" I said. "We're from Manhattan."

"I presume you're Catholics?"

Neither Liz nor I was a church person. "No, we're not Catholics."

"Well, then, you can't be married here."

We went back to Bob Kerr and told him what a gaffe we had made. He laughed and said, "I think I can fix you up. How about Episcopal?"

"Sounds all right to me," I said, and Liz agreed. She had been raised in the Episcopal church, and my parents were Episcopalians, though I had never belonged to any church. He took us to the Episcopal church in Great Neck and brought his wife along, having thought of something that hadn't occurred to me: we would need witnesses. The rector there gave us no trouble, perhaps because he knew our witnesses, and twenty minutes later we were as completely married as we are today.

For our "honeymoon" we drove back to Manhattan, where we had dinner at 21. That being a hangout for radio and advertising people, a lot of our fellow diners knew us, and as soon as they found out we were married they began gathering around, drinking toasts to us. Niles Trammell, the president of NBC, was there, as was John Loeb, another old friend, and I don't know who all, but we were feeling no pain by the time we finished dinner.

We then flew to Los Angeles, where I introduced my bride

to my family. My father staged a big welcome party at the Town House, on Wilshire Boulevard, after which we flew back to New York, where Liz had to work, while I had to wait for my navy orders.

By the time the navy did call me, spring had sprung and the flowers were in bloom. But the end of winter didn't change the country's gloomy mood. The submarine warfare had become so intense that it was now called the Battle of the Atlantic, and we were losing it.

The sea war had come almost to the mouth of New York harbor. In late January, just 60 miles off Montauk Point, a 10,000-ton tanker was sunk by three torpedoes, and a day or so later, another tanker met the same fate only 20 miles off Southampton, Long Island, a popular summer retreat for New Yorkers. The U-boats were now attacking convoys in packs throughout the Atlantic. By late February, *Time* magazine sadly reported, these pack attacks had reached the coast of South America, off Venezuela, choking all exports from that country's rich oil fields. At the same time, the Germans announced without contradiction that seven ships totaling more than 50,000 tons were sunk in one short foray against a convoy off the coast of Canada. Secretary of the Navy Frank Knox admitted that in 54 days, Nazi subs had attacked 114 Allied ships.

When I finally received my orders that spring it was not a propitious time to join the navy. I reported to the Naval Training Station at Princeton, New Jersey, wondering how they could choose such a place. I asked that not because I was a Dartmouth man but because Princeton was 40 miles from the nearest water. As I soon learned, we weren't there to test our sea legs. It was an indoctrination facility for civilians receiving commissions without officer training. They put us through close-order drill and classroom work, with a touch of military discipline, to which I was not as adaptable as I should have been. One week I did something so far out of bounds—I think one shoe was not as well shined as the other—that they put me "on the tree," which was the navy's equivalent of being put in Coventry. After that, my classmates called me "Sylvester the Simian." We were whipped through a strenuous six-week course that included as much navigation and seamanship as they could teach that far from the ocean. Since I was already an experienced seaman and navigator from sailing a fairly big yawl, these were the two subjects in which I excelled.

Liz stayed in New York during those six weeks, but when I graduated and they sent me to Miami, she went with me. I had a week or so leave, which we spent with friends in Palm Beach, after which we rented a room in a comfortable old house on Biscayne Boulevard, in Miami, from which I took the bus every morning to my new assignment. The early-summer weather in Florida was ideal, and I was delighted that Liz could accompany me, but I wasn't exactly comfortable about this assignment. They had sent me to the Submarine Chaser Training Center. When I got my first look at a sub chaser I noticed how small it was and immediately wondered, what do we do if we catch a U-boat? Before I finished the course I felt much better about that. The sub chaser was a converted patrol craft with diesel engines, a lot of speed, and plenty of weapons. In case of a confrontation, the submarine crew would be less comfortable than we would be.

At the training center we continued our classroom studies, but now we also went to sea for learning while doing. By the time I graduated I was looking forward to being a sub chaser, since there was no shortage of quarry. Then I saw my orders. They had looked up my radio background and decided I would be a communications officer on a destroyer escort. Any ex-serviceman can understand how that could happen.

Knowing they would need communications officers, the navy made sure I was trained as a sub chaser. I was new enough and rash enough to protest, reminding them that I also had an extensive ocean-sailing background. "I'm a sailor," I insisted. Wonder of wonders, they actually listened and changed my orders. They made me the executive officer, second in command, on converted patrol craft 492, Fourth Fleet, Destroyer Squadron Nine, headquartered at Recife, Brazil. Not until after they gave me this assignment did I realize what a chance I had taken by protesting. The navy had only two groups of the type of escort vessels for which I was trained. The other group was in the frigid, stormy Aleutians.

I bade Liz a loving goodbye and flew to Puerto Rico, then picked up another plane to Trinidad, where convoys formed up for trips south. As it happened, the convoy my vessel was escorting had left Trinidad either that day or the previous day, which meant, I was told, I'd have to wait six or eight weeks for its return. Though that wasn't a bad prospect, Trinidad being as beautiful as it was, I heard about a sister ship of the 492, the 609, which had been delayed by engine problems but planned to leave at midnight and catch up to the convoy. I rushed over to the 609, where the captain welcomed me aboard and promised to deliver me to the 492 on the return trip, when we reached Recife.

In two days we did catch the convoy, but not in time to do it any good. A pack of submarines was attacking as we approached. Though we didn't get close enough to do any fighting, and didn't even see any of the subs, it was obvious that they had sunk several of our ships, because the water was full of floating bodies and debris.

When the convoy reached Recife I transferred my gear to the 492. Its captain, a man named Edward Newman, welcomed me, made me feel at home, and allowed me to settle into an unlikely little stateroom that had been used as a storeroom. I wanted it because it had a desk, it was right on deck, and there were no rooms nearby. It offered me a bit of privacy. Strange quarters for the executive officer, but Captain Newman just shrugged and let me take it.

Our relationship was ideal. He taught me everything an executive officer had to know, including how to take command if anything happened to him and exactly what procedures to follow if we were to catch one of the subs we'd be chasing. We didn't come close to any subs on my first convoy trip north from Recife. It was an uneventful voyage until, on our way back, we were sent to Charleston for repairs. There, Newman was relieved and replaced by a man named Dunn, who soon made all of us regret the loss of his predecessor. I sometimes think Herman Wouk must have been secretly aboard that ship, because Captain Dunn was the perfect prototype of Captain Queeg in Wouk's classic *Caine Mutiny*. Dunn was so cold, mean, and needlessly demanding, not so much to me as to the crew, that I sometimes feared we might actually have a mutiny.

We had to put up with him for nearly a year, and it was an unpleasant one. Toward the end, I was so worried about the unrest, I quietly warned the crew that if the captain were to disappear into the sea one night, all of us would be in deep trouble. At the same time, I cautioned Captain Dunn never to go on deck alone at night. He scoffed at the notion that he might be in danger from his own men, but I noticed that he never did walk the deck at night thereafter.

In the middle of 1943, he was transferred to another billet, which I suspected he might have arranged for himself. In any case, the crew celebrated his departure, and so did I, though not as noisily as they did. Besides being happy to see him go, I was pleased to learn I was the new captain.

If anyone were to ask me what I considered the most

pleasant job a man could want, I'd say ship captain. If you have a good crew, you have almost no work to do. My decisions were easy to make. I had only to follow the navy's orders and use common sense. I had good, loyal, and well-trained people doing everything else. My executive officer, Russell Iseli, arranged all the inspections and gun drills. I had only to pay attention and make certain the men were as relaxed as they could hope to be, cooped up on a tiny ship in the middle of the ocean during a desperate war with enemy submarines all around them.

Whenever we had a submarine scare I would laugh it off (though I wasn't too comfortable myself) and say, "Believe me, fellows, you have nothing to worry about. Any U-boat commander who wasted a torpedo on our little craft when he could get a nice fat freighter loaded with airplanes for the African front would be court-martialed and hanged by Hitler. And don't worry about airplanes, either. They wouldn't come after us even if they could reach us, because they wouldn't have enough gas to get back to base." Actually, a submarine might torpedo us because we were a threat to all submarines. I never mentioned that to the men.

In the middle of my tour of sea duty I came due for leave—ten days, I think—which was especially welcome because Liz was in Hollywood at the time, which provided an opportunity to see her and the rest of my family at the same time. She was there to make a movie, *Tonight and Every Night*, starring Rita Hayworth and Lee Bowman. She had a small part that should have taken only three weeks to film but, by a quirk of fate, took ten weeks, during most of which she didn't even have to report to the studio. She happened to be in a scene with Marc Platt, the dancer, that required him to jump off a grand piano. When he did so he broke an ankle, forcing postponement of the rest of the scene. This meant Liz was paid for ten weeks instead of three, and it also enabled us to spend my entire leave together.

I then returned to my sub chaser but at the same time began plotting with a friend at the training center in Miami to get me the command of a destroyer escort. In late October 1944, my 492 accompanied a merchant ship to Guantánamo Bay, after which we proceeded to the Miami Naval Yard to be refitted. While there, I was ordered to report to the Sub Chaser Training Center, so I turned the 492 over to my executive officer, fully expecting to become the captain of a destroyer escort—a considerably larger vessel. But when my new orders arrived, they weren't what I had expected. Instead of taking over a destroyer escort, I was to report to the Armed Forces Radio Service in Hollywood. I guess that if I hoped to captain a destroyer escort, I should have pressed the navy to send me to Hollywood. My more than two years of sea duty had come to a sudden end without any Nazi submarine ever having come within view.

In November I reported to Armed Forces Radio Service at Gower Street and Santa Monica Boulevard, in Hollywood, where I found a staff loaded with so many Young & Rubicam people, I almost felt I was back on Madison Avenue. One of them, Tom Lewis, who had worked for me at Y&R, was now a colonel in command of this large operation, the entire function of which was to provide radio news and entertainment to American servicemen all over the world. This included the biggest shows on radio—Jack Benny, Bob Hope, Bing Crosby, Edgar Bergen and Charlie McCarthy, Fred Allen, Burns and Allen, the NBC Symphony Orchestra, important baseball and football games, several of the big-name bands, and noted commentators like Lowell Thomas, H. V. Kaltenborn, and Gabriel Heatter. It also included our own shows, the best known of which was *Command Performance*, a weekly one-hour program some critics have proclaimed the best in the history of radio. It was produced by Bob Welch, who had also worked for me at Y&R. He was still producing it when I arrived, but Tom Lewis put me to work supervising it, perhaps because he realized Welch would soon be leaving for Guam, where General Curtis LeMay and his B-29s were stationed, preparing the final air assault against Japan.

Lewis was married to the film star Loretta Young, whom I had known as Gretchen Young ever since I dated her sister during my school days in Los Angeles. I believe I introduced Gretchen to Tom, after she took the name Loretta and became a star. It was probably he who had talked the navy into transferring me to this outfit, though I don't remember him ever explaining how it happened.

I found us a nice duplex apartment up Cahuenga Pass just off Barham Boulevard and began thumbing my way down into Hollywood every morning. Reliable cars were not easy to find during the war, when no autos were being manufactured, but we must have bought one fairly soon. Even then it was very difficult to live in Los Angeles without a car.

The AFRS office was a busy place with more than a hundred people on the staff. We produced about fifteen hours of our own shows each week and broadcast them from the new CBS and NBC studios on Sunset Boulevard, though I think we also did a few from our own headquarters. One in particular, *Mail Call*, featured a young woman with a sexy voice who answered letters from servicemen everywhere. I remember her doing that show right from her desk in the office, but our big productions had to be staged at the networks, because they drew large studio audiences.

We had a musical show called *G.I. Jive*, presided over by a young female disc jockey who called herself G.I. Jill; another music show, *Jubilee*, with variety segments; a comedy quiz, *Are You a Genius?*, conducted by Mel Blanc; and several others, including *Command Performance*. This show was based on an inspired concept: servicemen everywhere were invited to "command" their favorite stars to perform on the program, and the stars would comply, as if the command had come from the President of the United States or the King of England.

To make that work, AFRS had to recruit a talent-procurement department composed of high-powered Hollywood agents. George Rosenberg was the head of this department, which also included such prestigious agents as Lester Linsk and Baron Pollen. They delivered just about every star our servicemen "commanded."

The most famous *Command Performance* show was "Dick Tracy," with an all-star cast, produced by Bob Welch under my supervision. Bing Crosby played Tracy, Bob Hope was Flat Top, Jimmy Durante was the Mole, Judy Garland was Snow White, and Dinah Shore was Tracy's long-suffering girlfriend, Tess Trueheart. Frank Morgan was also in it, though I can't remember his role. It was so good and so funny, we quickly realized it couldn't be contained in one hour, so we made it our first—and maybe our only—two-hour show.

One reason the Dick Tracy production turned out so well was the quality of the writing; we had many of the best radio scribes in Hollywood. Bob Hope's chief writer, Jack Rose, was one of them. Others wrote regularly for Crosby, Burns and Allen, Benny, and all the biggies. They were privates and corporals, but nobody felt sorry for them, because they had almost complete freedom and were still getting paid a thousand or more a week from the stars, for whom they continued to work.

The biggest laugh I recall from those shows came one night when Frank Sinatra was the star. He had a segment with Bing Crosby's toddling twin sons, who were then only three or four years old. Sinatra asked them what their dad was doing.

One of them said, "He's out in the garden."

"Oh," said Frank. "What's he planting this year?"

"Same as last year. Your phonograph records."

I took over from Bob Welch in the early spring of 1945, which meant that I produced the *Command Performance* shows on V.E. Day and, best of all, on V.J. Day. The one on V.E. Day was a rather restrained celebration, because we were still at war with Japan and it looked as if we would have to stage a bloody invasion to win it. We knew nothing, of course, about the atomic bomb our government was developing. We had commentators talking about what a marvelous job our troops had done in Europe and in the Atlantic. The V.E. Day show included our forty-piece orchestra, conducted by Meredith Willson. Many of our stars appeared in skits and songs. Everyone was delighted that the menace of Hitler had been eliminated, but no one was yet ready to cut loose in uncontrolled elation.

That came on August 15, when the Japanese, awe-stricken by two atomic bombs, decided not to force the invasion issue, even though their army was still intact and well placed to resist us.

When the Japanese surrendered, I remember walking into the writers' room that day to find them drinking and singing, drinking and shouting, drinking and dousing each other with liquor. Though I wasn't excessively sober myself, I realized, at least, that we had to go on the air in a few hours. I never did restore order among those writers, but I did quiet them enough to hear the only line that came to my mind: "For God's sake, fellows, control yourselves a little bit. You'd think we'd never won a war before." We did get on the air that night, though I don't know how.

Meanwhile, in January 1945, Liz had learned she was pregnant. Since it looked as if my AFRS assignment would be my last before peace broke out, we had decided it was time to start our family. When she told me she thought we had taken the first necessary step, and it was obvious we needed a doctor, I realized I no longer knew any physicians in Los Angeles. I asked Tom Lewis to ask Loretta to recommend one, and she did, but when the war ended we didn't want to spend the next two or three months in California, as I was eager to get back my old job in New York.

The day after the Japanese surrendered I called a friend in the Navy Department in Washington and said, "Will you please get me out of here? I want to get back to New York in time for Liz to have our baby."

At the end of the war, the order of discharge was based on a point system that depended on time of service plus time in combat. Since I had been in the Atlantic combat zone for two and a half years, I apparently had all the points I needed—within three weeks we were out of there and on our way to New York. Goodbye World War II. I was once more a civilian, in the market for new suits and shirts and ties.

10

AS FAST AS WE COULD GET THERE WE WERE BACK IN NEW
York, where Liz found a highly recommended doctor named
Harbeck Halstead, while I found an apartment on East Fif-
tieth Street. Neither of these accomplishments should be min-
imized. A moratorium on private construction unconnected
to the war effort made apartments scarce by 1945. The one
we found wasn't ideal, but after a few weeks we came upon
exactly what we wanted, at Sixty-fourth and Madison, where
we were to live for several years. As for doctors, so many of
them were still in the services that the rest were swamped
with patients. Fortunately, Liz was healthy, and on October
20 she delivered, with Dr. Halstead's help, a healthy baby
boy whom we named Trajan, after one of the greatest and
most benign of the Roman emperors. I had not lost my interest in Classical civilizations.

We now had a third mouth to feed without any income,
since my navy pay had been terminated and Liz was inactive
as she recovered from her delivery. I went down to the Amer-

ican Tobacco Company, where, happily, my old job as advertising manager was waiting for me—and at a substantial salary. I would now make $35,000 a year—a glorious sum in 1945.

The main concern at American was the health of George Washington Hill, its guiding light. The cigarette business had been good during the war, and Lucky Strike was still number one in sales, but a semiparalysis seemed to permeate the company, because this dynamo who had propelled it for so many years was now barely propelling himself. He was only occasionally at the office, and when he did appear you would wish he would go home to bed.

On my first day back he tipped his hat to me—from him, a gratifying gesture—and conducted one of his famous staff meetings. He opened with his same old line, though in wheezy tones.

"Tobacco is what it's about, gentlemen."

He meant the tobacco business, though he might well have been talking about his illness. Tobacco was what his sorry condition was about, too.

As usual, he extracted two packs of Luckys from one of his patch pockets and slammed them down on the table, but before he lit his first cigarette, he produced an atomizer and sprayed his throat with some kind of medicine. When he took his first drag he still drew in as much smoke as he could, but it was not much compared with his old habit.

"L.S.M.F.T!" he gasped. "Lucky Strike means fine tobacco!"—a slogan which, I believe, he invented himself.

After those few words he panted for air as he exhaled smoke, but he refused to surrender. Tapping out the rhythm with his ring on the glass-topped table, he kept repeating, "L.S.M.F.T! L.S.M.F.T! L.S.M.F.T!" pausing after each repetition until he could collect enough air in his lungs to continue smoking and talking.

He had lost his capacity but not his determination. He

took me to lunch at the Vanderbilt Hotel, where he wheezed and gasped and tried to talk, while I, feeling guilty, ate my food. He wanted me to know about all the great plans and projects he was about to launch. I listened with nothing but sadness in my heart, because despite his flamboyant bluster I had always entertained deep respect for the man—and, as I now realized, considerable affection. He had treated me nobly. Knowing how much I loved to ski, he had invited me each year, before the war, to take off the entire month of February and head for the mountains. Many times, when I asked him for an extra day off after working myself into exhaustion on one project or another, he would say, "No. Take three or four days. Take a week."

Now, as I listened to him while I ate my lunch, I realized that he simply didn't have it anymore. None of his projects made any sense to me.

He did say one thing that sounded good. He declared himself so pleased with me that very soon I would be a vice president in charge of marketing, at a salary of $250,000 a year.

With that in mind I began taking on duties in the sales department, but my chief occupation continued to be advertising. Lucky Strike was now sponsoring the Jack Benny show on radio, and with the anticipated dawn of television, I wanted to make sure we were ready for his visual debut. Partly to test his impact in front of the camera, we shot some short films of Benny, copies of which we sent to our salesmen. These films were amusing, and they also managed to put across the "Lucky Strike means fine tobacco" message, but, most important, they convinced me Jack Benny would be effective on television.

In the realm of advertising I quickly managed to introduce an interesting new personality to radio: in 1946 I put Jack Paar on the air as the summer replacement for Benny. And

I rewrote a lot of the advertising copy to reflect the optimism and opportunities peace had engendered.

By this time, George Washington Hill was so ill he almost never came into the office, and though his son, George, was his heir apparent, he didn't have his father's authority. The result was that no big decisions were made and no big projects launched.

Meanwhile, I continued getting overtures from Young & Rubicam. Like most of the ad agencies, Y&R was caught in two no-man's-lands at the same time: the present transition from war to peace and the anticipated transition from radio to television.

The latter was the more bewildering. Changing the focus of ads and commercials to fit the peacetime mood entailed a lot of work and thought, including heavy research to determine new aspects of public taste, but the issue was well defined and could be done. The questions raised by the expected emergence of television were much more difficult to answer. There was no certainty that television would become the force many of us believed it could be. This uncertainty created a conundrum: how could you get people to buy television sets, which were then expensive and not very good, unless there were programs worth watching? At the same time, how could you develop programs worth watching, with the expensive talent and production costs they would entail, if TV sets were so scarce you could hope for only an infinitesimal audience? This problem had not arisen in the early days of radio because sets could be made cheaply and the public had had no expectation of being entertained by star performers.

Taking such questions into account, should an agency prepare its clients for a new age of television or a continuation of the golden age of radio, which as yet showed no signs of coming to an end? Was it possible that radio's primacy would continue even if a golden age of television were to emerge? Would there be enough advertising revenue to support both, in addition to newspapers and magazines? Somewhere there was a limit, but nobody knew how to define it.

The people at Young & Rubicam were probably no more confused by these questions than those at any other agency, but because of their great prewar and even wartime success, they had more to lose than most agencies, and therefore were more eager to find solutions. They were already suffering a drop in business, because clients were as confused as the agencies were. I was probably only one of several people to whom they were turning for answers, but American Tobacco was still dangling that $250,000 vice presidency in front of me, and George Hill, Jr., gave every indication that I could expect the promotion even if his father died. Since George had been one of my boosters from the day I arrived at the company, I would have no need to worry after he took control as the new president. It might even open the way for an idea I had been trying out on his father without getting any response. I wanted the company to launch a new venture, to be called something like American Pleasure Products, which would sell not only our tobaccos but items like gum, candy, soft drinks, and anything else people would enjoy. It seemed to me that George junior would go for this idea.

Sometime around Christmas 1946, George Washington Hill died after a stubborn fight against what must have been lung cancer, though I don't recall that the cause of death was ever announced. In those medically squeamish days cancer was seldom mentioned openly.

The accession of George Hill, Jr., to the throne at American Tobacco was considered a mere formality. There were several other vice presidents, and there were the presidents of two subsidiary companies, Pall Mall and American Cigarette and Cigar, but they were all creatures of George Washington Hill, as were the directors, and he had no doubt made certain before he died that they would choose his son to succeed him. That's what everybody thought—but "everybody" did not include the board of directors. They picked a man named Vincent Riggio.

The shock was felt throughout the company. Riggio had always been considered a nonentity, an amiable puppet George Washington Hill had fashioned for his own amusement. For several years, he had been the old man's barber. Hill enjoyed his conversation and was impressed by the fact that this barber remembered the names of every one of his customers. Hill told me one day that Riggio had the awesome ability to call several thousand cigarette-store people by name. It sounded to me like a talent that would serve him better in politics than in business, but Hill must have thought otherwise. He gave Riggio a job in the company, where his affability and knack of addressing everyone by name made him popular, and promoted him gradually to vice president in charge of sales. When Hill died, Riggio proved my suspicion that his talent was for politics: he talked the board members into selecting him as president rather than George Hill, Jr.

Despite his shock, George put a good face on it, and so did the rest of us. We even joked about it. I've mentioned that whenever George's father wanted to see me, his secretary, Doc Bowden, would say, "Could you give Mr. Hill a minute?" We speculated that whenever our new boss, the ex-barber, wanted to see us, Doc would simply say, "Next."

Beneath the surface, I didn't see much humor in the changeover. Despite my resolve to carry on as before, I soon realized that I wasn't getting much done, and my ideas were not likely to prevail under Riggio. A few months into 1947 I got another call from Sigurd Larmon, who had become president of Young & Rubicam after Chet LaRoche left the agency to form one of his own.

"Will you at least talk to us about coming back?" he asked.

"Well, all right, I'll talk," I said, trying to hide my interest.

My lack of confidence in Riggio was not the only reason I was now willing to leave American Tobacco. I had put myself in an embarrassing position there.

As usual, I had taken off the whole month of February, which Liz and I spent skiing at Sun Valley. Though I ordinarily consumed three to four packs of Lucky Strikes a day, we were so busy on the slopes I didn't get a chance to smoke. I guess I was even more addicted to skiing than to smoking, because we put in full, strenuous days on those hills. When we got back to our quarters I was always so tired I'd fall into the sack and sleep until lunch or dinner time. By nine o'clock, most of the time we were so tired, we simply went to bed.

As a result, I was deeply tanned and feeling fit when we returned to New York. On one of my first days back I had lunch at the Union League Club with an executive from Young & Rubicam who was involved in the campaign to re-enlist me. I arrived early and had just finished the day's first pack of Luckys when lunch was served. Suddenly I was so dizzy I thought I was going to fall into my oysters.

After that incident I didn't need a doctor to tell me what was wrong. In the days since returning home I had resumed my heavy smoking habit. I had often tried to cut down, using all kinds of gimmicks as incentives, but nothing had worked. The only way to stop, I decided, was to quit cold turkey, so I did. At the same time, I realized that this created a moral issue. How could I continue to work for a company if I didn't believe in its product?

A week or two later I went into George Hill's office and said, "I'm resigning. If you want to know why, it's not just because I find it so difficult to work with Riggio. It's also because I'm embarrassed."

He was puzzled. "Embarrassed about what?"

"I've stopped smoking."

I could see the amazement on his face, but I wasn't expecting what he said next. "You did!" he exclaimed with a smile. "How the hell did you do it?"

Was my abstinence from smoking permanent? I haven't smoked since the day I quit. Of course, that was only forty-six years ago.

IN JUNE 1947, I returned to Young & Rubicam as vice president in charge of radio, television, and movies; also as a member of the plans board, a stockholder, and, most important, a member of the five-man executive board that ran and owned the agency.

There was some concern about the agency's prosperity. We didn't seem as well organized as we had been before the war, owing partly to the uncertainties of the transition to peacetime and television, but also to administrative problems. Harry Ackerman, who was in charge of radio and television operations in New York, told me a story that illustrated these problems.

After the war, Tom Lewis returned to the agency from Armed Forces Radio Service and took over the radio division, but ran it from Hollywood rather than New York. He refused to move east for an understandable reason: his wife, Loretta Young, had what you might call a pretty good job in Hollywood. But with all the networks and many clients or potential clients centered in New York, Lewis was at a considerable disadvantage. When he tried to compensate by periodic trips east, it didn't quite work, as Ackerman's story demonstrated.

During one of Tom's sojourns in New York, he and Ackerman and Sig Larmon hosted a lunch at the Union League Club for a major client company plus one of its subsidiaries, which also sponsored a Young & Rubicam program. Important aides on both sides also attended. Tom sat at one end of the table talking earnestly to the man next to him. When the luncheon broke, he hurried over to Ackerman and said, "Harry, tell me about this fellow I've been doing the selling job on. Is he the head of the parent company or the subsidiary?"

"You mean the man on your right?" Ackerman asked.

"That's the one. I think I made some points with him. He seemed to agree with everything I said."

"He'd better agree with you," Harry replied. "He's from our merchandising department."

Tom Lewis was a very capable man, and so was Harry Ackerman, but with one of them in New York and the other a continent away, coordination was almost impossible. Lewis left Y&R shortly before I arrived, for reasons that had nothing to do with me, but I was involved in Ackerman's departure. It was obvious that if I did everything Larmon and the executive board had assigned to me, I would need someone like Everard Meade, so I went to Harry and mentioned how well Hubbell Robinson, an ex-Y&R man, was doing with the television department at CBS.

"You know, Harry, TV will be different from radio, but you'll soon catch on to it, because you're a programming expert. What you should do is go join Hubbell and help build CBS into a giant TV network."

Harry was not enthusiastic about leaving the agency, but he took it pretty well. He did join Robinson at CBS, where they both prospered, and he always remained friendly to me.

My title as director of movies in addition to radio and television may sound ridiculous, inasmuch as we didn't make any films and had no intention of ever competing with Hollywood. Movies were included in my domain simply because my eyes were focused on grand visions of television's future.

It was one of the reasons I had decided to return to the agency. Y&R had been experimenting with film to determine what kind of visual commercials we could offer our expected television clients, and I continued these experiments because when I took over, my department developed the commercials as well as the shows. Everyone assumed the agencies would own television programs, just as they already owned radio programs, with the networks simply providing the time slots. Though I already had strong reservations about this system, it didn't seem to bother anyone else, especially the other agency people.

For a while after my return, my grand visions about television were nothing more than that. The birth of the new medium as something more than a fascinating gadget hadn't yet taken place. At the end of 1947, there were only 200,000 TV sets in the entire country. Just twenty or so stations were operating, mostly in the larger cities, but the orthicon camera tube was now in use, bringing better picture resolution without the intense lighting that had made the studios feel like ovens. Coaxial cables were being laid to enable connections between cities, and at least fifty more TV stations were under construction. The television manufacturers predicted that there would be more than a million sets in American homes by the end of 1948.

But in 1947, with only 200,000 sets extant, there could be no thought of expensive productions. We were still just fumbling, extolling to our clients the marvelous prospects ahead. We put a few small projects on the air that summer, but nothing memorable. I did, however, get full support and encouragement from Sig Larmon to move ahead with plans for the 1947–48 season, beginning that fall, though we both knew it would cost a lot of nonreturnable money to jump in that early.

Most of our TV shows that fall were simply simulcasts of

such established radio hits as Arthur Godfrey's *Talent Scouts, The Goldbergs,* and *The Life of Riley*. I tried but failed to put together an ethnic-comedy night, including *The Goldbergs* (Jewish), *The Life of Riley* (Irish), and *The Aldrich Family* (WASP).

The only good new live show we were able to assemble was *The Bigelow Show,* which featured Joseph Dunninger, a great storyteller and magician, plus Paul Winchell, a ventriloquist, who was also such an accomplished medical scientist that he later invented the first artificial heart. His dummy, Jerry Mahoney, was very funny. This show, sponsored by Bigelow's Mohawk Carpet Company, was ideal for the time, because the two stars provided a sharp contrast, and each was interesting and entertaining in his own right. More important, they didn't need scenery, stagehands, supporting cast, or music. All they required was a camera plus a background curtain. As soon as one of them finished a scene, the other would come out and do another. It cost so little to produce that it was easy to sell, and it was a hit because they performed so well.

Our big financial successes at the time were still on radio. Fred Allen had gone to CBS, but we had Burns and Allen, Danny Thomas in his first starring radio show, and Jack Carson, plus Arthur Godfrey, *The Life of Riley* with William Bendix, and *The Goldbergs.* Early in 1948 we acquired Bob Hope's Swan Soap show, on which he was supported by Doris Day and Les Brown's band.

The big television events of the 1947–48 season were the debuts of the Ed Sullivan and Milton Berle shows. Nobody knew the Sullivan program was a big event, because it didn't seem very impressive when it began. I thought it was just so-so, a fill-in until television could afford something better. Maybe I'd have looked at it differently if we had owned it.

I did look differently at Milton Berle's show. We didn't

own that, either, but we came close to acquiring it when I found out that Berle's sponsor, Texaco, had a rather insecure hold on him. After some backstage maneuvering I was able to bring good news to one of our biggest clients, a pharmaceutical manufacturer who had a rare quality for those days: he was actually eager to get into television.

"Did you see Berle last night?" I asked him.

"Yes, I did," he said, "and I think it's a very good show. Why do you ask?"

"I thought you'd be delighted to learn he has only a short-term contract with Texaco. I have in hand an ironclad option on the show starting next fall."

I spoke my piece, then waited for him to jump at this terrific opportunity. I could scarcely believe his reply.

"Much as I like Berle," he said, "I won't buy any show in which the star is more important than my product."

Since I couldn't find another big client eager to get into television, our opportunity to pick up the Berle show faded away.

While we were developing new programs, trying to feel our way into the television age, I was also reading some remarkable books that had recently appeared. One was *Cybernetics*, by Norbert Wiener, about the coming computer technology and the amazing advances it would bring. We were approaching what he called the Information Age, in which television would be an enormous factor. I was also reading Arthur Clarke, who described manmade satellites that could be placed in orbit by rockets, several kinds of which were already under development. After the performance of the buzz bombs the Germans used against England in World War II, no one could doubt the possibilities rockets offered. Clarke believed that satellites would give television the same worldwide interconnection that we already had in radio.

I was fully aware at the time of audio recording tape that was good enough for one of the networks to accept, and I knew that video tape was in the laboratories, destined some-day to be on the market. All the technical elements necessary to make television a major force were either available or about to be, but would television ever become a major force if, like radio, it offered the public only what General Foods or General Motors or Bristol-Myers found useful in selling products?

For some time I had been disturbed by the question of whether advertisers and their agencies should exercise so much control over what went on the air. Yet if advertisers and agencies were stripped of this control, who should be in charge? I didn't want the government to assume such powers. I was not an enemy of the free-enterprise system, nor had I forgotten how the German, Italian, and Japanese dictator-ships had used government control of the press and radio to mislead their populations.

Only the networks, it seemed to me, were in a position to help television fulfill its promise. They were governed by the profit motive, to be sure, but that didn't necessarily disqualify them. The profit motive governs most of us, giving us the incentive to compete. Since there were already three major networks, with the possibility that others might develop as more and more channels became available, they would be forced into heavy competition with each other if they wanted to survive. And their programming policies would be deter-mined on a much broader basis than the need of any indi-vidual advertiser, whose chief aim was to sell his commodity.

As television really got underway in 1948, it was obvious that it would offer a total presence. While radio could provide shows that prompted the listener to exercise his own imag-ination, as well as musical or even news programs that one could enjoy while doing housework, driving a car, or reading a book, television could offer much more. It was in danger, though, of becoming just another stage on which to produce a flood of entertainment. Theatrical wrestling matches, for instance, had already become one of its staples. Much as I enjoyed and favored good entertainment (excluding such ludicrous pretenses as "wrestling"), I believed that entertainment should provide only one of many attractions open to this wonderful new medium. It had the potential to take us, by sight as well as by sound, out of our homes and across oceans in a moment, to any part of the world. It could allow us to be present at political events worldwide and could broadcast concerts, plays, operas, and educational features. It could take us inside classrooms and museums. It could introduce us to famous people and places we could never otherwise hope to see. If properly developed, it could raise the educational and cultural level of the entire nation. It could enrich the common man—make him the uncommon man.

When I began talking this way to my colleagues at Young & Rubicam, they looked at me peculiarly, as if I were threatening our agency and the whole agency system, but I had no such intention. It seemed to me that agencies could do better than ever without the financial risk of producing expensive television shows that might or might not succeed. There were no enormous production outlays in radio—no costumes, no scenery, no far-distant locations, no huge staffs, none of the costs that made movies so expensive—but many television shows would be much like movies in these respects. An agency could go broke dumping money into a few projects that fizzled.

If the agencies were determined to enter into TV production, they needed safeguards that would at least spread the risks. With this in mind I started speaking to the heads of other agencies, trying to interest them in setting up some kind of cooperative through which to produce shows. That idea aroused nothing but parochial responses. The people I solicited were afraid even to discuss it, because of the competition between agencies. One executive said that if anybody saw him talking about it with me he might be in trouble, because his agency had a client in direct competition with one of ours.

Having made no progress in the world of advertising agencies, I returned to my concept of network responsibility for the development of television. After losing control of radio, I figured, the networks should welcome a plan to gain control of television. I decided to approach Bill Paley, at CBS, partly because I had started my career with CBS in California and partly because I was his best customer at Young & Rubicam. Among the radio programs I bought from him at CBS were the Arthur Godfrey show and Lucille Ball's *My Favorite Husband*, which she eventually converted into *I Love Lucy*.

My relations with Paley had been good from the start. He was a tall, slender, handsome man, always impeccably dressed, with a slightly receding hairline and a disarming smile, but also with the kind of reserve one sometimes sees in very wealthy, aristocratic types. I found this slightly ironic because, wealthy as he was, Bill Paley could hardly claim to be aristocratic: his immigrant father had started a cigar factory in the stable behind the house in Chicago.

When I went to see him, I was unaware that he shared my ideas, at least partially. I've since learned about a letter he wrote to one of his CBS executives in 1945, when he was in Europe serving as a colonel in the army, telling of his postwar plans for the network. He had decided that instead of buying radio programs from the advertising agencies, CBS should create programs of its own, either by hiring established stars or developing new ones. This was exactly the point I was now trying to make to him about the approaching era of television. I tried to get him to form a television production company—not a new network, but a corporation that would be controlled by his network—which would ultimately own the programs it produced. I saw myself as the head of such a company. I soon noticed, however, that Bill Paley did not share my vision. He listened to me politely without showing any interest in my proposal. In 1949, Paley still seemed only minimally aware of television.

AROUND THIS TIME, in early 1949, Liz realized that another member of our family was on the way. We began looking forward to the birth of our second child, due in the fall.

After my futile attempt to interest Paley, I went to NBC, because Bobby Sarnoff, the son of General David Sarnoff and at that time working at the network, was a friend of mine. This began a complicated negotiation with him and Niles Trammell, the president of NBC. They weren't much interested in my vision of television's future, but it soon became apparent that they were interested in me. Trammell was an excellent salesman and a most amiable person, probably the top man in network radio. He would take me to two- or three-hour lunches at 21, and when I insisted that I had to leave, he would push another brandy at me. He and Bobby wanted me to manage NBC's new television department, which existed, as far as I could tell, little more than on paper. I told him that I would come if they'd set up a separate production company, called NBC Television, along the lines of what I had suggested to Paley. It would function as an independent corporation, with its own staff and administration. I insisted on this because I was already aware of General Sarnoff's reputation as a difficult man, and I was convinced that neither he nor anyone else at NBC had given deep thought to the nature of television or the opportunities it offered. They seemed willing to drift into it, as they had drifted into radio, presenting themselves as a facility for the use of ad agencies and their clients.

Both Trammell and Bobby Sarnoff were convinced that the general would never allow me to launch even a semi-independent corporation. He had never learned much about radio production because the agencies had always produced the shows on NBC, and he couldn't be expected to understand television production, which was certain to be more complex and expensive. But while Trammell and Bobby found it impossible to accept the idea of a separate corporation, they liked many of my other ideas, and as the weeks and months passed, they continued pressing me to take charge of NBC Television.

"I won't come to NBC just to sell time to ad agencies," I said. "I'll come only if we can create our own shows and own them, and if we can sell every kind of advertising to support the program service."

They had no objection to that, perhaps because they thought it was just talk. If I could carry it off, fine; they might even get some of the credit for it. If I couldn't make it work, no great harm would have been done, and presumably I would slide back into the old system of agency-advertiser control over programs and time slots.

Once they gave me the go-ahead and we worked out the lesser details, I agreed to join NBC as vice president in charge of television and director of its still-new television network, even though I had not yet discussed the job in detail with General Sarnoff, the real boss. Some of the minor details, including stock options and membership on the board of directors, were actually not so minor. We agreed to them only orally, which was my mistake, as I learned later.

11

WHEN I LEFT YOUNG & RUBICAM, I GAVE UP WHAT amounted to financial well-being for life. It was the second time I had taken off from Y&R, and I felt bad about it, especially because some of the people there now considered me a turncoat, betraying the advertising agencies in favor of the networks. If I couldn't convince them otherwise, at least I had the satisfaction of leaving the radio and television departments in top shape. I had done over $20 million worth of business, and the division helped return Y&R to financial strength. And, of course, its reputation in broadcasting—we often had five of the ten top-rated shows, both in radio and on television.

Nevertheless, I regretted my departure, because I liked the advertising business and the people I worked with. But I saw an opportunity to play an important, constructive role in the birth and development of something that seemed destined to become almost colossal.

Everard Meade, perhaps my closest associate through the years, told *The New Yorker*: "Pat was too restless to accept the true mission of an agency department head, which is to get his client a safe investment. . . . Pat saw the limitations of the agency business. He outgrew Y&R." With all due respect to Ev Meade, I have never thought I "outgrew" the agency business. I did, however, see its limitations, as he said, and television represented an opportunity I couldn't resist.

Because I was familiar with NBC's lack of enterprise in television, I was expecting to find the department in disarray on the day I arrived, in June 1949. There were some good people—Herbert Swope, Jr., Leonard Hole, Jack White, and others, plus Norman Blackburn, a very able person from the J. Walter Thompson agency, who was program director, but with little authority and a small staff. Most of the shows originating in their office were sustaining programs, without advertising. They spent much of their time servicing agency-produced shows, and few of those were very good. Milton Berle's *Texaco Star Theater* was NBC's only runaway hit, but two others were excellent—*Kraft Television Theatre*, produced by the J. Walter Thompson agency, and *Philco Television Playhouse*, under the brilliant Fred Coe.

On my first day at NBC I was greeted with a memorandum that informed me the network had just canceled a Sunday program called *Meet the Press*.

I waved the memo in the air and cried out, "What the hell is this?"

The person nearest to me said, "Well, you know, it's a sustaining program. We can't get a sponsor to buy it."

"Has Martha Rountree been told?" She was the producer and one of the owners of the show.

"Yes, sir, I think so."

I immediately got Martha on the phone. "Forget that stupid cancellation," I said. "You're not fired—you're hired. And if you want a new contract, come and see me about it."

That is why NBC today has the longest-running show in television—more than forty-five years of *Meet the Press*.

During the golden age of radio, NBC had been the dominant network, until Bill Paley "stole" some of NBC's biggest stars in what came to be known as "the Paley raids." Jack Benny was at the top of a list that eventually included Burns and Allen, Amos and Andy, and Red Skelton. In fact, Paley hadn't stolen any of these stars from NBC. Every artist he acquired belonged to somebody else. American Tobacco owned Benny's contract. Burns and Allen were with General Foods. Amos and Andy, who had been on NBC since 1929, were not owned by NBC; I believe they were still under some kind of contract arrangement with the Chicago station WMAQ, which was broadcasting their show locally when they went to the network. Red Skelton was with us at NBC for two years after I arrived, but we didn't own his contract. He went to CBS when I was unable to make a deal with his manager.

CBS was our only competition when I took over television at NBC. The Dumont network was too small to be a significant threat, even though it did have Jackie Gleason under contract for a while. If the Mutual radio network ever dipped into television, it wasn't deep enough for me to be aware of it. The American Broadcasting Company was much bigger than Dumont, but not big enough to worry us. It had been the Blue network of NBC until 1943, when the Federal Communications Commission forced General Sarnoff to sell one of his radio operators. Naturally, he kept the Red network, which accounted for most of NBC's profit, and sold the Blue, to Edward Noble, who owned the Life Savers company, for something like $8 million.

It was Noble who changed the name to American Broadcasting Company, but ABC did not become a force in the industry under his leadership. In 1951 he sold it to the United Paramount theater chain, of which Leonard Goldenson was president. Under Goldenson, ABC eventually became a strong, competitive entity, but not while I was at NBC.

What scared me most about the so-called Paley raids was the possibility that we might lose Milton Berle. In the latest ratings for the New York area, which was then the overwhelmingly dominant TV market, Berle was NBC's only show in the top ten. The Berle phenomenon was unbelievable. During his first two years, there were rating periods when the pollsters found that virtually everyone watching television was watching him.

Fortunately, his sponsor, Texaco, was unlikely to do what some others might have done. Take, for example, Charlie Revson, who ran Revlon. He was a friend I couldn't help liking, but he was a bit of a rogue and a very shrewd man. If he had owned the Berle show, he'd have been in Paley's office at the end of that first phenomenal year and said, "Bill, next year you can have Milton Berle from eight to nine on Tuesdays. All we want you to do is pay for the show plus the agency and station compensations, and give us the time before and after the show. We get that and you get Berle. It's all we want."

We were so alarmed at the possibility of losing Milton that my whole staff romanced him. I talked to him backstage at every opportunity and even gave him what I called a "lifetime contract" at NBC, which was nothing more than a token of appreciation for his contribution to the network's welfare. I had no authority to offer him an actual lifetime contract, but he never forgot my gesture. A few years ago at the Beverly Hills Hotel, when I received the first Media Innovator Award from a group of old-timers called the Nostalgia Network, he reminded the audience and me of my "generosity." "In

1950," he said, "Pat gave me a lifetime contract at NBC. I found out seven years ago it had expired."

I wish I had had the time to become more intimately acquainted with Milton and some of the other great stars we had at NBC during those years, but I was too busy struggling to bring about my envisioned network revolution. I did become drinking buddies with Sid Caesar, and we had many a good time together—sometimes almost too good. One night, after signing Sid to a long-term contract, I took him to one of our favorite pubs, the Elbow Room, where we got down to some serious celebrating. After a while, celebrating became one of the few things we could still do. We weren't even ambulating very steadily.

It was our good fortune that Milton Berle was also at the Elbow Room that night and, as always, ready to help friends in need. He loaded us into a taxicab and made sure we got home safely. He also, of course, used the occasion to pull one of his gags. The next day, we both received telegrams from him: "DON'T FORGET THE HUNDRED DOLLARS YOU BORROWED FROM ME LAST NIGHT." Caesar, who didn't know Milton at that time as well as I did, actually sent him a check.

Sid was gracious and even quite modest about his sudden success in *Your Show of Shows*, but that didn't mean he lacked an appreciation of it. After his first season of stardom, when he couldn't walk down the street without being mobbed by fans, he and his wife, Florence, decided to spend the summer in Paris. Liz and I went down to the pier with champagne to wish them bon voyage, and I had never seen him so relaxed and happy. Yet two or three weeks later, they were back home in New York.

"What happened?" I asked. "Why aren't you in Paris?"

His explanations were somewhat vague, but Florence and his producer, Max Liebman, both of whom knew him much better than I did, were well aware of what had bothered him in Paris. "He had become so accustomed to being hailed continuously on the streets of New York," Max told me, "with everyone laughing at whatever came out of his mouth, he found the total lack of recognition in Europe too depressing."

If we had lost Berle to CBS during my first year at NBC, it would have put all of our shows in jeopardy. He was our anchor—the only one we had in a brand-new but already expensive medium. Without the revenue he was bringing in, I doubt if General Sarnoff would have given me the money I needed for the plans I was nurturing.

I must confess, incidentally, that the whole subject of the Paley raids laid upon me a certain embarrassment, which I didn't mention to people at NBC. As it happened, while I was at Young & Rubicam doing business with CBS radio, before television became a factor, I had suggested to Paley that his network would thrive if he could lure away some of NBC's most popular stars. I can't say it was I who put that idea in his head. He might already have been planning such a move, though he didn't say so during our talk. We were discussing the fact that the agencies often preferred to sell their programs to NBC, because it had many more station outlets than CBS.

"If you were to outbid NBC for some of those shows and put their stars under long-term contracts," I told him, "it might be costly in the beginning, but you'd soon find new respect from the agencies, and more stations all over the country would be rushing to affiliate with CBS."

I didn't dream that the time would come when he would do so, and that I would be at NBC, trying to recover from the losses.

Fortunately, Milton Berle was a man of good conscience who seemed more interested in his work than in seeking top dollar from CBS. Like most of us, he appreciated money, but performance apparently meant more to him. He pushed himself constantly, never refusing to entertain anyone within earshot. He was also great on the element that was missing from recent television—live comedy.

For all Berle's wild costumes and crazy stuff, his main focus was on the comedy lines. No one, not even Henny Youngman or Morey Amsterdam, could top Milton with one-liners. When he looked at the audience and said "Do married men live longer than single men, or does it just seem longer?" it was guaranteed to get a roar. I recall a bit he did with a joke so ancient I couldn't believe he would have the nerve to tell it on national television: The doctor says to an old man, "Listen, Mr. Smithers, I've called you here, emergency, because I just heard you are going on your honeymoon with your new wife. She is nineteen and you are eighty. You must understand that is very dangerous, very." And the old man replies: "If she dies, she dies!" Berle had millions of them, and they spilled out whether he was on the stage or on the street.

One night in the fall of 1949, I went to see him after his show and found him in his dressing room looking absolutely exhausted.

"I'm worn out," he moaned. "I can't keep this up. I think I'm dying."

He looked like it. I was so concerned, I told him to get some rest and quickly backed out of the room. Later that same night I went backstage to see Jerry Lester, who was starring in *Broadway Open House*, the first of my own comedy shows to go on the air at NBC. I found him using the same dressing room Berle had used earlier that evening.

"Let me tell you about Milton," Jerry said to me. "I came in tonight and here he was, sprawled out on the couch, looking like a corpse. He opened one eye and said, 'I can't keep up this pace. I'm exhausted, used up, at the end of my rope. I've got to stop before I'm a goner.'

"Then he did stop for a minute, and I was beginning to worry about him when he suddenly sat up and said, 'By the way, Jerry, are you using any music on your show tonight?'

" 'Well, yes,' I said. 'We need an opening number, but we haven't yet figured out what to use.'

"Next thing I knew, he was on his feet, singing a song and going through a whole dance routine to accompany it. When he finally finished, looking fresh and full of energy, I said, 'I've never heard that song. Where did you get it?'

"He hemmed and hawed and finally said, 'I wrote part of it.'

" 'In other words, you own a piece of it.'

" 'You might say that.'

" 'Lucky for you,' I said. 'That song just brought you back from the brink of death.' "

In my early days at NBC, I didn't see much of General Sarnoff, though I had known him for some time through his son, Bobby. Liz and I sometimes had lunch or dinner with Bobby and his wife, Esme, plus the general and his wife, Lizette. Sarnoff was always cordial to me then, and he remained so on the few occasions I had to see him. Usually, however, I dealt with Joe McConnell, who had replaced Niles Trammell as president of the network. I got along well with Joe and appreciated the fact that he left me alone. When I came up with a new project I would tell him how much money I needed and he'd say, "Okay, you've got it." Dealing with him also saved me from having to deal with the General.

When I took the job I counted on having Bobby Sarnoff as a shield against his father. I thought Bobby would know enough about the business and have enough influence to talk his father out of creating problems for me. One day, however, I received a call from the General that gave me a glimpse of how he managed to get whatever he wanted.

"I'm calling," he said, "because I just found out you were

promised a seat on the board of directors when you came here."

I told him that was true, and that I had also been promised stock options.

"If that's what they told you, and it influenced you to come here, I'm certainly going to honor it. I'll put you on the board, but I should let you know that the only member I can think of to drop so there'll be room for you is old Gano Dunn. He's eighty-two, in very frail health, and the only thing he lives for is to come to the board meetings."

"General," I said. "I don't want to get in the way of Gano. I'm sorry you can't live up to the promise, but I understand." There went my seat on the board. I thought I'd get it after Gano Dunn passed on, but that wasn't the way the general did business.

Incidentally, you might wonder why we all addressed him as "General." That was because he had virtually ordered everyone at RCA and NBC to do so. He did, in fact, hold the rank, having spent three or four years in the army during the war, putting together the communications network for the invasion of the European continent. He had a remarkable grasp of the technical aspects of the business and by all accounts did a splendid job in the preparations for D-day. His reward was a brigadier general's star. To make sure everyone knew it, he circulated a postwar directive to all of his employees on the proper way to address him.

His accomplishments in other aspects of the business were a mixed bag. He failed to capitalize on the remarkable developments by the RCA Laboratories in such innovations as radar, computers, miniaturization, and several other technological wonders. After the war, Sarnoff was far ahead of Thomas Watson, who was making typewriters at IBM, but Watson beat him so badly in the computer business that when RCA finally did get into it, eight or ten years late, the company piled up big losses. What held RCA back was the fact that Sarnoff, brilliant as he was at technology, concentrated too much on hardware, too little on people and trends. He didn't understand the full importance of cybernetics in the coming age of information. Because he saw and grasped only isolated aspects of it, he failed to run when he had the ball.

He did, however, understand the commercial possibilities of television hardware. His factories were turning out TV sets by the hundreds of thousands, which was one reason he had hired me to develop television programs for NBC. If he wanted to sell all the sets RCA was manufacturing, he had to make sure there was something on the air for buyers to watch. I think that was why he gave me a fairly free hand during my first three years at NBC.

In 1949, when I arrived, there were 2 million TV sets in use. I remember telling someone at the time that until there were 10 million sets, television would not be a major medium, but that once that goal was passed, TV would become an enormously powerful force in our lives. I was constantly aware of my responsibility in helping to sell the additional 8 million sets.

I had to bring about some vast improvements in the network's program service, but to do so I had to overcome the constantly increasing cost of creating new programs. I touched on this in a speech to network affiliates at Greenbrier, Virginia, in September 1949. "With shows of major standing now budgeted at over a million dollars [in a market] with only 2 million sets," I asked, "what will happen in three or four years? How many advertisers are there who can or will or should pick up a check for several million dollars [when the market increases to eight or ten million sets]? How can the smaller advertiser get into attraction television, the glamorous nighttime television that will reach virtually everyone with a set, plus their thirsty friends? And how can we take most of the circulation risk out of television? It was bad enough in radio to lay an egg and have to settle for an under-ten rating with a high-cost show; how can we survive a much higher priced show picking up a neat two in television? Your ulcers get ulcers."

At that time I was already arguing with the RCA auditors over program costs. My idea of cost was the expense of creating and maintaining a program, compensation for the stations carrying it, communication fees to the phone company, and a few smaller items. That was the outgoing money. How much did we receive from our advertisers? If we took in a lot more than we paid out, I thought we were doing all right. The auditors didn't agree, because they used the theoretical book figure on how much we should get for each program and based their calculation on that. But it seemed to me that those were arbitrary, even imaginary figures. I never knew how they were established and didn't give a damn. All I wanted to know was how much we were paying out and how much was coming in.

While I could disagree with the auditors, I couldn't beat them. The only solution was to overcome production costs, which were constantly on the rise. That was where my "magazine" concept of multiple advertisers came into being. Even some of the biggest companies were already feeling the pinch of sponsoring an entire program. I could envision the day when no corporation would be able to afford a whole hour, or even a half-hour, in prime time week after week. I had stipulated before coming to NBC that I be allowed to sell advertising to multiple sponsors instead of time slots to individual companies. However, my plan would work only if the networks, rather than the ad agencies and their clients, owned the programs.

Though I never blatantly announced my intentions, it

didn't take long for the agencies to get wind of what I was doing and to launch a counterattack. As *The New Yorker* reported, advertising executives were at the point of taking arms against what I seemed to be creating.

"I'll fight this to the death," one unnamed executive announced. "Who does Pat think he is, anyway? Hell, in the old days he was the greatest believer in agency programming! What does this plan offer the agencies? What does it offer my agency, with millions of dollars in billings? The chance of making commercials, that's all! Does Weaver think all the creative ideas come out of the network? No sir, this plan will not work."

The president of another agency, also anonymous, exclaimed: "Our reasoning here revolves around expenditures and results of those expenditures. . . . The client wants his money's worth. He wants the largest possible audience at the lowest possible cost. If he doesn't get it—bingo. Off the show goes. When you buy half an hour of network time for three minutes of sell, that half hour has to have impact. This magazine concept of Weaver's is bound to decrease the effectiveness of the sales message when several advertisers have commercials on the same program. What about the gratitude factor—the public's association of an artist with a particular product, the implicit understanding that a ticket of admission to the program is a purchase of the product advertised? This gratitude factor is vital in broadcast selling—vital! Look at Jack Benny. Most people still think of him as a Jell-O salesman. What happens to the gratitude factor when you have half a dozen advertisers on one show and the star doesn't even sell? . . . As I say, the client wants his money's worth. I don't see Weaver giving it to him."

Despite my continuing assurances that ad agencies would actually benefit from my innovations by avoiding the huge costs of television production, this controversy continued.

Even when it became public, however, I heard no criticism from General Sarnoff. On the other hand, neither did I sense any support or encouragement. That was not his way. He hardly ever sent me a note or a memo about our programs, or any other subject, nor did we have meetings, except under extraordinary circumstances. His interests were the sales figures for his cherished RCA hardware, especially television sets, and the bottom-line profits of both RCA and NBC. I don't know how active a role he played in the everyday workings of RCA, but I do know that he didn't appreciate any of my suggestions about NBC's parent company.

I was convinced, for example, that audio books for the blind and the elderly would become a major entry in the electronics field. I persuaded C. S. Forester to give us his latest ocean adventure about Horatio Hornblower so we could see what the market might be for it, read by a famous actor. But after approaching the RCA engineers with the idea, I soon heard from the General. He made it clear that I should stay away from his laboratory people.

I didn't always heed the General's edict. During my navy service I had devised an idea for an invention that would improve the techniques of antisubmarine warfare. It would require some rather precise electronic machinery that did not yet exist but that seemed to me well within the current state of the art. The RCA Lab people were very receptive to the concept, but later, when I tried to find out how they were progressing, they told me it was classified so they couldn't talk to me about it, even though I had originated it.

I don't know whether General Sarnoff played any role in that matter. I guess I shouldn't have ignored his ban and approached his lab people with the idea, but what would he have said if I had sold it to some other electronics lab?

In my early days at NBC I once did try to discuss with him the likelihood that cable television would eventually threaten the networks, bringing with it one form or another of pay TV. He didn't seem interested. His concerns were centered on the immediate future of commercial television, NBC's role in creating more demand for RCA sets, the development of a color system, and the profits he could hope to realize from all of this.

He didn't seem to care how I managed NBC Television, and I gathered from conversations with Joe McConnell that he was just as uninterested in the details of the entire network operation. That was agreeable to me, because I didn't relish the thought of him looking over my shoulder. My methods weren't exactly conventional, except that I did write a lot of memos, keeping everybody in the office aware of what we were trying to do.

Continuing with a principle I had followed in one job after another, I made no effort to dismiss or replace NBC employees who were there when I arrived. I simply brought in my own additional people, mostly for creative jobs like programming. The administrative positions I left to those who already held them. I did hire my own controller, though—I just couldn't adjust to the RCA methods of accounting.

Programming was almost always a communal effort. The people I hired had been trained, like me, at large agencies that owned the biggest programs on radio. As a result, they were all expert in the two most important aspects of commercial television, advertising and entertainment. These were the people who helped me develop the concepts for new TV shows, and then helped me sell those shows.

In our first years at NBC, the pace was frantic, and the office sometimes seemed like an insane asylum, but I don't think anyone considered it an unpleasant place to work. Most of the people who were there when I arrived, as well as those I hired, were still there when I left, which testifies, I think, to the fact that they enjoyed themselves. We had a lot of exciting times in those early days of television—not only in creating programs but in selling and maintaining them. Our best-laid plans often went awry, demanding immediate backup ideas and emergency repairs.

We had meetings quite often, but they were never long. I've always hated interminable meetings where people drag on and on with litanies of dull details. Even I tried to control my tongue during our sessions. I had attended too many conferences where I heard long exchanges about administrative matters that could have been settled in five minutes on the telephone. Successful management depends more on the development of better ideas than on tidy administrative procedures.

We seldom met for over an hour, at least fifteen minutes of which might be devoted to horseplay. It seemed to me that laughter produced more creative ideas than solitary brooding cogitation. I would simply announce the most pressing projects and problems of the moment, then listen to the ideas and solutions the staff proposed. We seldom settled anything at these meetings, but we broadened everybody's thinking about the problems. Then we returned to our offices, where we kept dropping in on each other to exchange more ideas. Out of this came television programs America would be watching for years to come. When I mention that I put this or that show on the air, I don't want anyone to forget all those who helped me do it.

One of our big projects arose from a plan I had brought with me to NBC. I had decided on a strategy of comedy every night at eight o'clock, right after the news, and drama at nine. At eight, the kids were still up, and they controlled the sets. They liked to be in on things, and if our four-year-old son, Trajan, was any example, they loved comedy, because comedians are the real insiders, the conveyers of in-jokes and in-ideas. Kids are not, however, enthusiastic about serious drama. I figured that they would hold on to the TV sets until nine, when they would either go to bed or do homework, leaving the grownups free to watch drama, or whatever else we were offering. Comedy at eight would get us the major audience after the news (7:45).

When my mind turned to comedy, I naturally thought of Fred Allen, who I was convinced could be as great on television as he had been on radio, if he were given the right kind of program. He had retired from radio in the summer of 1949 after a final show that I should remember because it featured a skit about Jack Benny, his last guest star, and myself. Fred included it in his book *Treadmill to Oblivion*. He and Benny were reminiscing about the times they had come across each other early in their careers. The first encounter was supposedly in Mason City, Iowa, during vaudeville days; the second was on a movie set in Hollywood; and the third was during radio days in New York. Each time, Allen was a star, while Benny was a bum called Gypsy Jack. It was in this third meeting that Allen involved me—not in person but as a character. Benny, of course, played himself. I don't remember who played me. Allen opened the scene:

ALLEN   I remember, that day I got the call from a man named Weaver. A big shot with the American Tobacco Company. I entered Mr. Weaver's office—
        (Door opens and closes.)

WEAVER   Gad! Fred Allen! We've been waiting all afternoon.

ALLEN   I got your note, Mr. Weaver.

WEAVER   We've got a big radio program all lined up for Lucky Strike Cigarettes—and we want you to be the star.

ALLEN   I'm sorry.

WEAVER   Wait till you hear this setup—we've got Don

Wilson to announce; Rochester, Dennis Day, Phil
Harris . . .

ALLEN But I've just signed to do a program for Tender
Leaf Tea and Shefford Cheese.

WEAVER Well, that does it. Without Allen we might as
well pull Lucky Strikes off the market. We'll
close the plantations, put LSMFT back in the al-
phabet, send old F. E. Boone [the tobacco auc-
tioneer] back to Lexington, Kentucky.

ALLEN There must be somebody else you can get.

WEAVER Who? Singin' Sam wants too much money. The
Street Singer went into the real estate business.
And what a program we had lined up!

ALLEN I'm sorry.

WEAVER We had this quintet hired to do the commercials.

ALLEN A quintet?

WEAVER Yeah. Show him, boys!

CAST HMMMMMMMMMMMMMMMMMM.

ALLEN Wait! The guy on the end—aren't you Gypsy
Jack?

BENNY Yes, Mr. Allen.

ALLEN Jack, you in a quintet?

WEAVER (*Sotto*) His wife, Mary, is in the show. We did
her a favor.

ALLEN Look, Mr. Weaver, the star of this Lucky Strike
show—does he have to be funny?

WEAVER No. We've got Rochester, Dennis, Phil—plenty of
comedians.

ALLEN Does he have to have any talent?

WEAVER All we need is a slob the others can bounce jokes
off of.

ALLEN Then here's your man—Jack Benny!

WEAVER Okay, Benny—you're hired.

BENNY Fred. I'll never—never be able to thank you
enough.

Jack Benny remained very much in radio after Allen re-tired. Fred was now idle and, as usual, in delicate health. The night of Judy Garland's celebrated opening at the Palace, in an ill-fated revival of vaudeville, I settled into my seat and discovered that Fred and Portland were directly in front of me. During the interval between acts I began talking to Fred about shows he should do on television.

Suddenly Portland turned around, gave me a withering glance, and said, "Why don't you just leave him alone?"

She was one of the most amiable people in the world, but she was very protective of her husband. That closed the conversation for the time being, though it seemed to me that Fred's health was no more fragile than usual. I was still convinced he could be a great star in television.

Meanwhile, we were working up a comedy show for kids, 4:30 to 5 p.m., called *NBC Comics*, and another one for nighttime viewing, by children from nineteen to ninety. I also had in mind a late-night comedy show, an early-morning program for people getting ready to go to work, and a day-time home show for women, but these were simply ideas in my head, although outlined in my memos.

The evening comedy broadcast turned out to be *Broadway Open House*, featuring Jerry Lester and Morey Amsterdam on alternating nights. It was not the kind of vehicle Fred Allen could have handled, because it was on the air five nights a week. Lester and Amsterdam were ideal, since they were both standup comics and the show was fairly impromptu. Jerry had worked for me at American Tobacco, and Morey had been on one of my programs in California in the early thirties. Jerry starred three nights a week, and Morey two. They were supported by a small musical group and a young lady named Dagmar, who became a sensation by doing vir-tually nothing except displaying her wondrously impressive bosom. Knowing the talents of Lester and Amsterdam, I figured the show would work, though I didn't expect it to be a blockbuster. I was wrong. It was a runaway hit from the beginning, and I had my first big success at NBC.

A few months later, on October 8, 1949, Liz and I had a second big success, at home. Four years after our son, Trajan, arrived, our daughter, Susan Alexandra, was born, healthy and even then, in my opinion, beautiful. She wasn't actually born at home, of course, but in the Leroy Hospital, at Park and Sixty-first, the same place her brother had come into the world. Before Susan's birth we were both worried, because Liz had considerable difficulty carrying her. But after one look at her we relaxed.

Not many readers are likely to recognize Susan's adult identity under her given names, since she grew up to become a well-known movie star under the name Sigourney Weaver. She was a well-behaved child, and sometimes embarrassingly perceptive. The day after I left NBC, for instance, when she was six years old, she saw my picture and the story of my resignation on the front page of the *New York Times*. Already a voracious reader, she pored over the article to the very end, then looked up and said, "Mommy, why can't Daddy hold a job?"

After graduating from the Chapin School, in Manhattan, at the age of thirteen, she enrolled at Ethel Walker, in Connecticut. Because she was tall for her age, her smaller prep school classmates decided she was too big to be called Suzy, so they nicknamed her Amazon. After brooding about this for a while, she decided to call herself Sigourney, after a character in a Scott Fitzgerald story.

When Sigourney wanted to change her name from Susan, she had our wholehearted support. We told her that if she still liked the name after two years, she should make it legal. I telephoned her boarding school and talked with the headmistress, who was most understanding and promised cooperation from everyone at the school.

When Sigourney chose a career in show business, she also

had our endorsement. We are very proud of her, and very proud that she chose this path. She is married to James Simpson, who taught at the Yale Drama School before launching a successful career as a director. Their little girl, Charlotte, born in 1990, has completely won our hearts.

12

AFTER THREE MONTHS OF OB-
servation and assessment at NBC, I wrote my first memo to
the staff, a short essay (short for me, anyway) called "The
Course to Be Followed." I began by outlining some preliminary possibilities in the growth of television, which was then
still an infant medium.

"In my judgment," I wrote, it would depend "not on what
we all think about it but what a few people do about it.
. . . There is no inevitable pattern which it will follow, no
inexorable development. Rather, some of us will determine
and direct the advance of the medium. The only inexora-
bility, in my opinion, is that television will go into the American home, and rapidly."

After mentioning the growing costs of production, the advantages of network program ownership, and the need for
the "magazine" concept of sponsorship by multiple advertisers, I touched upon what I considered to be our most

immediate requirement—the development of our own programs. Programming was my top priority. To me, a real network was, or should be, nothing but programming, which is basically a creative job. You think about what the public—or, at least, some segment of the public, such as children, housewives, sports fans, or late-night viewers— could be attracted to watch, and, having determined this to your satisfaction, you try to design a program that will give them not only what they want but also something of lasting value. Then you turn your concept over to creative people —writers, performers, producers—who have the skills to bring such a program to life. Once you've chosen the creative people and put them to work, you leave them alone. You wouldn't tell Milton Berle what jokes to use. You wouldn't tell a producer like Fred Coe how to climax a dramatic story for *Television Playhouse*. At least I never did. The fact is, I watched drama only once in a while, and I hardly ever watched daytime TV. I watched comedy regularly because I love it. After all, I started as a comedy writer.

I had already brought in Fred Wile from Young & Rubicam to build up the program department. We were of one mind about what was needed, and he would follow exactly the plans I outlined. His mind was sharp, and he was dependable.

Fred was one of the advertising executives I recruited in the first year or so, all from agencies, to take charge of the programs we were launching. I hired ad men because there was no other place to find people with wide program experience.

These people had the further advantage of knowing all the major advertising clients, their needs and personalities. After Wile, I hired George McGarrett, who had already distinguished himself at CBS, Young & Rubicam, and Foote, Cone and Belding. Sam Fuller had been head of radio and television at the Sherman and Marquette agency. Merritt

Barnum had produced the Phil Baker show, with Lucille Ball and Patsy Kelly, at Y&R, after which he became the number-two man at Ruthrauff and Ryan. Carl Stanton, who had gone to high school with me in California, had been the original producer of *Amos and Andy* when he was with Lord and Thomas and later worked for me at American Tobacco; I made him the head of talent at NBC. Tom McAvity had run the Lord and Thomas agency several years earlier. It was he who had helped me get my initial job in New York, writing the *Evening in Paris Roof* show in 1935. He was one of the first people I tried to hire, but I didn't get him until 1951, because he was busy on other projects. In addition, I had Norman Blackburn, who was already at NBC when I arrived, doing his best with a hopelessly inadequate programming department.

One of my problems in enticing ad men to NBC was the $15,000 yearly salary limit the RCA personnel department imposed. Every one of them was making much more than that. I simply put each on the weekly budget of the program he supervised at $1,000 per show. The personnel people had conniptions about this, but I got away with it, and my staff ended up earning plenty of money, which was as it should have been because they were worth it to NBC. They had all the skills necessary to help us catch up to CBS in a hurry.

The first major actor I signed to an NBC contract was Robert Montgomery, and that was a triumph. Until then, big stars signed contracts not with networks but with ad agencies or their clients, and there were several prestigious clients trying to get Montgomery. He had moved from Hollywood to New York in an angry mood, which I believe was partly the result of the Los Angeles Country Club rejecting his application for membership. This was not, as one might expect, because he was a member of some racial or religious minority. He was an Anglo-Saxon Protestant from a highly

respected family, and of a very social temperament. He belonged to several desirable clubs in New York. His only problem was that he was an actor, which was enough to blackball
him at many of the elite country clubs.

In those days, the question of admitting Jews, blacks, or
other minorities to such clubs had hardly even been raised;
it was taken for granted that they weren't "suitable." But
the idea of admitting show people was often advanced, especially in Los Angeles, where most of the wealthy film stars
and executives lived. (In fact, Jews there created the Hillcrest
Country Club because they were banned from other clubs.)
Even some hotels were still turning away actors—a holdover
from centuries past, when "mummers" had little money and
were reputed to be notorious about sneaking out without
paying their bills. There was a story about Jimmy Stewart
trying to check into one of the best hotels in London sometime after World War II. Under "profession" on the regis-
tration card he wrote "actor," whereupon the clerk said that
he was sorry, but actors were not acceptable. Stewart, so the
story goes, crossed out the word "actor" and replaced it with
"retired air force general," which he was and still is, and
was promptly welcomed.

The Los Angeles Country Club, the most expensive and
exclusive on the West Coast, was no exception to this form
of discrimination. My own brother, Doodles, a prominent
comedian, was a member only because our family belonged.
I've been told that Randolph Scott, who came from a prominent old Virginia family, was the only other actor then in
the LACC. I imagine there must be a few more by this time,
but not in 1949, when Bob Montgomery was rejected.

When Bob came to New York he had in hand an excellent
and already well-developed plan for a show he wanted to do
on television, a one-hour drama called *Robert Montgomery
Presents*, which he would produce and introduce each week,
sometimes also starring. I liked his idea so much, I said

immediately, "All right, Bob, I'll buy it, but only if you'll go under contract to NBC. I would refuse to sell any more than half the show to any one sponsor. We would get another sponsor for the other half."

After I explained to him the facts of life in television production costs and what I was trying to do, he quickly agreed, signing a contract which assured me that no sponsor could ever move him to another network. *Robert Montgomery Presents* was for a long time one of the most successful dramatic programs on television. With Fred Coe's *Philco Television Playhouse* and the *Kraft Television Theater*, it gave us strong representation in drama.

It was comedy, however, that brought in the high ratings and big profits. Unfortunately, we had only Milton Berle on Tuesdays and *Broadway Open House* five nights a week late at night. I considered it incumbent upon me to turn up the volume on laughter.

This brought me to my old idea, which I called *Saturday Night Revue*. As I explained in an article in *Variety* on July 26, 1950, it was the final crystallization of several plans, which were based on two concepts. The first was that we had to find a way to let the average-budget advertiser participate in high-cost programming, so that the base of the network's television income could be broadened. We were caught in a vicious circle. Unless we brought in more money, we couldn't afford the higher expenditures for the better talent and more ambitious production we needed to attract the larger audiences that would enable us to bring in more money. That was one reason I insisted on multiple sponsorship—it was the only way to get around the conundrum. I couldn't see anything wrong with it. Magazines had always accepted a wide variety of advertisements, some of which were in direct competition with others just a few pages away.

The second concept was that of all-evening programming.

This was an idea I had tried and failed to achieve at Young
& Rubicam when I proposed a package called variously "The
City" or "The American Scene," combining segments of several programs into a connected evening of entertainment,
integrated by an emcee, and thus holding the audience from
the early news show to the close of programming, which in
those early days of television was eleven or eleven-thirty.
Another version of the idea called for a movie, a live stage
revue, a party, and comedy, the most important of these
being comedy.

When I worked out the idea of *Saturday Night Revue* it
was in the hope of getting more people to spend their entire
evening at home with NBC rather than doing what they
usually did on many Saturday nights—going to dinner and
a stage show or movie, then perhaps a nightclub or a ballroom with a dance band. If I could give them television
entertainment of equal or perhaps even superior quality, they
wouldn't have to go out and pay a lot of money for it.

This brought me to a producer named Max Liebman,
whose work I had first seen at a summer resort in the Catskills
called Tamiment, where he staged an exceptional, ever-
changing comedy revue with a sort of repertory company
that included some unknown people with strange names like
Sid Caesar and Imogene Coca. I had been so impressed by
the Tamiment show that I had tried to bring Liebman and
his company of comedians, dancers, and singers to Young
& Rubicam in the hope that General Foods would sponsor
them on television. But the sponsor chose instead a Benton
and Bowles show called *Lambs Gambol,* which turned out
to be the flop of the year.

Meanwhile. Liebman sold his show to the Admiral television manufacturers. *The Admiral Broadway Revue* was
successful. though not as great as Sid Caesar later remembered it to be. It did. however. give Liebman's company its

first television experience, and under his guidance they used
it as an opportunity to refine their comedic talents. It was
on CBS.

I had never lost sight of Max Liebman. I knew how smart
and innovative he was, and I decided I had to put him under
contract to NBC. I went to him, explained my idea for all-
evening programming under the title *Saturday Night Revue*,
and told him I would modify it if he would fill two and a
half hours, which I proposed to call "The Max Liebman
Saturday Night Revue."

He didn't feel he could spread himself that thin. "I'll give
you a first-class Broadway-type revue, ninety minutes every
Saturday night," he said, "but you'll have to find someone
else to fill the extra hour."

I couldn't blame him. Even ninety minutes is an enormous
hole to fill each week, especially with comedy. It's like producing a new Broadway show every week. However, in a
book titled *Producers on Producing*, edited by Irv Broughton,
Liebman indicated that he had not been frightened by the
task. "I had no qualms about that," he said. "I have changed
schedules after a dress rehearsal. I have fired an emcee after
a dress rehearsal [though] we had to go on an hour after
that. I had absolutely no qualms."

About Max Liebman, I can believe it. He was a remarkably
cool operator, always in control. But with a stock company
as capable as his, it was a bit easier for him to relax than
for other producers. He brought to NBC a group of dancers
and singers, as well as solo dancers and singers. But above
all, he had Sid Caesar, Imogene Coca, Carl Reiner, and Howard Morris. As he said himself, he had in his company "all
the elements that are usually gathered in a Broadway show,"
including a choreographer, a scenic designer, and a writing
staff, headed by Mel Tolkin and Lucille Kallen, that was
destined to be celebrated in show business.

He even had at his disposal a Sanner dolly, because he had prevailed upon me to buy one for his use when he was doing the Admiral show—or so he said. I don't recall it. What was a Sanner dolly? It was a fairly long-armed crane on wheels, mobile enough to shift in all directions—left, right, up, and down—with the camera on the end of the arm and the cameraman seated behind it. A man named Sanner devised it, and Liebman had seen it in a small Hollywood television studio. All the movie studios had one, or its equivalent, but I think ours may have been the first in New York, and I owed Max a bushel of thanks for talking me into buying it for him, if I did. We saved a lot of time, which was money, by being able to make all kinds of camera moves without interrupting the action.

We decided to call Liebman's ninety minutes *Your Show of Shows*, and we completed our Saturday night coverage by preceding it with a Jack Carter production comedy, which turned out to be pretty good but not great. Though Jack was a talented comedian the show never really took off, perhaps because his writers were not as good as Liebman's, and also because, funny as Jack was, he could hardly match the antics of Sid Caesar, who was a true comedic genius. With Caesar, Coca, Reiner, and Morris, plus a team of writers that included, besides Tolkin and Kallen, Mel Brooks, Neil Simon, Larry Gelbart, and eventually Woody Allen, *Your Show of Shows*, with its sequel, *Caesar's Hour*, was destined to become a unique experience in television.

I put George McGarrett in charge, and he made sure Liebman and his people were free to do their thing without interference. The way George handled clients and ad agency people at rehearsals was typical of his operating methods. They would all gather in the client's room to watch the dress rehearsal, pencils and paper in hand to write down their suggestions. After it was over, George would collect all the notes, agree with every one of the comments, covertly chuck them in the wastebasket, then take the assembled company over to 21 for drinks and dinner. It must have worked, because Liebman told Irv Broughton, "I have never found, outside of minor things, that I was ever interfered with by the network or the sponsors."

During the planning stages of our Saturday-night programming I became increasingly concerned about the rising costs. I could imagine myself traipsing up to the fifty-third floor of the RCA Building and watching General Sarnoff's face as I told him how much money I needed for just two shows. I didn't think Joe McConnell, who was even newer on his job as network president than I was on mine, could approve an expenditure of more than a million dollars.

Then one day McConnell asked me in general terms about the programs I was planning. "How about that big Saturday-night project you've mentioned?"

"We're working on it," I replied. "I'm getting it underway, but it looks as if it'll be pretty expensive. What will I have to do to get approval on a project in the millions?"

"I'll give you the approval right now," he said, thereby taking a load off my mind. I much preferred having him announce the cost to the General than me. Despite Joe's approval, however, I feared that I hadn't heard the last on the subject. In fact, I had. The costs were covered, and there were no complaints. I hate to think what might have happened, though, if *Your Show of Shows* had flopped.

From the day I first imagined the show I was worried about selling it, because it was on this program that I intended to introduce my concept of large-scale multiple sponsorship. I wanted to launch it with rotating commercials, which would guarantee every sponsor at least one exposure during each half-hour segment.

The Federal Communications Commission refused to approve that plan. In 1950, there was still a scarcity of television stations in the country. Even some sizable communities had only one or two channels. In such places, a station could choose its programs from any of the four networks—NBC, CBS, ABC, and Dumont—and didn't have to take an entire show. If there was only a single station in Omaha, for instance, it might want to broadcast one or two half-hours of *Your Show of Shows*, then switch to CBS for another program, or to one of its local shows. If we were to rotate each sponsor's commercials throughout the ninety minutes, these stations would have to take the whole show or none of it; otherwise, some sponsors would be paying for commercials that would not be seen in those markets.

Though we could have corrected the situation by refunding the sponsors for unused commercials, the FCC, dominated by radio people who didn't understand the exigencies of television, refused to let us do it, so we had to sell commercial time within half-hour segments, three minutes per half-hour. I felt this would work for *Your Show of Shows*, but I was by no means certain of it, because I couldn't yet say for sure that the ad agencies and their clients would even accept the multiple-sponsor concept.

I couldn't have been excessively nervous about it, however, because in February, when the show was scheduled to open, Liz and I took off on our usual ski vacation, this time to Switzerland. While there, I received a cable from McConnell that said, in approximately these words: "Must come back for *Show of Shows* opening. Promises to be biggest thing ever on television. Come soonest."

Liz and I were having such a good time in St. Moritz that we didn't want to be anyplace else, but we made plane connections as quickly as possible. This wasn't easy in those days, with airlines just beginning to expand, and transatlantic flights still at least slightly adventurous. When we arrived in New York it seemed as if everyone in television and advertising was talking about *Your Show of Shows*. The word had leaked out, either accidentally or on purpose, that it was an event to rival the invention of the electronic tube.

The demand for tickets to the opening from the ad agencies and their clients was so overwhelming, we soon ran out of seats, whereupon they began asking for tickets to the dress rehearsal, which also played to a packed house. The reaction of almost everyone was glorious. Burgess Meredith was the guest of honor on that first show, and he was as good as you would expect him to be; but Caesar, Coca, and company were spectacular. Even though they had done about twenty TV shows for Admiral, most people had never seen them, and, as anyone old enough to remember can tell you, they were a revelation, a sensation, something new—not just to television, but to the art of comedy.

I think it was on the first show that Sid and Imogene introduced a bickering married couple who might well have been the inspiration for *I Love Lucy*, Jackie Gleason's *The Honeymooners*, and every other domestic farce in the last forty years of television. Sid also exposed the audience to that wondrous ability of his to speak Japanese, German, French, Italian, and Russian so convincingly, you would swear he really knew those languages, until he started dropping in English words, which made you realize it was all comic nonsense. He did a skit in which Howard Morris, as his valet, was dressing him in a German general's uniform. As Morris made one mistake after another, Caesar, in his phony German, found a dozen ways to tell him what a dummkopf he was, and even though the words had no literal meaning, Caesar conveyed with them his real, comedic meaning. When the "general" was finally dressed, he gave Morris the back of his gloved hand, then marched stiffly out of the room like a proper German general and through a fancy hotel lobby to the front entrance, where he took up his post—as a doorman.

It was an unfortunate inaugural for the Jack Carter show on two counts. First of all, the shortage of studio and theater space in New York forced us to open in a rented Chicago theater, where Jack was out of his element and the facilities were limited. Space in New York was so scarce and difficult to rent that I had begun buying theaters for NBC's use as we continued to expand production.

What hurt the Carter show more than the limited facilities, however, was the inevitable comparisons with *Your Show of Shows*. Caesar, Coca, and company were so brilliant, nobody would want to be compared with them. As a runaway hit, the show eliminated my concern about multiple sponsors. Within a few days, *Your Show of Shows* had sold all its commercial time for thirty-nine weeks.

The whole country seemed to be talking about *Your Show of Shows*, and, equally important, it was buying television sets to be able to see it. By now there were 3.5 million sets in the United States, but the medium was still small. Radio continued to be the networks' major source of revenue, and there were concerns in the industry that earnings from radio might dwindle before television revenue increased sufficiently to replace it. The success of *Your Show of Shows* stimulated more of that speculation as Caesar and Coca began appearing on the covers of national magazines, and even the remarkable comedy writers who put the show together inspired articles. Were new stars like these about to kill off the old radio favorites who were still bringing in so much money?

The *Your Show of Shows* writers were on their way to becoming legends themselves. Rumors arose that they were even funnier than the programs and that their work sessions were uncontrolled riots of laughter and high jinks. Not so, if my observations were correct. Funny and talented as they were, I found the writers a sober, industrious crew, conscious at all times of their frightening task of filling ninety minutes with high comedy each week.

Max Liebman himself confirmed that in his interview with Broughton. "We were not, as seems to be the myth or the legend, a barrel of inebriated monkeys, screaming and yelling. In fact, Fred Allen used to come Saturday morning to the theater when we were blocking the show for the evening's performance, and he would sit in the back and said it was like a church. If anybody raised his voice, he was stopped, and if he did it too often he didn't last very long."

Liebman himself was not one of the writers. As he saw it, he had another function to fulfill. "I had a great deal of respect for any writer who worked for me for any period of time," he said, "and any one of them would tell you that my forte, more than anything else I did, was the element of being a stalwart editor."

He didn't hesitate to veto skits or gags. "Very often I would say, 'I don't think this will work,' but even then I would say, 'Well, okay, do it,' and then someone would say, 'Uh huh, Max is handing us the rope.' " This meant, of course, the rope with which to hang themselves.

"I admired them very much," he added, "or I wouldn't have them. It was my experience that gave me the edge in guessing what would and wouldn't work." Judging from the finished product, he must have had a fine sense of what was workable.

After each show, he recalled, there was a lot of celebrating, "but it was very sad at times. Maybe because I had to say, 'What are we going to do next week?' The idea of getting into the next show . . . was always a new challenge."

It was a challenge that he and his people were to meet, week after week, for the four remarkable years during which the show continued at the top of the ratings.

The desire to advertise on *Your Show of Shows* broke down some of the agency and client opposition to the concepts of multiple and alternate sponsorship, but not all of it. I continued to have problems with agencies that still considered me a turncoat for joining a network, and that included a few influential people at Young & Rubicam. It was not one of the agencies that rushed to buy time on *Your Show of Shows*. Some ad men had not yet abandoned their arguments about sponsor identification and the gratitude factor among radio listeners and television viewers. To answer that argument and their resistance to one-minute commercials, I would say, "Look, you've all used radio spots. You know how effective they are. If you have a good selling message that makes sense to the audience, they'll buy the product. If you give them a message they can believe, they'll listen to it and act upon it. That's the really important factor in advertising. You have to think about the other things, but it's the credibility of the message that makes the difference, not the gratitude factor or sponsor identification."

This was an argument that continued for some time and found its way into the public's consciousness. It was even referred to on several television programs, including *Your Show of Shows*. One night, after the first part of a skit between Caesar and Shirley MacLaine, guest star Art Carney promised the viewers they could see the second part of the play in three weeks. He described the whole thing as "an original repeat of a drama presented by our alternate sponsor, who brings you next week's show on an every-other-week basis, and who is this week's cosponsor but in three weeks will be the regular alternate sponsor."

All jokes aside, the revolution I had envisioned in the whole system of ownership, sponsorship, and control of television programming was underway.

13

IN THE EARLY SPRING OF 1950, AS SOON AS *YOUR SHOW of Shows* was renewed, I was planning my next comedy program, which I tentatively called *The Comedy Hour*. I had penciled it in for Sunday nights, as one more step in the direction of providing comedy every night of the week. As I envisioned it, *The Comedy Hour* would be a weekly show with four or five of the nation's top radio or movie stars, each of whom would appear as the headliner once a month. No one had ever rotated comics this way on the same show, but I thought it would work if I got the right performers.

Though we still had a long way to go, we were making gains on CBS by this time. We now had three strong comedy anchors—Milton Berle on Tuesdays, *Your Show of Shows* on Saturdays, and *Broadway Open House* late at night. We also had several other projects in the works.

A show we did do, *Cads and Scoundrels*, grew out of my belief that the most fascinating people in fiction were the villains. It was the story of a honeymoon couple at Monte Carlo. The groom lost all his money, as well as his bride, to a cad in the casino. Jack Lemmon played the cad and Grace Kelly, in one of her earliest acting appearances, the bride. Tommy Phipps wrote the piece, and Michael Arlen, the famous writer, narrated.

The strongest show we launched that spring was called *Mr. Omm* (short for Omnibus, Omniscient, Omnes, or whatever anyone preferred). Mr. Omm, a storyteller, appeared in a series of vignettes, which varied in length. In the first scene of each story, he set the stage; then, as the action began, he moved off. Merritt Barnum produced the program, which also featured the brilliant photography of George Hurrell, who had taken most of Liz's still photos when she was working in films. One of our proudest possessions is a large portrait of Liz with Trajan when he was four or five. It is now in a huge golden frame at his home in Salt Lake City.

(During Trajan's teenage years, incidentally, he joined the Mormon church, which surprised but didn't displease us. I've liked all the Mormons I've known. We attended his initiation into the church by the bishop of Long Island, who was also a captain with Pan American Airlines.

Tray entered Ricks College shortly after this, went on his traditional two-year mission a year later, returned to Ricks, then met and married a splendid woman named Karen Young, a descendant of the Mormon patriarch Brigham Young. They both graduated from Brigham Young University, after which Trajan worked for the Latter-day Saints organization. He also did some acting in radio and on television but finally settled into an independent advertising and marketing business. He and Karen have four wonderful children—Wynelle, Diane, Patrick, and Christopher.)

We began our NBC evening programming for the 1950–51 season with *Kukla, Fran and Ollie*, the classic puppet show for both kids and adults, at 7 p.m., followed by various singers for the fifteen-minute 7:30 segment before the news. Dinah Shore and Perry Como did these, although not together. The rather weak *Camel News Caravan* with John Cameron Swayze was at 7:45. On Mondays at 8 p.m. we had the ventriloquist Paul Winchell with his dummy, Jerry Mahoney, and a mentalist in a good but not sensational comedy format, and for Thursdays we had secured Groucho Marx in *You Bet Your Life.* He was marvelous, but not yet consistent; he sometimes needed editing.

With our production expanding, we were feeling an acute need for studios or theaters from which to televise programs. In New York we had the use of the large Center Theater at Rockefeller Center, besides which we had bought one theater, had leased another, and were in the process of acquiring more. But the real problem was not in New York. Most of the major radio stars we were hoping to lure into television lived in California, which meant that we would need stage facilities in Los Angeles. Unfortunately, there weren't many legitimate theaters in L.A., so we had to build such facilities or buy them, perhaps from the movie studios. We were eager to get this problem solved before January 1952, when the coaxial cable, permitting coast-to-coast transmission, was scheduled for completion. We weren't likely to attract the stars we wanted if they would have to fly to New York to work for us, especially if by that time they could stay at home and work for CBS. In addition, Hollywood had the world's greatest pool of film technicians—the very people we would soon need for television, I decided that our Hollywood facilities should be at least as extensive as those in New York, and I began lobbying for such an expansion through Joe McConnell.

The movie studios gave us trouble from the start. They fought us as fiercely as they had fought radio. The studios resisted the very notion of producing programs for us. We actually should have been grateful. Had MGM, for instance, gone into the television production business, with all the acting, writing, producing, and technical talent at its disposal, the studio could have started a network of its own that would have been very difficult for us to match. Any ambitious person with vision would have jumped at the chance of making MGM a force in television. There was no cosmic design which dictated that the big radio networks would now become the big television networks. Indeed, radio people couldn't match movie people in visual expertise. Television executives like myself—and even General Sarnoff, if he had been aware of it—had reason to worry about the latent power locked up in Hollywood and the possibility that the studios might invade our limitless but chaotic new medium.

I was not, however, as concerned as I might have been, because I believed we could count on the continuing woolly-headedness of motion-picture executives. I considered this almost a sure thing, unless the bankers, who really called the shots in Hollywood, were to compel the picture companies to start making sense in the field of television. I didn't think this would happen, because I couldn't imagine the banks worrying that much about the future of the movie companies. Even if the big studios failed, as long as movies continued to be made, whoever produced those movies, either for theaters or for television, would have to keep coming to the banks for financing. The bankers would get their piece of television whether it was controlled by the movie companies or the networks.

For all of these reasons, I was only minimally concerned about the studios' possible threat to the networks, but I was quite concerned about our need to use some of the assets that lay idle in Hollywood. Besides wanting to rent or buy some of their sound stages for television production, we hoped to hire their stars for guest appearances on the big shows. We also wanted to arrange single or perhaps periodic showings of films like *Gone With the Wind, Goodbye, Mr. Chips, Going My Way, Snow White, Citizen Kane, Casablanca, The Informer, The Lost Weekend,* and other great pictures that were sitting on the shelves of studio libraries. I made trip after trip to Hollywood in the hope of negotiating agreements on such matters—but all for naught.

On one of those trips I was talking to Walter Wanger. He sympathized with my plight but could do nothing to help me, even though he was an important producer at the time. "How can you be so naive about what's going on out here?" he asked me. "You must be aware that movie people, especially the theater owners, fought against the introduction of sound, of color, of improvements in both, just as they're fighting now against the use of the big screen. They have resisted every new development that threatened to create any kind of change or improvement. And you know how they fought against radio, even after it became obvious that selective radio advertising and guest appearances by stars could make their movies more prominent and profitable than ever."

I did, indeed, know all of this, yet I continued butting my head against the studio doors until it was almost laughable. Sometimes it was laughable. During one of my trips to Hollywood I gathered my staff and said to them, "Ladies and gentlemen, you're stationed here in Hollywood because you know and I know how important this place will be in the development of television. You also know that I haven't been able to get the movie studios to listen to my proposals. But I think I've figured out how to get through to them, and today I plan to try it.

"You're all aware, I suppose, of a man named Isadore Schary, who came out here from New York and spent year after year fighting the good fight, doing his damnedest to get someplace in movie production. Alas, he couldn't seem to break down the doors, until, one day, he decided to cut his name in half. He became Dore Schary, and before he knew it he was head of MGM, just about the biggest studio in town.

"The success of Dore Schary has got me thinking about myself. I must admit that up until now, Sylvester Weaver has failed miserably in Hollywood. But all that is about to change. Starting today, Vester Weaver will begin making the rounds of the studios, and before you know it, we'll get what we want."

I can only wish it had been that easy. Not until the collapse of the star system and the breakup of the studios in the 1960s did the powerful men in Hollywood realize what an opportunity they had missed in television.

By the middle of 1950, television was growing so rapidly that, as I told a group of Pittsburgh industrialists, "all prognostications about it seem to fall behind the actuality." It was now available in forty of the forty-eight states and in all but two of the forty-two cities with more than a quarter of a million residents. It was within reach of three out of every five U.S. families. On the basis of homes with sets, compared with the circulation of the nation's ten leading magazines, it had jumped from number eleven to number one. A study found that in New York, for example, the number of homes with TV sets was double the circulation of the most popular magazine, which at that time was *Reader's Digest*. Another study indicated that two out of three persons who did not own sets nevertheless watched television in public places or at the homes of friends. Almost all of these people were expected to break down soon and buy sets of their own. And *Your Show of Shows* had established an all-time record of circulation per set, overtaking Milton Berle. Sid Caesar, Imogene Coca, and company were reaching almost four times as many viewers as there were sets. As in the early days of radio, whole families were gathering in front of the set to watch their favorite programs.

All of this was especially good news to those of us who worried about creating more revenue to pay for increasing production costs. Two studies of public buying habits in the tristate greater New York area were even more reassuring. These studies compared sales figures of seventeen consumer and durable goods advertised on television with thirteen competing brands that did not use television. The researchers validated their findings by actual studies of product use in the homes of consumers.

The studies found that the sale of television-advertised products increased by 40 percent per home after a set was installed, and in the same homes at the same time, sales of products not advertised on TV decreased by 37 percent. One of the studies concluded that television ads produced an average of twenty dollars in sales for every dollar of cost.

However, not everything in television was progressing in accordance with my hopes and plans. Quite a few critics and intellectuals were accusing the television networks, including NBC, of appealing to the lowest common denominator of public taste. While acknowledging that we had done some good things, they pointed out that there was still a lot of junk on TV. Though I didn't agree with all their claims, I couldn't deny that there was some truth to their charges, and I was especially sensitive to their barbs because of public statements I had made about the great potential of television for elevating public taste, and about my hope to make the common man an uncommon man by exposing him to all kinds of cultural experiences. I was more sharply aware than the critics that this noble ambition could not be realized overnight. Though I had been at NBC only a little over a year, I knew how hard it was to bring about any substantive changes.

I had several ideas for upgrading the quality of television, or what I once called making television "the shining center of the home," but I knew I would have to introduce them gradually and carefully, one step at a time. I would have loved, for instance, to telecast opera performances or ballet, but I wasn't stupid enough to think I could just go ahead, do it, and sit back while congratulations poured down on me. (That's not what would have poured down on me.) My main job at NBC was to develop a program service that would attract total cumulative audiences. One cannot build a large network by beaming programs to small, special groups. You wouldn't drop in a French lesson right after Milton Berle, however important it might be for Americans to learn foreign languages. Every show in prime time must aim to reach as many people as possible, and I was aware that neither opera nor ballet would do that. They're not mass-appeal arts, though both are splendid entertainment, and millions of people would find that out if they were properly exposed to them.

By way of introduction, I intended to insert an occasional aria or a scene from a popular ballet like *Swan Lake* into high-quality variety revues. I hadn't abandoned that plan; I was simply waiting for the right spots on the right shows. Through gradual exposure I hoped to broaden interest in those arts, just as radio had increased the demand for classical music. It might be a long time before opera could break into prime time, but if it were brought along gradually, it could one day fit into less expensive time slots or special programs.

In this frame of mind, I had begun work, shortly after my arrival at NBC, on the development of a cultural project, tentatively titled "Operation Frontal Lobes." It grew out of the scientific observation that the human race had evolved and achieved mastery of the animal world because of the frontal lobes of our brains. No other animal had well-developed frontal lobes. I appealed to our creative people at

NBC to conceive of programs that would use entertainment to enrich, inspire, and enlighten viewers. We would have to preempt a succession of prime time shows to do it, though each no more than once a year, but when the sponsors realized the scope and quality of the attraction, I felt confident they would accept it—perhaps reluctantly at first, but ultimately with some enthusiasm.

I began with a proposal I thought would easily win sponsor approval. One of our NBC children's programs, *The Roy Rogers Show*, starring Roy Rogers, his horse, Trigger, and his wife, Dale Evans, was sponsored by General Foods. It was not a prime time show, to be sure, but it was very popular, and General Foods was the kind of big sponsor I would have to convince if this Frontal Lobes idea was to succeed. I went to General Foods, explained the educational value of my concept, and suggested that, on a onetime basis, the sponsor set aside the usual Roy Rogers format and have him instead lead a group of children to Washington, D.C., where they would visit Congress, the Supreme Court, the White House, and some of the great monuments, while Rogers explained to them how our government worked, how our system had developed, the accomplishments of the great people whose statues they saw, and the significance of the historic documents they could read and almost touch, especially the Constitution and the Bill of Rights. I still think it was an excellent and highly promotable onetime idea for a children's show. But the General Foods people didn't like it—not even a bit.

While I was disappointed, I wasn't defeated. In December 1950, I announced publicly the Frontal Lobes project, which I had been planning for almost a year. During a Chicago address to the Speech School Broadcast Conference, I said, "NBC wants America to see operas in English, the NBC Symphony [conducted by Arturo Toscanini], great theater performances . . . [and] Sadler's Wells Ballet. . . . In addition to music and drama of the finest, we want to create a new kind of reporting for the American people. We want to present the issues of our times with enough showmanship so that most people will be eager to watch."

As examples of what subjects we hoped to treat I mentioned individual rights, which could be argued by a philosopher like Bertrand Russell or illustrated by dramatizing the life of an average man to show the limitations placed on his freedom. I suggested the possibility of a show based on Dartmouth College's Great Issues course, or one that would trace the changing attitudes of Americans from the Revolution to modern times. I pointed out the plenitude of enormously important themes—historical, social, political, scientific, religious—that could be presented so dramatically and promoted so well that they would attract wide audiences. The speech teachers to whom I was speaking received my message with such enthusiasm, I felt a surge of new encouragement about the prospects of Frontal Lobes, but at the same time I realized that speech teachers were not program sponsors. Only time would tell whether I'd ever be able to put Frontal Lobes on the air.

AFTER A SUCCESSION of problems, I finally managed to launch the Sunday-night *Comedy Hour*. My first difficulty had arisen from the fact that I was after legendary comic talents like Eddie Cantor, Fred Allen, Bobby Clark, and Bob Hope, few of whom had ever before agreed to appear on television. It took some persuasive campaigning, not only with them but with their agents, before I could get the above-mentioned signed, as well as the new comedy team of Dean Martin and Jerry Lewis. Even though Allen and Cantor were no longer working on radio, neither of them seemed eager to try television. I think Eddie was just a bit tired after a long stage, radio, and film career. Fred professed to dislike television, he had health problems as usual, and his wife didn't want him to work for fear it might kill him. Portland hadn't changed her mind since my talk with Allen at the Palace Theater, but I sensed that Fred might be bored with his retirement.

Martin and Lewis were not yet legendary, but they were so popular in nightclubs, they were certain to become stars, and I knew I could get them. I wasn't sure I could get Bob Hope, who was still a star in radio and films, but I was a friend of Jimmy Saphier, his agent, and we did make a deal. While I was trying to sign these people I was also romancing Danny Thomas, whom I had launched in his first radio show when I was at Young & Rubicam. Since Danny was already committed elsewhere, I turned to Bobby Clark, a great stage comedian who had never made it on radio because his humor was as visual as it was vocal. For this reason I figured he'd be ideal on television.

I knew I had a tough selling job to do, and I soon found out that even the comedians' agents were against the idea. Finally I figured out the right approach. I went to the agents, one after another, and made a firm proposition. First, I said, we'd offer his client a weekly salary to match his top radio pay. But on radio he had to work every week for his money, while on the *Comedy Hour* he'd have to work only once a month, because we'd be rotating our stars. Second, to get the agents to go along, knowing how treacherous and duplicitous all of them were, I'd let each of them package his client's show, from which the agent could have 10 percent off the top for everything except our network costs. I had no trouble selling that to them.

As soon as I had my stars signed, and word of that accomplishment spread through the advertising industry, Colgate jumped in, eager to buy the whole show, which may sound good, but which I didn't want. If Colgate sponsored the entire program, Colgate would, in effect, own it, thus overriding my resolve to keep the show under network control. In addition, and only slightly less important, Colgate's chief executive officer, Edward Little, was a dictatorial operator whom I had found to be difficult in previous contacts.

To hold my own against Little, I quickly sold the Bob Hope and Bobby Clark weeks to General Motors for sponsorship by its subsidiary Frigidaire. This left the Fred Allen, Eddie Cantor, and Martin and Lewis shows under Colgate sponsorship. Though I would have been happier without Little, I couldn't ignore an advertiser as big as Colgate, so I settled for an arrangement with which I thought I could live. As I eventually learned, there was no possible arrangement that would make life with Little comfortable. In addition to being irascible, he was also ignorant. He may have known all there was to know about soap and toothpaste, but he knew nothing about show business. I remember him once asking me, "Who is this Abbot N. Costello you keep talking about?"

Fortunately, during my career at NBC I ran into no other sponsors like Little, perhaps because I had early instructed my producers that if any sponsor interfered with the program, they were to say, "We'll relieve you of your contract if you're unhappy."

That just about eliminated the problem. I do recall one strange case, though, when I was at Y&R. Eric Sevareid was doing a news show for Metropolitan Life Insurance on CBS radio, whose only "commercial" was a one-minute institutional spot about ways to maintain good health. One day I received from Metropolitan a "we have a problem with the series" phone call. Their problem? They were worried because their sponsor identification kept going up, and they didn't want the public to think they were "advertising."

The *Comedy Hour* itself was a delight and an immediate success, although the five stars did not share equal popularity. Bob Hope, who was at the height of his appeal, and Martin and Lewis, who were rising rapidly, won higher ratings than Cantor, Allen, or Clark. Even though Mike Todd produced the Clark shows, Bobby, for some reason I've never been able to understand, simply couldn't match on television the success he achieved during his many years on the Broadway stage.

My first major disappointment concerning the *Comedy Hour* came when Fred Allen dropped out. He simply couldn't find a groove in which he felt comfortable. Perhaps it was because he was in poor health, and television was more demanding physically than radio. You couldn't just stand still and talk into a microphone. You had to take into account stage movements, camera angles, acting style, and the sometimes complicated production demands. As a onetime stage star, he could have managed all of that, if he had concerned himself only with his own performance. We had plenty of very competent people who could handle the production details, but one of Fred's problems was that he worried about these people, especially the technicians—"That couch is too heavy for you to drag over here," or "Why don't I move instead of making you shift the camera," or "We don't need another set when we can easily do both scenes on this one."

That, however, was not Allen's major difficulty. I think it was that he was doing the wrong show—or perhaps I should say the wrong shows, because he was never allowed to settle on one format in which he could feel at home. I used to get angry about that, but I didn't want to interfere, because I stuck close to my policy of leaving production to the creative people. I thought Fred should be doing the same show on television that he had done with me on radio many years before—*Town Hall Tonight*, or *Allen's Alley*, which followed *Town Hall*. The producers could have created picturesque settings around these concepts into which he could have comfortably fitted all of his great supporting personalities— Mrs. Nussbaum, the Jewish housewife; Falstaff Openshaw, the Shakespearean actor; Beauregard Claghorn, the Southern senator; Socrates Mulligan, the ignoramus; and Titus Moody, the down-to-earth New Englander. They tried the *Allen's Alley* format one week, staging it with puppets, then gave up on it. Nothing good happened for Fred on that show, and Little began to complain. Fred, who was one of the most sensitive men I ever met, decided it was time for him to retire once more. His friendship with me, however, never faltered. I saw him and Portland as often as possible until his death in 1956. I went to his funeral, though I have a monumental distaste for funerals. He remains my favorite person in show business.

When Allen bowed out of the show, I replaced him with Jackie Gleason, whose career I had followed closely since the mid-1930s, when I used to go see him with Frank Hires and Jack White at Club 18. Later I thought he was great on the Phil Silvers radio show I produced at Y&R, and I hired him to play the good-hearted slob on *The Life of Riley* on TV. I loved his performance, which, incidentally, certainly helped his portrayal of a very similar character in *The Honeymooners.*

I thought Jackie would be a magnificent replacement for Fred Allen, and he would have been, were it not for Little, the swamp fox at Colgate. The day after Jackie's debut as a *Comedy Hour* host—which opened with his patented pratfall and closed with a big ovation after a performance that won him excellent reviews—I got a call from Little, who sounded belligerent as usual.

"About your Mr. Gleason," he said. "I don't want that fat man on my show anymore."

Despite my protests, the verdict from Colgate terminated

Jackie Gleason on *The Comedy Hour*. Money talks, and Little
had a huge chorus of it behind him. We still had Jackie on
The Life of Riley, doing his pratfalls, exploding into outrageous bombast, and sheepishly fading into his embarrassed
apologies, but now I had to put aside the plan I had had to
star him in his own hour-long show if all had gone well on
The Comedy Hour. A year or so later, Jackie's agent, Bullets
Durgom, came to me with an almost identical proposal. I'd
have bought it in a minute, but by that time the price was
so high I had to go upstairs to get General Sarnoff's approval.

When he heard how much it would cost, he asked, "How
much of that does Gleason himself get?"

Reluctantly, I told him how many hundreds of thousands
of dollars it would be. I can't remember the exact figure, but
I do remember how it impressed the General.

"That's more money than I make!" he exclaimed.

"But General," I impulsively declared, "you can't do the
pratfall."

Apparently Gleason's salary was less than Bill Paley's,
because CBS grabbed the show, and I was again frustrated
in my attempt to land one of the outstanding talents of our
time.

Even without Allen or Gleason, *The Comedy Hour* became
a triumph, but it was not my triumph, even though I received
a lot of credit for conceiving it and putting it together. To
replace Gleason I wanted another great comedian, Phil Silvers, who later gave full scope to his many talents in his
long-running portrayal of Sergeant Bilko. Everyone in the
business knew how good he was—everyone, that is, except
Little of Colgate, who refused to accept him. He did, however,
agree to Donald O'Connor and Ray Bolger, which surprised
me, because they were both so talented, I couldn't imagine
what he could have liked about them.

Meanwhile, I wasn't the only person having trouble with

Little. His relations with his cosponsor, Frigidaire, were such that they eventually canceled, which was what I did not, and Little did, want. He now had the whole *Comedy Hour* for himself in prime time every Sunday night, and before I could do anything about it, the program had become *The Colgate Comedy Hour*—exactly what I had been trying to prevent from the beginning.

14

THOUGH, THANKS TO THE TAKEOVER BY COLGATE, I couldn't consider *The Comedy Hour* a personal triumph, I was proud of the show and its quick commercial sale in the spring of 1950. Just as I had taken advantage of the *Show of Shows* success to sign the *Comedy Hour* stars, I now set out to use its success in an effort to acquire the talent for my next project, which was to be virtually the same show but with different stars, a different title, and a different time slot. I called this one *All-Star Revue*, and I scheduled it for Wednesdays at 8 p.m.

With that title I would need some giant performers, so I went to Las Vegas, where Jimmy Durante, Lou Clayton, and Eddie Jackson were performing at one of the hotels. Durante was still resisting television. Despite the attractive financial incentives that were now being offered, many headliners still avoided television, because they felt that exposure on the tube would make their acts too familiar to the public, thus diminishing their demand and their huge salaries in night-clubs and hotels. Joe E. Lewis, for example, never did appear on television, and Durante had not yet done so.

After romancing Durante for a week in Las Vegas, I began to wonder how much more time I could waste there before giving up hope. He was the element I badly needed. I was almost certain I could get Danny Thomas, who was now available, as were Jack Carson and Ed Wynn, the old Texaco Fire Chief of radio, who was one of the great performers of the 1930s but was no longer that big a name. Thomas and Carson hadn't yet fully grown into the stardom I felt they would achieve. Durante, on the other hand, was then considered one of the most compelling entertainers in the history of show business.

I had just about run out of persuasive arguments to use on Schnozzola when his old partner, Lou Clayton, who was then mortally ill and died shortly thereafter, walked into the room where we were talking. He listened to me for a while, then turned to Jimmy and said, "I think you should give it a try."

I don't know whether it was because Durante was tired of fending me off, or because of his love for his dying partner, but he finally agreed to appear once a month on *All-Star Revue*.

I had no trouble signing Thomas, Carson, and Wynn, especially when I offered them, their agents, and their writers the same deal I was giving the principals in *The Comedy Hour*—the agents got 10 percent, the stars and others got their weekly radio salaries, even though they would have to work only once a month.

The next thing I did was to find three sponsors (I eventually came up with six or seven), because I wanted to make certain there would be no repetition of Colgate's domination of *The Comedy Hour*.

When I sold *All-Star Revue*, I accomplished my aim to telecast a comedy show every night of the week at eight o'clock. On Sunday we now had *The Comedy Hour*; Monday, Paul Winchell and Jerry Mahoney; Tuesday, Milton Berle; Wednesday, *All-Star Revue*; Thursday, Groucho Marx; Friday, various tryout comedies; and then *The Saturday Night Revue* which included *Your Show of Shows*, with Caesar and Coca.

As I said many years later in an article for *Advertising Age*, "Comedy was vital to what we were trying to do. For instance, our Nielsen [rating] for the first year of *The Comedy Hour* was a 99 percent cumulative [i.e., reaching 99 percent of the total potential audience] per month. People who might have hated Eddie Cantor loved Bob Hope. The basic fundamental I laid out at NBC—and this is pure advertising training—was total reach. . . . I wanted [our] researchers looking for people who didn't watch so we'd think up things they would watch."

Comedy has a greater appeal than any other form of entertainment. Attractions like drama can do very well, but the major hits are comedy, and that's true in the theater and films as well as on radio and television. Movie executives made a profound mistake when talking pictures came in, because in their push to develop realistic dialogue and story lines, they left most of the great slapstick silent comedians out in the cold. There were a few exceptions, like Laurel and Hardy, but not many. People like Buster Keaton and Harold Lloyd became passé, despite their enormous talent. And Charlie Chaplin almost finished himself when he abandoned his immortal tramp persona. In the best of his talking pictures, *City Lights*, he portrayed for the last time the heart-tugging hobo that had made him famous. Only a couple of his subsequent talkies approached this masterwork.

The result of the changeover to sound has been that most

of the good film comedies stand out not because of great comedians but because of good writing. Hollywood simply stopped developing comedians, or even properly using those who came up through vaudeville and radio.

In the late 1940s, Phil Silvers summed up to me Hollywood's treatment of comedians: "You can be the biggest star on Broadway"—which he was at the time, in *High Button Shoes*—"and the biggest draw in nightclubs"—which he also was—"and accepted as one of the top comics in the country, but when you go to Hollywood, you know the part they'll give you—the girl's brother."

One of the few exceptions was the pairing of Bob Hope and Bing Crosby in the "Road" movies. The two of them were so popular on radio and so powerful, they could decide for themselves what they were going to do, and what they did was their radio palaver. From one of those pictures to the next, the plot line kept lessening in importance, to the point where nobody even recalls what the stories were. We only remember Hope and Crosby doing their funny stuff.

Phil Silvers's most famous role was as Sergeant Bilko on television. He never did get to prove his talents in movies. Neither did Sid Caesar, for which I guess I should be thankful, because it gave us the opportunity to take full advantage of his gifts on television.

As *Your Show of Shows* grew from week to week, not only in popularity but in comic maturity, people began to realize that what they were seeing in their homes on Saturday nights was better than most of the Broadway comedies. The show became the talk of the town, then the talk of the whole country. At NBC its effect was profound. Coming at a time when we were second to CBS in both ratings and talent lineup, it galvanized our entire organization and prompted us to pursue our plans with new confidence and vigor. Under the leadership of Max Liebman, *Your Show of Shows* con-

tinued to surprise and delight everyone. He even incorpo-
rated one of my preachments into the show by mixing the
comedy with some wonderful cultural entertainment. Among
the *Show of Show* guests—some of whom returned several
times—were Gertrude Lawrence, Yehudi Menuhin, Isaac
Stern, and many great stage stars. The opera singers Robert
Merrill and Marguerite Piazza were in the cast every week.
Finally I was realizing my hope of getting at least a taste of
opera into prime time.

I was such a fan of the show myself that I went to the
rehearsals. I would simply sit there in the back, laughing at
the jokes, then come back at night to watch the show itself
and laugh again at the same jokes. In those days almost all
TV shows were telecast live, and the same was true in radio.
The networks had dictated that no recordings could be
played on the air. In my early radio days, if a program ran
short we had to fill it with organ or piano music, which also
had to be live. This meant that the cast, and even the announcers, had to be on their toes, with adrenaline flowing,
to avoid boo-boos. And all of that still applied up to the time
I left NBC.

Sid Caesar was one comic who felt he had to be funny all
the time, and he could turn on the laughs in a spontaneous
stream whenever he felt like it. With that malleable face, he
could make you laugh just by changing expressions. I never
got to know Imogene Coca as well as I knew Sid, but I always
found her to be friendly. The two of them might be going
yet on *Your Show of Shows* if it weren't for her manager at
the time, who decided, after four fabulous years with Sid,
that she had to have a show to herself. In 1955, we finally
let them go their separate ways, even though we still had
both of them under contract.

In the fall of 1951 our television network was doing so well
that General Sarnoff added to my duties the control of the

radio network, which had begun to fall off as television gained ground. Though NBC Television was now operating at a profit, the revenue wasn't even remotely sufficient to carry the entire network. We were sharply aware of the danger that radio might die before television became big enough to replace it. I had addressed this problem first in a memorandum to top management two years earlier, in September 1949: "The future of radio is anything but static. It, almost as much as television, needs unified command. It needs imagination and daring. . . . This being the case, I naturally oppose any enlargement of the management area. It is quite clear to me that one serious difficulty in present NBC operations is the large number and superfluity of executives. This enables people to avoid making a decision. . . . I think the future clamors for an autonomous, driving team leader."

Perhaps that was why radio was added to my television duties. Perhaps Sarnoff remembered this memo and took me at my word, dropping the problems of radio upon me. Having written so boldly about the need for "imagination and daring" in radio, I realized I had better show a little of each.

One ironic aspect of the situation in radio was the fact that the number of sets in the nation kept increasing while the popularity of the medium precipitously declined. In 1945, at the end of the war, when radio seemed to be at its zenith, there were 56 million sets in the country. By 1951, there were 99 million, but, thanks to television, there weren't as many people listening to them, as the New York–area Hooper ratings for June of that year illustrate. Jack Benny's 1948 rating of 26.5 had fallen to 4.8; Bob Hope's 16 was down to 3.2; Groucho Marx had dropped from 12 to 5; Bing Crosby, from 18 to 3.8; *Amos and Andy*, from 13.6 to 5.9; and Arthur Godfrey's *Talent Scouts*, from 20.3 to 5.9.

At all three networks executives were worrying about the fate of radio and wondering how to save it. We had already resorted to quiz shows and morning giveaways, with mixed success. With its larger audiences, television could afford to give away just as much or more, and it could show its viewers the gifts it was offering.

The first thing I did at NBC when I took over radio was to introduce the same magazine concept of multiple sponsorship that I had established in television, and it worked fairly well, mostly, I think, because the big radio sponsors had now entered television, dividing their advertising budgets and making it too expensive for them to control entire programs, as they had previously done. The advent of television also left the ad agencies with less time and personnel to think creatively about radio programming. If any new ideas were to arise, it was up to us at the networks to think of them.

The first sizable one I came up with was a forty-hour weekend program with comedy, news, information, commentary, and music. *Monitor* lasted two decades on NBC and saved the radio network from disaster for most of those years.

During our press conference announcing the plans for *Monitor*, I explained at some length what kind of show it would be, whereupon one of the reporters said, "What I want to know is this. Most shows are simple enough that they can be defined in two words. Can you tell me in two words what *Monitor* will be?"

"Easy," I said. "Monitor will be, in two words, a kaleidoscopic phantasmagoria."

One of the superb performers on *Monitor* was the inventive comedian Ernie Kovacs. I still remember a pre-Christmas skit in which he said: "All I want for Christmas is a large towel and a wet girl."

Another thing I did for the radio division was to shift the emphasis from programming to the advertising strengths of the medium and set up new approaches to the sale of commercials. We stressed the fact that radio and television were complementary media. They needed each other. You could advertise on a TV hit that millions of radio listeners would never see. To reach a complete audience, you had to advertise on both.

Though radio was consuming more of my time than I wished, I managed to keep bringing new people to television. I used the success of *All-Star Revue* to launch Kate Smith in a five-day-a-week late-afternoon program produced by Barry Wood and Tommy Loeb. It was an opulent show with major guest stars, special-interest departments, and comedy, much like her radio program, which I had supervised when I was at Young & Rubicam. We also used the show to introduce and develop new talent. Bud Abbott and Lou Costello had their first big television success on the Kate Smith show, and *The Aldrich Family* television format was a spinoff from it.

For children, we already had *Howdy Doody*, which was doing well despite the fun adults made of it. Clarabell, a clown on *Howdy Doody*, was played by Bob Keeshan, who later created *Captain Kangaroo*. It was also about this time that Dr. Frances Horwich's *Ding Dong School* began, for younger children.

In October 1951, I felt a personal satisfaction when my old agency, Young & Rubicam, finally gave in to my multiple-sponsor policy by making one of its clients, Goodyear, a cosponsor with Philco of Fred Coe's *Television Playhouse*, which eventually became the *Alcoa-Goodyear Playhouse*. With the surrender of Y&R, we now had all the major ad agencies participating in NBC-owned programs—perhaps not because they were enthusiastic about it, but because their clients demanded it. They couldn't resist investing in the hit shows we had developed.

The multiple-sponsor movement had been a pivotal struggle, because if we had lost it, our future would not have been in our hands. By the autumn of 1951, just two years and four months after I came to NBC, our contractual control was such that none of the shows we considered important was vulnerable to raids by other networks. The programs on which our ratings depended were all NBC-planned and -controlled. Though there were still some agency-produced shows on our schedule, they were either middle or lower bracket, and their loss would give us opportunities to strengthen our lineup. While there continued to be pockets of resistance to our system of network ownership, we had, in effect, won the battle.

It was no time to relax. Many innovations in my plan were yet to come, and there were problems I still had to solve. Television news presentation was one of the most important.

The shortcomings of our news programs were not the fault of those involved. We had some first-rate people down on the fifth floor, beginning with Davidson Taylor, whom I hired away from CBS, and including men like Bill McAndrew, vice president in charge of news; Gerald Green, who later became famous by writing such fine novels as *The Last Angry Man*; and Reuven Frank, who was destined to serve two terms as president of NBC News. McAndrew is long since dead, but Green and Frank, still living in the New York area, may be surprised at my praise, because, as Frank mentioned in his 1991 book, *Out of Thin Air*, I was not happy about their output during those early days. The fault, however, lay not in themselves but in the facilities with which they had to work—the technical state of the art of television.

NBC's TV news department wasn't born until 1948 (only a year before my arrival), when Young & Rubicam made an arrangement with *Life* magazine to televise that year's political conventions, over the NBC network, with Ben Grauer as anchor. After the Democrats nominated Harry Truman and the Republicans Tom Dewey, the *Life* people packed up and returned to their magazine, leaving the network's fledgling news department virtually devoid of newsmen. Within a year or so, someone had the good sense to hire Green away from International News Service, and he lured his Columbia Journalism School classmate Frank away from the Newark *Evening News*, where he had been night city editor.

As an example of the low regard in which television news was held at the time, Frank reports that when he took the job in 1950 for $110 a week, he asked, "Why me? All you know is I'm Green's friend and I type faster. NBC is a worldwide news organization. Why didn't you get someone from radio news downtown?" (Television news at that time was tucked away in the Pathé Laboratories, on 106th Street.)

"To be honest," the man who hired him said, "nobody down there who's worth a damn thinks this is going to last. They hate it."

As a onetime radio newsanchor in San Francisco myself, I, too, had a low opinion of television news, because with the equipment available at that time there was no way to cover properly an important breaking story. The cameras were too heavy. The sound equipment was so cumbersome, it was difficult to get close enough to pick up the action on your microphone, especially with scornful print reporters crowding around and gleefully elbowing all the television upstarts out of the way. Even if there was film worth using, it took so long to bring it back to the lab and have it developed, the news was stale by the time it went on the air.

Radio, by contrast, had split-second, point-to-point communication all over the world—and it still does. If something was happening in London, your announcer simply said, "Come in, London," and your correspondent there had only to say, "Ladies and gentlemen, Winston Churchill is about to address the House of Commons." A moment later you were listening to Churchill's voice, live, from England. (Even now, breaking news may have to be covered by television through an audio feed.) For radio we had world coverage on a regular basis. Such key television developments as lightweight, hand-held cameras and satellites for picture transmission were simply ideas in the minds of brilliant scientists. Through the fault of no one at NBC, our evening telecast, the *Camel News Caravan*, was little more than a radio newscast in which you could see John Cameron Swayze at a desk, reading the items.

It was for this reason that, even before I came to NBC, I developed my own ideas about what TV news should try to do under those difficult circumstances. Instead of concentrating on spot news, I believed we should develop real world coverage—a wide view of trends and developments, national and global, that would have greater significance than any one day's events. CBS, with reporters like Edward R. Murrow and Eric Sevareid, was far ahead of us in this arena. NBC at that time had not yet developed the likes of David Brinkley, Chet Huntley, John Chancellor, and Frank McGee. I kept after Bill McAndrew, whom I had brought in from Washington, to hire correspondents able to compete with Murrow's team, assembled during World War II, but, in truth, it wasn't easy then to find such people. Meanwhile, I wanted to concentrate on values like enlightenment and education. It wasn't that I opposed spot-news coverage. I simply realized that at the time, television couldn't manage it.

When major stories broke we covered them with cutaways to a correspondent and ran additional coverage at night. One of our first big real-world telecasts was the House Un-American Activities Committee hearings, in which our viewers could watch Alger Hiss and Whittaker Chambers have at each other. They might also see an obscure California congressman, Richard Nixon, accusing Hiss of Communist affiliations.

The Senate hearings on organized crime was also important, with Senator Estes Kefauver confronting Mafia boss Frank Costello, but it couldn't be shown entirely because Costello had agreed to testify only if his face wouldn't be shown. As a result, everyone in the hearing room was on television except Costello, whose hands alone were seen.

The most important of all early-fifties television events, the Army-McCarthy hearings, didn't produce NBC's finest hour. Though we covered them well enough, ABC cleared its schedule and presented every minute of them, live. And CBS beat us later on the same story when Edward R. Murrow gave America his brilliant dissection of the McCarthy hysteria.

I finally put together a Sunday show called *Commentary*, with Scotty Reston of the *New York Times*, columnists Marquis Childs, Joseph and Stewart Alsop, plus Alistair Cooke, who was then the overseas correspondent for the Manchester *Guardian*. Each of them had five or six minutes to analyze the most important story or situation about which the American people should be aware that week. It was a worthwhile show, but it was strongly opposed by our news people, who didn't believe we should use print journalists on television.

The weakness of television news was the strongest factor prompting me to forge ahead on our early-morning program, which would be called *Today*. I had originally conceived of it as simply a rise-and-shine show. Since then I had converted it, in my mind, into a coverage program that would not only entertain but would tell early risers all kinds of things they should know as they faced the day. We hadn't been able to start it when I had first thought of it in 1949, because we couldn't talk the network stations into opening that early. There was an almost universal belief that no one would watch television right after they got out of bed. I didn't share that sentiment, but two years later, in 1951, many people still did.

I was loaded down with warnings that such a show, even in the enlarged version I now imagined, would not be accepted by the public. I plowed ahead despite a lot of thoughtful advice.

During the early planning of the *Today* show, I wrote in a memo to the staff: "Seventy-five percent of all homes use radio between seven and nine [a.m.]. A great deal of that usage is music and news as one gets dressed, or entertainment that requires a low attention factor. We want to bring that audience over to *Today*. Hence we must have music and news."

In another memo I wrote that the show should follow the basic morning radio format—giving the time, weather reports, highway tips for commuters, news bulletins, and music, plus entertainment, especially light comedy. I knew that radio formula well, because I had used it in San Francisco. It was rather like Don McNeill's *Breakfast Club* in Chicago and Tom Brenneman's *Breakfast at Sardi's* in Hollywood, but with the additional visual appeal for those who had time to watch as well as listen.

I worked out several quick visuals, including the morning's newspaper headlines and wall clocks to display the exact time at various places around the world. I decided to insert short interviews with authors of new books, stars of new plays or films, and people in the news. I didn't ignore breaking news events. I asked our news department to cover spot stories during the previous evening or night, early enough to have the film developed, edited, and on the air by 7 a.m. or shortly thereafter.

In my original conception I had pictured a wide-awake, rapid-fire master of ceremonies, but as I enlarged the scope of the show, I decided we should have someone more relaxed and low-keyed, with an offbeat sense of humor. In Chicago, NBC had developed such a person—Dave Garroway, who was not highly regarded by network executives in New York, where he had tried out without great success as an announcer. Maybe that was why he had been sent to Chicago. I had always liked his casual style, especially after he somehow maneuvered himself into a show of his own, *Garroway at Large*. I was also slightly partial to him because of his experience in Chicago, where stations had done a lot of their own programming, as we had on the West Coast. Hugh Downs was another Chicago talent whom I had eyed. One thing I liked about both of them was their wide interviewing experience in radio as well as on television. They both knew how to bring people out and make them tell their stories. Pauses and silences are deadly on radio, and the *Today* show was to be, in effect, a radio program with visuals, which viewers could either watch or ignore as they bathed or shaved or ate breakfast.

After choosing Dave Garroway to preside over the show, I added Jack Lescoulie to clown around with the sports and weather, and, in general, to have fun as a foil for Dave. It was not until *Today* had been on the air awhile that I added the renowned critic, chimpanzee J. Fred Muggs, who shocked the other critics but amused everyone else.

I assigned Mort Werner to produce this grand goulash and brought in Richard Pinkham, circulation manager of the New York *Herald Tribune*, to help him.

I had hired Werner shortly after coming to NBC. I had known him during my radio days in San Francisco, where he came to the station every day after school to work as a gofer and to play the piano during station breaks, all without pay. Toward the end of the war I worked with him on Armed Forces Radio, where he was a producer and his wife was the disc jockey GI Jill. At NBC I soon gave him the assignment of shaping the show that would eventually become *Today*. He understood the concept and loved it.

Pinkham was an excellent newsman and highly intelligent. He was executive producer of *Today*, then later of the *Home* and *Tonight* shows. I had known Dick since his graduation from Yale, followed by several years at *Time* magazine and at the Lord and Thomas ad agency. During the war we were both in the navy, and it was Dick who tried to get me the command of a new destroyer escort after I was relieved as skipper of a smaller escort vessel. I was the godfather of his first child, Penny, and he was the godfather of our son, Trajan. Liz and I spend a lot of time with him and his wife, Bunny. Dick should write his own book, because he went on to have a distinguished career in television and was chairman of the Ted Bates advertising agency.

Bill McAndrew didn't much like what I was doing. He thought I was treating the morning's news too lightly, so I made Gerry Green *Today*'s managing editor of news, confident that he would understand what I was up to. He was, and is, a man with a great sense of humor as well as a sharp news sense.

By January 14, 1952, the *Today* show was ready to be unveiled—or so I hoped, because we were opening it that day at 7 a.m., not only on the air but practically on one of the sidewalks of New York. The studio we had fashioned for it was right on the Forty-ninth Street level, with a huge window enabling people to see a live telecast as they walked past the RCA Building. This was no small attraction in those days of television's infancy. Everyone was curious about it. We also piped the sound out onto the street, causing a sensational reaction among the crowds of pedestrians who stopped to watch and listen. I wish our opening had created that much of a sensation among viewers at home. Alas, there were so few of them, they created only a sensation of emptiness in the pit of my stomach.

15

I WATCHED THAT FIRST *TODAY* SHOW WITH LIZ FROM OUR bedroom. I drank my coffee with considerable delight, even though my friends and associates had warned me that no one would watch television at that hour. I knew how strong radio was at that time of day.

Most of the NBC station managers seemed to agree with the pessimists. No more than half of our affiliates were willing to go on the air early enough to carry *Today*, despite a fifteen-minute fight talk I had given them on a closed-circuit channel, describing the program's merits and the fabulous future I envisioned for it. In New York, the advertising agencies were equally skeptical. *Today* didn't quite start as a public-service sustaining show. We had some commercials, but hardly enough of them to support the program.

As I watched that first morning, however, I knew I was still a believer. To me the potential was obvious. Though there were some opening-day glitches, and the set was very busy, with too many things happening at once, all this could be corrected, and when it was, we would have a great beginning for our planned eighteen-hour schedule. Dave Garroway and the rest of the cast were excellent, and I loved that ground-floor studio with its windows on the sidewalk, inviting passersby to watch and listen. Already that first day, they were beginning to take notice.

The studio was actually a part of the RCA Exhibition Hall, and I had grabbed it the minute I found out it was available. I was sure we'd get a rush of publicity plus word-of-mouth about it, and we did. The crowds increased as soon as people realized we might be aiming our cameras at them, and then the signs and banners began to appear. Almost everybody wants to be seen on television.

That storefront studio produced an amusing incident, thanks to our associate producer, Joe Thompson. On about the third day of the show, he went out onto Forty-ninth Street to be one of the gawkers looking in at us. Suddenly he adopted what came to be known as "the look." It was a bemused expression that seemed to say, "What are those idiots doing in there at this time of day?"

It fractured everyone in the studio. Dave Garroway doubled up with laughter. One morning about two weeks later, on a day when the show seemed to be dying, Thompson went outside and again gave the look to everyone inside.

As it happened, I was watching with network president Joe McConnell that day, long before he became converted to the show. We turned on the set at the very moment Thompson, outside, was displaying his stupid look. McConnell watched him, then turned to me.

"I told you," he said, "that this show will attract nothing but idiots."

The critics also had great fun at my expense. Most of the heat was beamed at me because I was the idiot who had come up with the idea. It would be a while before that heat subsided.

I don't want to criticize the critics for their reviews, however, because through the years they have been kind to me. John Crosby and Jack Gould come to mind. Crosby, syndicated through the *Herald Tribune*, was an exceptionally entertaining writer, though I wasn't so fond of his wit the day after *Today* opened. "An incredible two-hour comedy of errors," he called it, perpetrated as "a new kind of television."

Gould, the television critic of the *New York Times*, had a strong sense of fair play and in my view slightly better judgment, though I don't recall that he was very kind to *Today* either. Jack Hellman and George Rosen of *Variety* were slightly less acerbic. And I still recall the favor Hellman did me on another occasion, when he asked me whether General Sarnoff had approved the deal that would have made NBC a major stockholder in Disney. I looked at him and said, "Why should a rat buy a mouse?"

Hellman could have published that line, to my great embarrassment, but he resisted the temptation.

The reviews didn't help to convince our affiliates that they should go on the air early, and many people continued to scoff at the idea of watching TV while getting ready to go to work. They hadn't caught on to the fact that *Today* could almost be a radio broadcast. You could hear enough to follow it and enjoy it even if you were too busy showering or shaving to look at it. But as *Newsweek* reported on April 7, 1952, *Today* had not yet proven "that video by dawn's early light will pay." I was still calling on possible sponsors, trying to convince them it would pay.

While ratings continued to be low, those who did see *Today* apparently loved it. The fan letters were so enthusiastic, we thought of a new way to use them. Instead of opening them, we began giving each of our salesmen a hundred of them, still sealed, which he would dump on the desk of a prospective advertiser with an invitation to open and read what an unsorted sample of viewers thought of the show. These letters were convincing enough to have an effect. And at about the same time, we introduced on the show J. Fred Muggs, the unpredictable chimpanzee. I don't know whether it was the chimp or the letters or simply the increasing entertainment value of *Today*, but a few months after its opening, it began to roll. After its first full season, *Billboard* ran a big headline announcing: "*Today* is the biggest one-year grosser in Show Business." It had outgrossed all other TV shows and hit films, including even *Gone With the Wind*. My NBC pals had that page bronzed, with the comment: "And they called it Weaver's Folly."

As time passed, Dave Garroway also became increasingly popular, but at the same time increasingly peculiar. He's a hard man to describe. He kept a schedule that was so strange, you never saw him until just before the show, and he disappeared right afterward. He had a lot of hobbies, including old cars, but I don't think he ever invited me to see his collection. He was known for using downers and uppers, the latter of which he called his "doctor." He used to offer them to Mort Werner and Dick Pinkham, but they were afraid to partake of that pleasure. Though Dave was with NBC for several years, I can't say I ever did get to know him.

As most people know, *Today* is still on the air, and doing well, four decades later. That makes it the second-oldest television program, behind *Meet the Press*. I made a short appearance on *Today*'s anniversary show in 1992.

By 1952, I had begun work on another idea—the presentation of special programs, both entertainment and cultural, of either ninety minutes or two hours, which we would call NBC "spectaculars." Leland Hayward agreed to produce thirteen of them, Fred Coe would do another thirteen, and David Selznick would do several, based on his *Gone With the Wind*. The project didn't materialize that year because it ran into the same problem that had blocked my Frontal Lobes program—refusal by sponsors to accept onetime pre-emption without what I considered unreasonable compensation. I had to set aside my spectaculars, but I didn't bury them.

BY THIS TIME our news department had developed at least the rudiments of how political conventions should be covered on television. After watching *Life* magazine's people at work in '48, I had a better idea of what was needed in '52, and so did Bill McAndrew. He chose Bill Henry as our anchorman, and we had several correspondents with walkie-talkies working the aisles, interviewing the important delegates. Neither McAndrew nor I was completely satisfied with the coverage, partly because the technical facilities were limited (the networks had to rely on pool cameras rather than their own), but we were learning. The one thing we badly needed was a more compelling personality to anchor the coverage.

We were then in the middle of the McCarthy era, which was fearsome to many people in show business but only a minor nuisance to us, because I refused to take it seriously. We required no loyalty oaths, and I told my staff that if anyone came in from *Red Channels* or some other witch-hunting group, they should simply tear up his literature and tell him to go to hell. If a client began complaining about our selection of talent, or claiming that one of our stars was a Communist, we simply told him that since he didn't think we were doing the right thing, we'd relieve him of his contract. We now had so many hits on the air, sponsors were reluctant to back away from us. They knew that if they had a spot on *Your Show of Shows,* for instance, or the *All-Star Revue,* and they decided to drop it, a dozen other clients would jump at the chance to pick it up. In this respect we had an advantage over CBS, which was no longer so strong. It was Edward R. Murrow at CBS, however, who, in 1954, made television's most effective attack on McCarthyism. Still, no one at NBC, including General Sarnoff, tried to overrule my position.

My struggle to upgrade the quality of programming by broadcasting cultural attractions was not always successful, but I never abandoned it. One of my more notable triumphs was a program titled simply *Wisdom,* which aimed to find the world's greatest thinkers and achievers, put them on camera, and let them tell us what they were doing or thinking, where mankind stood at the moment, and where we were going. During the run of the show we were able to present dozens of celebrated people, including Frank Lloyd Wright, Robert Frost, and the biggest brain of all, in my opinion, the British philosopher Bertrand Russell, a brilliant maverick who did not toe anyone's line but his own. He rejected my written invitation to speak on the program, so I flew to London in the hope of persuading him.

He told me that his reluctance stemmed from his low opinion of British television programs he had seen. "All the more reason for you to appear," I said. "The whole purpose of *Wisdom* is to raise the cultural level of American television." He finally agreed, and the show debuted with him talking for an entire, fascinating hour. Though we had a moderator, he was instructed to step in only if the guest seemed tired or hesitant. No such thing happened. At the end of the show, Russell was ready to continue his learned dissertation.

Wisdom was one program that I think even General Sarnoff liked. His lack of interest in television was so pronounced, he seldom watched any of our attractions—with the exception of NBC Symphony Orchestra, conducted by Arturo Toscanini, whom Sarnoff had brought to the network. The General had a distinct vision of himself as a cultured man, and he was one, I believe, despite his impoverished beginning in a Russian slum. He might even have seen himself as the equal of some of our guests on *Wisdom*. He did have a remarkable career. Perhaps I would have encountered less trouble with him later if I had invited him to appear as a guest on the show, but the thought never occurred to me.

Sarnoff's love of publicity, legendary at RCA and NBC, impinged on me personally for the first time when I was quoted someplace about the technical advances that were needed—satellites, for example—before television could reach its full potential. He quickly informed me that any hardware or other technical developments at RCA were his province, and he would make all announcements about them.

I don't think the General ever liked me. Though he never said so, he did tell me once that he was certain I didn't like him. "I know what you think of me," he told me. "I can see it in your eyes."

By that time I guess he knew about my nickname for him—General Fangs. It was actually no more than a playful jibe. In our business, everybody had a nickname for his boss. I'm sure my staff had fun describing me among themselves. I thought up crazy names for all the bosses I ever had. George Washington Hill at American Tobacco became Monstro around the office after I saw a Disney movie about a whale with that name. I remember when Lew Wasserman at MCA, which took over Universal studios, was called "Positive" Wasserman, in imitation of one possible result of the Wassermann venereal disease test. Abe Lastfogel at William Morris was called Abe Firstfogel. It's all in fun. Most bosses are aware of it, but some of them, I'm sure, don't see it for what it is and don't like it. Sarnoff, I'm afraid, was among the latter.

While I worked on *Wisdom* I was also planning a history project, but before I was very deeply into it, I had a stroke of good luck. Henry Salomon, a college friend of Bobby Sarnoff, walked in with a ready-made history project. Salomon—whom everybody called Pete—had been the right-hand man of Samuel Eliot Morison, the author of the monumental *History of United States Naval Operations in World War II*. Morison had provided Pete with the listings of all navy films made during the war, and Pete saw in this material the makings of an extraordinary television series. The navy had filmed all the war action, defeats as well as victories, mostly from decks of ships in the middle of battle. Almost all of it was available. As fast as I could pick up a pen, I signed Pete Salomon to do the series called *Victory at Sea*. It keeps returning to the screen endlessly in reruns.

By the latter months of 1952 I was feeling good about my situation. When I joined NBC in June 1949, the network was far behind CBS, both in radio and in television, and it was not in control of its own destiny. Since it had been producing few, if any, shows of its own, it was at the mercy of the advertising agencies and had to take whatever they offered. In my first three and a half years, I had turned that around. We now produced and owned nearly all of our programs, and we had so many hits that we had surpassed CBS and begun to show sizable profits. Though I was still frustrated by my inability to facilitate some of my ideas, I was confident I would soon bring most of them to fruition. So altogether, the future looked rosy for NBC Television and for me. Joe McConnell was about to vacate the NBC presidency because Colgate had made him a compelling offer, and I knew I would miss him. I liked him and found him always helpful, but I couldn't pretend his absence would hurt me. I was almost certain I would be named to replace him as network president.

Then one day, shortly before Christmas, my joyous holiday

mood was shattered by the announcement that Frank White, a nice fellow whose expertise was in business and finance, would be the new president of NBC. I would no longer control even the television and radio programming. I was being kicked upstairs as vice chairman of NBC, whatever that title might mean.

Needless to say, I was as stupefied as I was angry, and I was about as angry as I had ever been, especially when I began receiving consolation visits from the people I had brought to NBC. My first impulse was to submit my resignation immediately, but all of them pleaded with me not to do so. "If you leave tomorrow," one of them said to me, "all of us will be fired by New Year's and replaced by other people at half our salaries."

I knew that there was merit in this argument. I had lured these people to NBC from lucrative positions elsewhere, and I owed them some loyalty. Yet I couldn't just sit still and accept General Sarnoff's gratuitous insult as if I enjoyed it. Maybe I deserved at least a portion of the blame for his disliking me. I could have showed him more consideration and respect, I suppose. But this was business. He didn't have to like me. He had indicated in many ways that I was doing an outstanding job. Why would he suddenly banish me by kicking me upstairs with a totally meaningless title?

I picked up the phone and called him. One of his secretaries told me that he was busy. I called back, and he was still busy. I grasped the message—he didn't want to see me. But I was insistent. I went up to his office, and finally, reluctantly, he agreed to talk to me.

"I was planning to call you," he said, "because we have an important task I'd like you to handle. As you know, with the coming of color television, we're trying to have our system adopted for the whole industry. But with CBS campaigning for theirs, I'm not at all certain we'll prevail, even though ours is clearly superior. With your communication skills, I'm sure you can make the American public aware that if the CBS system is adopted, they'll have to throw away their black-and-white TV sets and buy CBS color sets immediately. That wouldn't be fair."

I knew all this, and I agreed with him. With the RCA system, color sets would be compatible with the millions of black-and-white sets already in use. But I had not come up that day to discuss color television. "General Sarnoff," I said, "how could you do a thing like this? Why on earth would you jeopardize a great network operation, which is a mutation from all previous network concepts, and which will make you much more money than NBC has ever before produced? Why would you endanger our whole structure by kicking me upstairs into a vacuum?"

He said, "You mean, why didn't I make you president of the network?"

"Yes, of course. I'm sure Frank White is a competent money man, but so are some others around here. Programming is what breathes life into a network, and he knows nothing about that. I was the logical choice."

"I'll tell you why I didn't choose you," Sarnoff said. "One of my dearest friends before he died was Albert Lasker. I used to visit him after he took sick, and one day when he was very ill—actually on his deathbed, as it turned out—he looked at me and took my hand in his. 'David,' he said, 'I have one favor to ask of you.'

" 'Anything you want,' I said. 'What is it?'

" 'Will you promise me you'll never make Pat Weaver president of NBC?' So I promised."

The memory of my encounter with Lasker ten years earlier came flooding back into my mind. I didn't doubt that Lasker had extracted such a deathbed promise from Sarnoff, but I did doubt that Sarnoff would honor such a promise if he didn't want to. It was difficult to ignore openly the request of a dying friend, yet Sarnoff was too practical and hard-headed to take it seriously. I felt certain that he had passed me over not because Lasker disliked me but because he himself disliked me.

"General Sarnoff," I said, "I can't accept that explanation. I'll submit my resignation in the morning."

"Before you do," he said, "I hope you'll give it more thought. We'll continue to enforce the terms of your contract even if you do resign. We wouldn't have to pay you, since you wouldn't be working for us, but you wouldn't be allowed to work for anyone else. On the other hand, if you decide to stay, we'll give you a new contract with several advantages. It will be for five more years, with a clause which I think is fair to both of us. We won't be allowed to fire you, and you won't be allowed to quit."

He was a cold, hard man. If I had ever before doubted that, I never would again. My head was reeling when I left his office. After talking it over with Liz and with my staff, I decided to sign his damned contract. Liz and I could use the raise in salary. It was better than being unemployed with no money coming in, but I was still puzzled as to why he wanted to keep me around and even increase my pay when I would be doing very little work. In time, I would learn the answer to that question.

16

General Sarnoff moved me, with irony I couldn't help appreciating, into the building's most impressive office aside from his own. He had the NBC boardroom converted for my use, and I rattled around in that huge, elegant "undertaker's chapel" for two or three days, twiddling my thumbs, as it dawned on me that after three and a half busy years, with all kinds of people and projects swarming around me, I was now sitting alone in this stunning office without even an occasional visitor to whom I could talk. It was apparent that my closest friends were reluctant to drop in, either because they were embarrassed about my exile or because they considered it unsafe to be seen with me.

Finally I called someone—I think it was Frank White— and said, "Look, I need an assistant."

In fact, I had no need for an assistant. There was almost nothing to do. What I needed was someone to talk to, so I chose a funny man named Mike Dann from the NBC press department because I had always liked him. (He would become CBS program chief in the 1960s.) He laughed at my jokes, and he told a lot of amusing stories himself. He was very intelligent and would be pleasant company.

The next day, before the two of us had settled in together, I decided that the first thing to do was to get the hell out of there for a while. Since I was doing nothing, I wouldn't be missed. I went to Cuba for the opening of a television network there and spent a week or two on the beach. Then Liz and I flew to France for five or six weeks of skiing in the Alps. Truman Capote was also there, writing one of his books. On the day he finished and mailed his manuscript, he invited us to an excellent dinner, with a superb bottle of champagne to celebrate the event.

When we returned to New York I learned that Frank White was ill and was spending little time at the office. The network seemed to be in the hands of his aides, few of whom I held in high regard. The people on my staff were still around, but none of them were in positions of authority. I was uneasy about this for a selfish reason: I didn't want to sit around helplessly and watch the gradual destruction of something I had built. Mike Dann and I had some good laughs about things we observed in this new administration, but I didn't really enjoy it. I figured that White and his people would be gone in about a year. Then who would the General find to replace them?

As vice chairman, I occupied at least a portion of my mind and my time by campaigning, at Sarnoff's behest, for the RCA color television system against the CBS color wheel. Though it wasn't what I wanted to be doing, I did consider it worth the effort, because our color approach was undoubtedly better and fairer to the public than what CBS proposed. The Federal Communications Commission was expected to make the final decision in the matter, and it seemed to be leaning toward CBS.

NBC had bought the Colonial Theater, on Broadway at Sixty-second Street, and made it into a center for experiments, exhibitions, and even a few actual telecasts using our color system. We herded people in and out constantly, selling them hard on what we considered not only the best but the only practical conversion to color. In the meantime, I made speech after speech, especially to our affiliates, preaching the importance of color in the continuing growth of the industry. I also composed an article for *Variety*, in July 1953, on the expected impact of color: "To the program man it means the opportunity to use an exciting new tool. To the broadcaster it means the opportunity to show people what really is at the end of the camera. Color shows you reality. When you see color you say, 'This is the way it is.' "

More important than any of my speeches, however, were the demonstrations to our clients. At the Colonial we took current black-and-white commercials, reshot them in color, then showed them to advertisers. Since these advertisers were large corporations with heavy influence in Washington, we encouraged them to make themselves heard by the FCC. They did so, and when the final vote was cast, our color system was adopted.

My prediction that Frank White's regime would last a year proved inaccurate. It lasted eight months (he resigned because of illness). And whom did General Sarnoff find to replace White? He found me. I now knew why he had raised my salary and prevented me from quitting when he stripped me of power at the end of 1952. He wanted to keep me on ice in case his experiment with White didn't work. In September 1953, all my powers were restored, and I became, finally, the president of NBC. So much for Sarnoff's solemn promise to Albert Lasker.

In the new setup, Bobby Sarnoff became executive vice president, which was quite all right with me. I had always found Bobby cooperative. In fact, I would never have risked going to NBC, knowing the General's reputation, if it weren't for my friendship with Bobby, and when I arrived there, I made sure he would learn everything I could teach him about the business. I made him supervisor of comedy programs, then executive producer of Pete Salomon's *Victory at Sea* series, and later head of the network's film division.

The real breakthrough for Bobby came when we began our big comedy shows in 1950—*Your Show of Shows, The Comedy Hour,* and *All-Star Revue.* He was in charge of all those stars and producers—Sid Caesar, Imogene Coca, Max Liebman, Bob Hope, Eddie Cantor, Danny Thomas, Ed Wynn, Jimmy Durante, Fred Coe, and many others—plus the major ad agencies. Needless to say, he would not have remained in charge if he had thrown his weight around, but he was much too intelligent for that. He got along with all of them, and his experience with them did much to deepen his grasp of show business and advertising.

There was no doubt that he would become the executive vice president when I became network president. That didn't bother me. I believed I could do such a good job at NBC that by the time General Sarnoff retired I'd get his RCA position. Then, as head of RCA, I could not only help Bobby run NBC, but I could also make the RCA Laboratories get to work in earnest on the projects I thought we should be tackling in cybernetics, computers, miniaturization, solid-state electronics, and other developments in communication and information that I thought were about to explode upon the world, as they did during the later 1950s and the 1960s. But I was simply dreaming about things like that. On the day I became network president, the reality of the situation there was not so pleasant.

My first meeting was with Havy Halvorstad, head of advertising with Procter & Gamble, one of our most important clients. "I'm here with some bad news," he said. "Due to the unfortunate situation that's been developing at NBC, my company has ordered me to cancel our commercials on all of your programs. But when this decision was reached last week, we didn't know you were again taking charge here."

The fact that P&G had decided to pull its advertising was a measure of the depths to which NBC had fallen in only eight months. I had a lot of pieces to pick up and try to put back together. Kate Smith's nighttime show had lost some of its zip and some of its popularity. Our ratings had dropped markedly. And, worst of all, the White regime had begun reverting to the old system of running the network simply as a facility that sold time to the ad agencies for their shows. It was during those eight months that *The Comedy Hour* became *The Colgate Comedy Hour*, and Colgate's agency began producing the show, which, it seemed to me, also needed some revamping.

At the end of the 1953–54 season, we had another loss. On Saturday night, Imogene Coca was leaving *Your Show of Shows*. It was rumored that she and Max Liebman had been having problems with each other. I remember chatting one day with a member of the production staff.

"Imogene was pretty distraught this morning," he said.

"About what?" I asked.

"I don't know. All I know is that she was so upset, she phoned Max and cried over the phone."

"So? How did Max react?"

"He cried right back at her."

I knew what was actually happening. Imogene's agent, Deborah Coleman, was determined to have Imogene split with Sid Caesar and launch a show of her own. When this happened, it brought to an end *Your Show of Shows*—an unfortunate development. Sid survived the separation nicely, continuing to exercise his talents on *Caesar's Hour*. And Liebman maintained his high standards, especially when he began producing Saturday-night spectaculars. Imogene, however, was less fortunate. Her own program on NBC lasted only one season.

Jerry Lester left *Broadway Open House* in 1951. It had been our first hit. I tried in vain to convince him that he should stay. We used several comics in his place, but none of them worked as well. He did make one appearance for us on *The Comedy Hour*, but Colgate rejected him as a continuing host.

One problem we didn't have was the *Today* show. By November 1953, it was reaching more than 50 percent of all homes cumulatively. I wouldn't be satisfied until it approached 100 percent, but it was moving in that direction. And following it in on our morning schedule we now had Frances Horwich's *Ding Dong School*, for preschoolers, a show I've always considered comparable to *Sesame Street*. It held its own against Garry Moore on CBS.

With the demise of *Broadway Open House*, which had proven the viability of late-night comedy, I activated my plans for the *Tonight* show. But before that, I launched another of my longtime visions, the *Home* show.

When I was at Young & Rubicam, I had conceived the idea of *Home*, and we had done research that indicated that at least half of American women who were at home during the day did not turn on daytime radio or television—women who presumably could not be seduced by soap operas or game shows. We also studied the women's magazines and found that most of their ads were for products that did not advertise on television—for example, furniture, carpets, cosmetics, clothing, and kitchen appliances. The *Home* show, I was convinced, would attract the makers of these products and the women who used them. Such products represented millions of dollars in possible revenue that television was not realizing.

The host and hostess of the *Home* show were Hugh Downs, a low-keyed but quick-witted anchorman who knew how to blend all the elements into a cohesive whole, and Arlene Francis, a sophisticated, amusing, beautiful actress who had already made a name for herself in the theater. Downs had proven himself on Chicago television. The two of them presided over a large, sprawling set that was unique in television at the time. It was divided into sections for each of the subjects that were staples of the program—cooking, fashion, furniture, beauty care, and others. Arlene would steer her guests from one subset to another, depending on what she wanted them to see. The *Home* show opened in March 1954, and before I left, it was attracting $10 million a year in commercials for products most of which had never before been sold on television. A few years after I left, the show was canceled, and all of that money was lost to television.

During my first years at NBC I had begun a comedy-development plan that was now paying us dividends. First, we sought out promising comedians whom we felt might make it big on television. Then, we provided them with first-rate writers. George Gobel, Jonathan Winters, and Alan King were among the comedians; Woody Allen was one of the writers. It seemed to us that Gobel was now ready to become a star, and in 1954 he proved we were right, when "Lonesome George" became a national sensation.

NBC radio had also declined in quality and revenue during 1953. Part of that was understandable, because television had now largely replaced radio in people's lives. But there was still a place for radio, and I hoped to make it as appealing and as profitable as possible. Twenty-five million American families remained without television, and they deserved the best radio coverage we could give them. They still had Arthur Godfrey, Groucho Marx, *Dragnet*, and some other good shows. I noticed, however, that the most popular radio programs were also shown on the tube. Maybe that was why they were so popular on radio. They were getting all kinds of publicity as TV shows, and this exposure was rubbing off on their radio counterparts, which received very little attention. So I suggested taping voice tracks of the *Today* show and converting them into a five-day-a-week Dave Garroway program for radio.

By the spring of 1954, NBC had recovered sufficiently to yield profits that were satisfactory to me, under the circumstances, but apparently not to General Sarnoff. He called me to his office and greeted me with a copy of the sales balance sheet in hand for the fiscal year that was coming to a close.

"I see here the NBC profits are about thirty-million dollars—eighteen million from the network and twelve million from our owned-and-operated stations," he said. (I can't vouch for those exact figures, but as I recall they're approximately accurate.) "Aren't you missing some opportunities? It seems to me you could clear more profit than that."

I said, "Certainly, General. I could clear a lot more. We now pay our New York station seven million a year in program compensation. I can pick up this phone right now, call the president of the Mutual network [which owned WOR-TV in New York], and sell him the right to put all those programs on his station for a million a year. We'll save the seven million we pay WNBC, and we'll pick up a million from Mutual. They'll jump at the idea."

It would be an unthinkable thing to do in the long run, even though it would mean an immediate jump in profits, but what amazed me was General Sarnoff's completely bewildered reaction. He didn't seem able to grasp my message, which was that we were paying our NBC-owned stations too much for using our network programs when independent stations would gladly compensate us for that privilege.

FROM THE MOMENT I first conceived of NBC spectaculars, before my eight-month exile, I never lost my determination to get them on the air, despite the opposition of sponsors, who didn't want me to create time slots for these special shows by pre-empting the sponsors' programs. The pre-emption argument continued until the end of 1953, when I decided it was time to stop arguing. I simply issued a notice that henceforth we would withhold from sale to sponsors either ninety minutes or two hours on Mondays, Saturdays, and Sundays of every fourth week. These time slots would be reserved for NBC spectaculars, which would be created by three individual producers—Fred Coe for *Producers' Showcase* on Monday nights, Max Liebman for *Max Liebman Presents* on Saturday nights, and Albert McCleery of *Hallmark Hall of Fame*, as producer of the Sunday spectaculars.

In the fall of 1954, we managed to put our first spectacular on the air, and it was indeed spectacular. So were most of those that followed. Despite the technical limitations of the fifties, we offered some remarkable productions. I believe that Fred Coe's Monday-night *Producers' Showcase* spectaculars were so good, they may have been the best ever on television, though Max Liebman made a good case for the thirty-two Saturday spectaculars he produced.

Max—who called the shows "specials" because he thought the word "spectacular" sounded boastful—did some brilliant programs. "Lady in the Dark" was one, starring Ann Sothern. Also "Zizi," with Renée Jeanmaire and her husband, Roland Petit. And he produced a revival of "Babes in Toyland" with Dave Garroway and a large cast. Max had a touch of genius in creating comedy. His sponsor, Oldsmobile, got love letters by the ton about his shows. I wanted to sell the shows to multiple sponsors, but the Oldsmobile people were so persistent, I allowed them to buy out his spectaculars. *Producers' Showcase* had two sponsors. I was especially pleased with the program's advertising punch. On one Sunday spectacular, Sunbeam featured an electric frying pan and sold over a million of them. Sunday had several other sponsors.

Much as I have always admired Max Liebman, however, I must say that Fred Coe was the most creative of all the remarkable producers of the early days of television, and this includes another man I greatly admire—Worthington Miner, who was at CBS in those days, producing *Studio One*. (I passed the word that we would welcome him at NBC, and he eventually came over to us, in 1953, producing, among other shows, the hit series *Medic*.) The 1950s gave rise to several good producers, but Fred Coe stands out among them. He developed his own group of writers and directors, whom he brought along gradually by working with them, eating with them, and staying up late with them. It was thanks partly to Coe's patience that Paddy Chayefsky wrote "Marty," a major hit on television that later became a popular movie starring Ernest Borgnine. In the sixties, Coe and his group abandoned television for the movies, where they were equally successful.

Among Coe's most memorable *Producers' Showcase* spectaculars were "The Petrified Forest," with Humphrey Bogart, Henry Fonda, and Lauren Bacall; Frank Sinatra in a musical version of *Our Town*, with Paul Newman and Eva Marie Saint (Sinatra sang "Love and Marriage," which he still sings); and "Peter Pan," with Mary Martin, which remained the highest-rated show for the next dozen or so years.

On *Producers' Showcase* we were also able to fulfill my dream of presenting ballet and opera in prime time. According to Nielsen, 30 million people watched the Royal Ballet dance "The Sleeping Beauty," with Margot Fonteyn in the starring role. Later, Fred Coe presented the ballet "Cinderella," then Sol Hurok's "A Night at the Met," with a host of great opera stars. On two Christmases, Fred gave us Gian Carlo Menotti's opera "Amahl and the Night Visitors," created for NBC by contract and still shown at Christmas on NBC.

Shortly after selling out all the commercial time on the spectaculars, I got a call from one of General Sarnoff's secretaries. He wanted a few minutes with me.

The network was swimming along so well, I got into the elevator with a smile on my face. Did he want to congratulate me for putting the spectaculars project together and selling it? Or had he decided finally to come through on the promise of stock options? I thought of this last possibility as no more than a joke. I had long since stopped deluding myself about stock options.

Sarnoff also had a slight smile on his face as he sat at his desk. Plaques and awards covered the walls of his office. His own private barbershop was in the room behind him. He seemed more cheerful than usual. I was beginning to look forward to this visit. Then he spoke.

"I understand you've finished all those bothersome details connected with programming and selling your spectaculars," he said. "Maybe now you'll have time to get down to business."

"Business?" I said with disbelief.

"Administration," he responded, rolling out the syllables.

I began to sense what he was driving at, and I wasn't sure how to handle it. To him, the nuts and bolts of office management constituted a large part of what he called administration—details I had always left to my deputies. "What is it you have in mind?" I asked, with some trepidation.

"I was thinking about personnel," he said. "It seems to

me your staff is getting a bit fat. Can't you skim off some of that excess? Don't you have anybody down there you can replace with someone who would cost us less money?"

I could hardly deny his charge, but every organization has a bit of fat on it. "I admit my people are well paid," I said, "but every one of them is worth what he earns."

He mentioned John West, an RCA man who was on our payroll because he had handled our purchase of the Burbank studios. "How much are we paying him?"

"I can't say exactly."

"I'll tell you exactly," Sarnoff said. "That man makes fifty thousand a year."

"And he deserves it," I said.

"But you could easily replace him for twenty-five thousand."

"Why replace him? He's not quite as busy now as he once was, but he's done this company a lot of good. I'm glad to have him. And I don't worry about his salary, because our network is about to go through the roof with profits. We can afford him, and we may need him badly one of these days." I stood my ground, and that was the end of it. Sarnoff didn't order me to fire West, but I was sure he wouldn't forget the incident, either. I wasn't exactly comfortable when I left his office that day.

MY FIRST PUBLIC mention of what would eventually materialize as the *Tonight* show had taken place at an NBC affiliates' convention in September 1949, a few months after I joined the network.

Summing up what at that time were nothing but my hopes, I said, "We have plans for a strip late at night, shot on an ad-lib basis as in the early radio days. The producer and cast will rehearse numbers that need rehearsing, then say good evening to the cameraman and go on the air. . . . We'll run for an hour with fun and songs and jollity and features and unrehearsed gimmicks. The idea will be that after ten or eleven at night, a lot of people will still want to see something funny."

I had to put that project aside shortly thereafter, because *Broadway Open House* became such a hit in early ratings and audience response that there was no room for a *Tonight* show. With the collapse of *Open House*, it was time to get back to that earlier idea, which seemed to me an almost certain success in roughly the same time slot.

The only people I can remember considering to host the program were Fred Allen, who was too big for the job, and Steve Allen, whom I had first seen perform in California.

I invited Steve to my home and explained that we were thinking about him for a show in which he would have to interview celebrities and cover openings of movies, plays, nightclubs, and all kinds of other things, but at the same time he would have to be very funny five nights a week. I said I liked his shows, but for *Tonight* on WNBC, he would probably need more comic characters, with a wider range of material, in addition to the strange audience-participation antics he was already performing. None of this frightened him. He was happily agreeable to all of it.

We began the *Tonight* show on September 27, 1954, using as our studio the Hudson Theater, just off Times Square on Forty-eighth Street. The opening shot that night and for some time thereafter was from a balcony about halfway up on the Times Tower, panning down on the square to give viewers the feeling that they were there while the announcer introduced the show. The camera then panned over to the Forty-eighth Street corner, to be picked up by a second camera, which zoomed in on the Hudson Theater marquee before dissolving to Steve onstage inside. He was so good, the show was a colossal hit from the very beginning.

Ronald Shafer, in a recent *Wall Street Journal* article,

reminded me of some of Steve's antics. Guessing a question to which he had been given only the answer—a gimmick Johnny Carson was to use to advantage in his Great Karnac routines—was a device Allen employed almost forty years ago, as the Question Man. To what question is "Et tu, Brute" the answer? "How many pieces of pizza did you eat, Caesar?" Maybe Merv Griffin—who later developed *Jeopardy* —was listening?

Allen also instituted the comic-monologue opening, which Carson and many others have since adopted, and his tricks included what he called "crazy shots"—closeups of two bare feet sticking out of an oven, or goldfish swimming in a water cooler. One night he even dressed in a policeman's uniform and began stopping cars on the street. He often conducted funny interviews with members of his audience, including, one night, a nondescript man whose neighbor in the next seat was Cary Grant. Steve talked to the man as if he didn't even notice the famous star beside him.

The only mistake Steve Allen made, in my opinion, was his insistence, in the summer of 1956, on hosting a Sunday-night variety show of his own, which went on the air against Ed Sullivan. He eventually had to give up the *Tonight* show to devote all his energies to the new one. Steve never again reached the level of popularity he had earned on *Tonight*.

A measure of the immediate success of *Tonight* was the fact that it made money for us from its first night on the air. *Today*, *Home*, and *Tonight* together brought in $14 million in 1954—a huge sum for those days.

17

I SAW NEW TROUBLE LOOMING IN THE SUMMER OF 1954 when *The New Yorker* magazine approached our press department about doing one of their famous profiles about me, though the magazine had never profiled the real publicity and fame seeker in our organization—General Sarnoff.

A lady I knew in New York, whom I won't name because I don't think she would like it, had told me about an incident during World War II when she was in England. At a London cocktail party she met Sarnoff, who was stationed there in the U.S. Army, putting together the vast communications network that would be needed for the invasion of the Continent. As the party was winding down, he asked her to go to dinner with him. She declined his offer and returned to her hotel.

About ten minutes after she arrived there, a man came to her door and introduced himself as General Sarnoff's aide-de-camp. "I don't think you realize who General Sarnoff is," he said, handing her a book about the man. She learned later that the book, which included flattering press clippings, had been commissioned by the General himself.

If that story hadn't been enough to disquiet me about the prospect of a *New Yorker* profile, another item, which came directly from the RCA press department, made it obvious that I should steer clear of the magazine. Sarnoff was a friend—or, at least, a close acquaintance—of Raoul Fleischmann, the publisher of *The New Yorker*, and had been trying for years, in person and through the press department, to get the magazine to profile him. Considering Sarnoff's remarkable accomplishment in gaining control of RCA, it wouldn't have been a bad idea, but Fleischmann, or perhaps his editor, Harold Ross, didn't seem to see it that way. Sarnoff never managed to get himself profiled by *The New Yorker*.

Meanwhile, I had already been on the cover of *Newsweek*, and *Life* had published a spread about what I had done at NBC. I didn't want to test General Sarnoff's patience any further.

When our press people proposed that I cooperate with *The New Yorker*, I said, "Listen, fellows, you know that all this publicity will only get me in trouble with the General. Why don't you try to have them profile him? I don't mind getting involved in publicity that will help sell one of our shows. But we've already sold out the spectaculars. I don't need any more publicity. What I really need is a moratorium on personal notice."

They had a powerful argument against me. "*The New Yorker* tells us," one of them said, "that they plan to do it whether you cooperate or not. And so much of you is on the record, there's no way they can be stopped, especially since there's no way you can keep your friends and associates from talking about you."

I couldn't fight that. If they were intending to do it anyway, I decided I'd better try to make them friendly. So Tom Whiteside began interviewing me. All in all, I thought he did a good job, showing my limitations as well as my accomplishments and dreams. Other people seemed to agree. Those two articles won Whiteside a Benjamin Franklin award for biography. I never heard a word of reaction from General Sarnoff, but I didn't suppose he was pleased. Of course, I wasn't in the habit of talking to him any more than was necessary. I can remember only two occasions when I visited his office around that time, and he didn't mention the articles.

The first time I went to see him was when I heard that the 30 acre Burbank studios, across Cahuenga Pass from Hollywood, was up for sale. It was John West, the RCA and later the NBC man on the coast, who told me about it. The problem of finding stage space for our productions was still acute. In New York I had induced the Rockefeller brothers, through my friend Nelson, to buy the plot of land across Sixth Avenue from Rockefeller Center, where the Time-Warner building now stands. The original plan was to create a Television City for NBC. Norman Bel Geddes had designed at my behest a wonderfully clever two-thousand-seat theater, which could be used for two or three shows each evening. In other theaters rehearsal needs would prevent such multiple use, but here each cast would rehearse on upper floors, and their sets would be shunted up or down by a massive elevator. When showtime arrived, the cast would walk onstage and find their set in place. It was a splendid dream, but it never happened. Television production kept moving west to what we loosely call Hollywood.

As soon as I heard that the Burbank property was available, I tried to talk Sarnoff into buying it. He was reluctant at first, but he knew we needed space someplace in Los Angeles. We were gradually becoming overcrowded at our Sunset and Vine studios, which had been designed and built for radio.

Finally I persuaded him to agree to the purchase by saying,

"The worst that can happen, General, is that you'll make a fortune from those thirty acres in Burbank even if we never do anything with it." The NBC West Coast studios were built on that property, which, years later, the *Laugh-In* show made famous by referring to it as "beautiful downtown Burbank."

The other time I went upstairs to see General Sarnoff was when John West and I were negotiating with Walt Disney and his brother, Roy, on a deal that would allow us to use their films and planned TV projects on television—a real coup if I could manage it. I soon found I had a bargaining chip I had not anticipated. The Disneys' brand-new recreation theme park in Anaheim, Disneyland, had cost so much to build that they apparently needed money. Walt and Roy finally agreed to do business with us, but one of the stipulations in the deal was that NBC would have to buy 25 percent of Disneyland.

To me, such a purchase was more of an opportunity than a requirement, but when I told Sarnoff about it, he frowned at the whole idea. "I can't do that," he said. "It would put me in show business."

I couldn't conceal my exasperation. "General, what business are we in now?" I asked.

"Communications," he said, bringing the subject to a close as far as he was concerned. I still wonder how much 25 percent of Disneyland, purchased with 1950s dollars, would be worth to NBC today.

After that incident, I resumed concentrating on programming, a pursuit in which I didn't have to consult General Sarnoff. Even before I had become network president, I had been talking about a show concept that I then called *The Wide Wide World*. I spoke to our affiliates about it in a speech I delivered on November 18, 1953: "*The Wide Wide World* is a show that takes the viewer across this great country of ours and shows him what other people are doing with their leisure time. . . . It's aimed for Saturday or Sunday afternoon, in ninety-minute form, and it's aimed as well as an extension of our life and interests through television."

It was not until 1954 that I was able to plan the program in earnest. I began with a memo to NBC executives and producers: "We must have the show that gets the most talk in the coming season, that wins the Peabody award, that enables me to keep carrying the fight to the intellectuals who misunderstand our mass media development, and that can be profitably sold without affecting any of our present business. *The Wide Wide World* is what its name is. It takes you OUT. It takes you THERE. It puts you in it."

Wide Wide World went on the air on June 27, 1955, debuting as one of the *Producers' Showcase* NBC spectaculars. After that, it ran on twenty alternate Sundays per year, produced by Barry Wood, who had been a singer on the Lucky Strike *Hit Parade* on radio and subsequently supervised the Kate Smith daytime TV series. Dave Garroway hosted *Wide Wide World*, as the camera switched to remote units all over the U.S. and beyond. On that first program we had cameras in three countries—Canada, Mexico, and the United States. This was such a daring feat in those days that some people accused us of having filmed the Canada and Mexico segments in advance.

From Stratford, Ontario, we telecast a scene during their Shakespeare festival. From Tijuana we showed part of a bullfight (though not the bloody part), with the great Mexican comedian Cantinflas in his very funny bullfight parody. From various locations in the United States our remote units telecast a variety of activities, though I can't recall what they were on that opening program.

I do remember—because I kept some of them—the reviews we garnered the next day. The headline in *Variety* was "Weaver Wanderlust a Whammo!" The *New York Times* said, "Television took a major step forward." And the word was equally enthusiastic outside New York. The Columbus *Dispatch* told its readers, "NBC really stretched its muscles, muscles it hadn't even used very much before, and it was a grand sight. Keep it up, Mr. Weaver."

Wide Wide World was still running, sponsored by several branches of General Motors, when I left NBC, but in 1958 it was needlessly allowed to die.

BACK IN 1953, when Pete Salomon finally finished *Victory at Sea,* I had talked to him about my desire to do other programs based on history. In the meantime, I had negotiated with Dino de Laurentiis to portray the history of the Roman Empire in a hundred hours of film. He was agreeable, but I needed help from some organization like the Ford Foundation for such an ambitious project, and I couldn't get it.

Salomon had a firm grasp of the kind of thing I had in mind. The result was *Project 20,* a documentary series that set out to show various aspects of our twentieth century. He did some brilliant documentaries, including "Three Two One Zero," on the atomic bomb; "Nightmare in Red," about Communism; a show on the rise and fall of fascism; and many others. The series was so well received that it continued for several years, during which it sometimes strayed from the twentieth century, with such shows as "The Real West," "Meet Mr. Lincoln," and one on the life of Christ.

ONE OF MY continuing concerns was our afternoon schedule. I was never enthusiastic about soap operas. When the soaps first began to run on television, I still hoped we wouldn't have to go the way of radio. I preferred to dramatize well-written and well-acted stories that were complete in them-

selves. As in many other matters, my hope was slow to materialize into reality. In arguing against soap operas I had
come up against evidence that I never figured out how to
counter. The damned things were too popular to ignore. The
soaps were soon entrenched, as they still are today, but I
didn't surrender to them completely. At the beginning of
1954 we instituted a 3-to-5 p.m. soap-opera block in
competition with CBS. We were only partially successful,
prompting me to go back to my belief that there was a place
in the daytime schedule for the dramatization of good stories
complete in themselves.

Al McCleery, the producer of *Hallmark Hall of Fame*,
agreed with me, so I put him in charge of the project, which
we called *Matinee Theater*. It was a concept that envisioned
a new, onetime drama every afternoon, five days a week.
This was a dauntingly difficult and complicated job, but
McCleery was ideal for it. He had a military background and
was a demon for organization, but he was also a solid creative
man.

In undertaking *Matinee Theater*, I was trying for something more important than finding an attraction to fill a time
slot and compete with CBS for afternoon ratings. I saw it as
a project that could strengthen NBC for years to come.

"Here's what you should do," I said to McCleery. "Tell
our soap-opera writers you'll use them if they can jump up
a mile and do what most of them have dreamed about
doing—write something really great, something that will use
every bit of whatever talent they might have. Tell our prime-
time writers that this will be a first-rate show, even if it is
for afternoon, and make them realize it's an opportunity to
do something better than anything they've ever done. Then
impress the actors with the same kind of message—make
them realize that this show is going to be a highway to
stardom for those who can prove they have what it takes.

Get all these people believing the message, and it will come true. You'll build a company of writers and actors, all under contract to us, and we'll eventually have a roster of our own stars, writers as well as actors, like MGM or the other major movie studios."

He did all of that so successfully, *Matinee Theater* was still on the air and doing well when I left the network. Unfortunately, it didn't last long enough to create any NBC stars.

SOMETIME DURING THE early summer of 1955, I attended a broadcasters' luncheon in California where the speaker was a prominent ABC correspondent in Los Angeles, Chet Huntley. By that I mean he was prominent in California, having gained recent publicity suing a witch-hunting woman because she had called him a communist. He not only sued her; he won the case. I didn't care about the suit. Huntley didn't have to prove to me in court that he was no communist. I was familiar enough with his work to have full confidence in him. He was an excellent journalist who happened to be liberal in his political views, and as everyone knew, it was actually the liberals at whom the red-baiters directed most of their campaigns. There simply weren't enough actual communists in the country to fill their insatiable crusading needs.

I can't remember the subject of his speech, but I do recall how impressed I was by the conviction, power, and authority in his full-toned voice, which I had never noticed before. When I returned to New York I went into Davison Taylor's office in the news department.

"I think I've found the newscaster we've been looking for," I said. "I want you to go to Los Angeles and hire Chet Huntley."

Taylor looked puzzled. "He's already working for ABC out there," he said.

"But I want you to get him under contract to us in New York. And don't listen to any nonsense about him being too liberal. He has exactly the voice we need."

Taylor and Bill McAndrew went to California and came back with Huntley under contract, thus laying the groundwork for a combination destined to become immortal in the history of television news—Chet Huntley and David Brinkley.

For a while now we had been planning to enlarge our sadly inadequate fifteen-minute *Camel News Caravan* into a twenty-five-minute nightly newscast, but these plans were delayed because Camel cigarettes had some time to go on its contract, and we lacked a replacement for John Cameron Swayze, whom I considered lacking in the power and conviction I felt Huntley could supply. (When we enlarged to twenty-five minutes, the remaining five minutes of the half-hour would be filled by the inimitable Bob and Ray in one of their devastating soap-opera satires. I think it was "The Life and Loves of Linda Lovely," but it may have been "Mary Backstage, Noble Wife.") After hiring Huntley, my intention was to develop him and somebody else as co-anchors, though I don't recall that I had any candidate in mind as a partner for him. I believe it was McAndrew who suggested Brinkley, who was at the time our chief Washington correspondent, with a wry wit quite unusual among broadcast journalists.

Before any of that could happen, though, we had to wait for the Camel contract to lapse. Meanwhile, we invented for the idle Huntley a Sunday-afternoon program called *Outlook*, which gave him his first opportunity at least to comment on the news for a network television audience.

Nineteen fifty-five had turned out to be a banner year for NBC. Though our radio division continued to diminish— saved from deficit by the success of the weekend *Monitor* program—our television operations flourished. We made high ratings and a profit of well over $30 million that year, which was considerably more than CBS. My position at the network had never seemed more secure. Then came December.

After a flurry of rumors about changes in the executive structure—rumors I didn't believe, because I was convinced that if they were true I would have to know about them—Bobby Sarnoff came into my office one day and told me exactly what was happening. His father had decided to make me chairman of the board because, he said, it was about time for Bobby, after his long apprenticeship, to take the job he was destined to fill—the presidency of the NBC network.

That was not a big shock to me. I had always known that Bobby would one day become president. It didn't really bother me as long as I could continue to wield the power of the chief executive officer. Then came the bad news. I was to lose not only my title but my authority. Bobby was obviously embarrassed about this. The troubles I had with his father had never affected my relations with him. I can't remember a time when there was any serious difference between us. Even the day of his revelations our meeting was amicable, despite the desolation I felt inside.

Though the Sarnoffs offered me another substantial raise in salary and invited me to keep my presidential office, I was once more tempted to resign. Again, however, I felt the nagging responsibility to the people I had brought to NBC. It took me a few days to make up my mind, during which time Bobby kept increasing the inducements to stay.

Finally I said to him, "I'll stay only if you give me your solemn promise that none of my people will be released without my agreement."

Bobby didn't hesitate to make that promise, and I'm sure he did it sincerely, so once again I agreed to remain, this time as NBC chairman, something of a promotion over my previous period of exile.

Shortly after my election as chairman of the NBC board of directors, we held our first meeting. Because I was busy elsewhere, I was the last to enter the room. The first thing I noticed was that General Sarnoff, as usual, was in the large chair at the head of the table. But in my view that was no longer his chair, it was mine. And since I was mad at him anyway, I decided I'd make a point.

I walked over to him, looked down at him from my considerable height, and said, "General, you're sitting in my seat."

I'm sure he was as shocked as everyone else in the room, but he sheepishly stood up, muttered something under his breath, and chose another chair.

For some time in the early months of 1956, I didn't notice much difference in my status. Because I was in the same office, people kept dropping in on me, and that included Bobby perhaps more than anyone else. Nothing seemed to change between us. He consulted me so frequently and followed my advice so often, I still had a lot of influence in the organization. For example, after Chet Huntley and David Brinkley were paired triumphantly as coanchors at the political conventions of 1956, there were still people at NBC who didn't think the two would work out as a team in a daily newscast. I kept telling Bobby to ignore them, and he did. Though it didn't happen until the fall of 1956, after I was gone, *The Huntley-Brinkley Report* was launched at last, and with it the rather rapid ascendancy of NBC News to preeminence over CBS and ABC.

Despite Bobby's continuing willingness to involve me, I became increasingly self-conscious about the fact that I actually had no power. I began wondering what it was that kept me there. Was I truly that concerned about the danger of my people at NBC losing their jobs? Bobby had promised to keep them, and not just as a gesture to me. He was likely to have held on to them anyway because they were topnotch executives and he needed them. Even if he were stupid enough to fire them, they would all do well wherever they went.

I began to ask myself if I was continuing at NBC because I hoped I would again regain power one day, just as I had in 1953, after my first exile. The future of NBC, and all of television, meant as much to me now as it had on the day I joined the network, and I was convinced I had much more to contribute. I was still questioning myself about such considerations that day in September 1956 when I learned that Fred Wile and George Frey had been fired by the Sarnoffs, which to me meant the General, not Bobby.

The game was over now. I could no longer protect anyone from dismissal, nor could I entertain any more idle dreams about emerging once again from the shadows to take charge of the National Broadcasting Company. It was this realization that made me pick up the phone and put in that final call to General Sarnoff.

POSTSCRIPT

ONCE THE DIE WAS CAST, LIZ AND I SAW OUR CHILDREN safely cared for and took off for a long trip to Europe.

I engaged an agent, Ted Ashley, but was soon informed that no network would negotiate with me for any kind of job and the major movie companies were not interested in me for their TV or movie operations. And the station groups were not big enough to offer me anything challenging.

My cronies in television and advertising all repeated in chorus that executives were very wary of taking on someone whose extensive publicity and creative credits might be a threat to them.

So I started my own network and called it Program Service. I outlined to independent stations and several ABC stations the kinds of programs we would be developing and distributing, and worked out fees for the outlets that would carry the shows. We shared office space with Joe Dine and Allan Kalmus, and I brought in NBC's Lew Marcy and Jerry

Chester. Within a year we had acquired *Ding Dong School,* which NBC had been dumb enough to drop, and had it widely sold, five mornings a week, with the veteran radio personality Mary Margaret McBride taking over the next half-hour. Our nighttime programming showed promise, particularly because we could offer sponsors who advertised with us a bargain: they would get two-thirds of the circulation offered by the networks and would pay only one-third the cost.

I wanted to concentrate on Program Service, but Mort Werner asked me to meet with Henry Kaiser, who persuaded me to accept a consultancy with him. Among other things, I oversaw *Maverick,* the big western hit show of the late fifties and early sixties.

In 1958, Nelson Rockefeller decided to run for governor of New York the hard way, as a Republican. I pointed out to him that other wealthy New York politicians, like Franklin Roosevelt and Averell Harriman, were Democrats when they entered politics. In the year before the election, Nelson was 60 rating points behind Governor Harriman in the polls. But in many ways Nelson was made for television, and we explored those ways. TV certainly elected him. I stayed on as his personal advisor for all his remaining campaigns, and finally when he was vice president under Gerald Ford.

I had also agreed to work with Marion Harper, the head of the McCann Erickson advertising agency, on renaming Standard Oil of New Jersey, one of his international accounts. (It eventually became Exxon.) Marion had been accomplishing many new and controversial things in a business I knew well. As the 1958 recession arrived, and Nelson was elected, I sadly had to fold Program Service. Marion offered me the managing role for all the McCann companies outside the United States. These included advertising agencies, public relations companies, and research outfits, and I would run them all as chief executive officer. Later I would assume the same role for the company that was set up to manage all of the company's radio and television activities in the United States.

McCann Erickson introduced many new ideas in the communications business. My early start in and knowledge of broadcasting, as well as my strong advertising background, made me understand Harper's innovations. We opened a Tokyo office, McCann Hakahoto, and it went from nothing to $350 million in billing by the 1980s. And we bought an agency in Australia. World-hopping was wonderful. Marion Harper decided that we should have a new name and selected that of one of our German PR companies, Interpublic. In the next few years, our agency in South America was the continent's largest, and we also owned the third-ranking agency. We were first by far in Europe and booming ahead in the United States. Along with Marion, I was also working with my old friends Emerson Foote, Bob Healy, and Paul Foley. It was great fun, and I was the second-largest stockholder in a superb enterprise.

I was still thinking about what the telecommunications revolution was going to mean as new concepts emerged, when I was approached in late summer of 1963 to take over the first major pay television operation. We would start in California, because the promoter Matty Fox had signed up the Dodgers and Giants baseball teams in Los Angeles and San Francisco, and we were partners with the manufacturer Lear Seigler, one of the giants in the electronics industry of the sixties. Reuben Donnelly, owned by Dun and Bradstreet, was to be the selling arm, and the board for the new venture included such well-known figures as Bunker Hunt and Robert Lurie. But the Wall Street issuance of our stock was menaced by ads from theater owners and some broadcasters claiming that they would put us out of business. Their position was that free TV and pay TV could not coexist.

Our opponents used the California referendum process to promote this theme and scare people into voting a prohibition of pay TV. But we offered so much to the customer that I believed we would win such a fight, and every attorney of stature agreed that the California Supreme Court could not permit a referendum that was plainly illegal to remain on the ballot.

Through phone company cables we provided three channels, with hi-fi sound and in full color. Channel one showed brand-new movies. Channel two covered the performing arts—the living theater, the opera, the ballet, the concert hall. Channel three carried sports, plus an array of special programs. Alfred Sheinwold gave bridge lessons, and there were language lessons by Berlitz. We showed potential customers our shopping channel in cooperation with Sears Roebuck. I wrote the basic sales call for prospective clients, and we expounded at length on the miracles to come. Each home had channels that were two-way, reporting what people were using, for automatic billing. Later, with the fast-approaching development of cassettes, we demonstrated how the subscriber could apply our code to intercept a flood of special material. Everything was priced in our monthly magazine, *Subscriber's Choice*. Most programs permitted a free viewing period before the charges were entered.

The cables were laid to fifty thousand homes each in Los Angeles and San Francisco, and by mistake, in areas with a median income below that for California as a whole. Our advertising (banned by ABC, the San Francisco *Chronicle*, and some other media) was vastly outspent by that of the theater owners, but 50 percent of the homes we were to pass in our first year subscribed to the service, showing that the public was ready for our kind of pay TV in the 1960s. The anti–pay TV referendum was placed on the ballot and won (it was not removed by the court), and we had to close down,

but the state Supreme Court ruled that the vote was illegal.
We won all successive appeals, but I had to take us through
Chapter II and sell to a miniconglomerate that was not in
the cable business. The company used our tax loss to make
big profits, and the stock soared from 1 to 17 or 18.

I decided to look for work in programming again. I was
lucky enough to sell my *Mad* show to Mike Dann, who was
now at CBS, for the 1966 season. He got Garry Moore to star,
but it wasn't as good as *Laugh-In*, which arrived the next
season and did the crazy stuff better. Mary Wells asked me
to come to Wells Rich Greene, her hot new advertising
agency, on a part-time basis, so that I could continue my
subscription-TV work. I joined the board of Rheem Manufacturing and was a consultant to Westinghouse, to Comsat,
and to Disney for the planning of Epcot. In 1980 I almost
started the first cable comedy network service, and I gave a
series of lectures at UCLA for the director George Sheaffer.
My program company also produced a comedy news show
five hours a week, which Mike Eisner bought for ABC.

Later I formed a partnership with the pollster Louis Harris,
and one of our projects may eventually be the talk of television. It is called Intercept TV, and it offers those with VCRs
(VCRs are now in 80 percent of all TV-owning homes) a
service that conforms to the results of Lou's longtime research on the size of audiences for the theater, the other
performing arts, and movies. One-third of all adults go to
the ballet, the opera, and concerts; two-thirds attend the
theater each year; and movies account for 90 percent of all
cassette rentals and sales. Our subscribers will receive the
best seats in the house at theaters, the opera, the ballet, and
the concert halls. Fifty-two weeks a year, seven days a week,
the viewer will have his VCR record each night's offering
during so-called dead time (2 a.m. to 5 a.m.). Opera and
ballet will be shown on the same night every week, as will

classical music. A third night will present a popular theatrical work; a fourth, a serious dramatic play. The fifth night will schedule a movie of the week. We expect to pay substantial fees to the film studios, who will pick the time for the first showings of their movies. Our hardware will contain an element that makes duplication impossible. On the sixth night there will be comedy, and the last night of the week is as yet undecided but will probably commence with movie classics. These shows will give viewers the best seat in the house in the greatest cultural and film centers of the world, and will provide them information about what it's like to be in Rome, Vienna, Tokyo, Sydney, and the rest of the globe. There will be no advertising, and I can't help thinking that we will attract a very large number of subscribers.

I AM PROUD of what I have accomplished in broadcasting and cable, but the future of communications is so fascinating, I wish I had another lifetime to help in realizing its potential.

A NOTE ON THE TYPE

This book was set in Bodoni, a typeface named after Giam-
battista Bodoni (1740–1813), a celebrated printer and type designer of Rome and Parma. Present-day Bodoni typefaces were
adapted from the original Bodoni designs and were cut for
Monotype machine typesetting in 1911. Bodoni's innovations in
type style included a greater degree of contrast in the thick and
thin elements of the letters and a sharper and more angular
finish of details.

Composed by PennSet,
Bloomsburg, Pennsylvania

Printed and bound by Arcata Graphics/Martinsburg,
Martinsburg, West Virginia

Designed by Brooke Zimmer